A CHURCH WITH A FUTURE

I gcuimhne ar Mháire Nic An Airchinnigh
Ar dheis Dé go raibh a hanam

Edited by Niall Coll and Paschal Scallon CM

A Church with a Future

CHALLENGES TO IRISH CATHOLICISM TODAY

the columba press

First published in 2005 by
the columba press
55A Spruce Avenue, Stillorgan Industrial Park,
Blackrock, Co Dublin

Cover by Bill Bolger
Origination by The Columba Press
Printed in Ireland by ColourBooks Ltd, Dublin

ISBN 1 85607 488 9

Table of Contents

List of Contributors

Paul Andrews is Rector of Manresa Retreat House in Dublin, and writes for the Jesuit prayer website, sacredspace.ie. He is a Jesuit.

Joseph Briody, a priest of the diocese of Raphoe, is Curate in Creeslough, Co Donegal.

Jim Cantwell was Press Secretary of the Irish Episcopal Conference from 1975 until 2000.

Niall Coll, a priest of the diocese of Raphoe, is Senior Lecturer in the Department of Religious Studies at St Mary's University College, Belfast.

Concepta Conaty is National Coordinator of Disadvantaged Initiatives with the Department of Education and Science in Dublin.

Paul Fleming, a priest of the diocese of Down and Connor, is Head of the Department of Religious Studies at St Mary's University College, Belfast.

Tom Layden works in the areas of spiritual direction, adult education and ecumenical ministry, and is based in Belfast. He is a Jesuit.

Richard A. Lyng is Tutor in the Department of History, National University of Ireland, Galway, and Parish Priest of St Augustine's Parish in Galway city. He is an Augustinian.

Feidhlimidh Magennis, a priest of the diocese of Dromore, is Principal Lecturer in the Department of Religious Studies at St Mary's University College, Belfast.

Séamus Murphy lectures in philosophy at Milltown Institute, Dublin. He is a Jesuit.

Máire Nic An Airchinnigh submitted her article shortly before her untimely death in 2004. Originally a research scientist, she pursued her interests in Ecumenical Theology as a student at the Irish School of Ecumenics, Dublin, 1997-8, and then by teaching at the Milltown Institute, Dublin and the Priory Institute, Dublin. She also served on the executive of The Irish Theological Association.

Breda O'Brien is married to Brendan Conroy, and they have four children. She is a secondary teacher and a columnist with *The Irish Times*.

Dan O'Connell is currently a doctoral student at Boston College. He has lectured in social ethics at All Hallows College, Dublin.
Christopher O'Donnell is Associate Professor of Spirituality at the Milltown Institute. He is a Carmelite.

Nuala O'Loan is the Police Ombudsman for Northern Ireland. She is a qualified solicitor and was the Senior Lecturer holding the Jean Monnet Chair in European Law at the University of Ulster.

Michael Router, a priest of the diocese of Kilmore, is the Director of Adult Faith Formation and Pastoral Development in the diocese.

Simon Rowe is the editor of *The Voice Today* and was formerly editor of *The Irish Catholic*.

Paschal Scallon works on the Vincentian Mission Team and is based in Belfast. He is also Secretary to the National Conference of Priests of Ireland. He is a Vincentian.

Martin Tierney, a priest of the Dublin diocese, is Parish Priest of Kill-O'-The-Grange and a columnist with *The Irish Catholic*.

Introduction

Timothy Radcliffe, former Master General of the Dominican Order, has boldly asserted that 'the one clear thing that the Bible tells us about the future of the church is that it *has* one.' Inspired by such a confident assertion, this collection of essays sets out to explore some aspects of how the Irish Catholic Church might best respond to the myriad challenges that face her today as she endeavours to proclaim the gospel in a culture which is increasingly secularised, and which is also traumatised by a steady stream of disclosures of sexual abuse perpetrated by clergy. It would be natural to feel profoundly disheartened.

This volume brings together nineteen reflections that describe current experience and which offer suggestions which may contribute to a renewal of the Catholic Church in Ireland. The volume is presented in three sections, dealing broadly with ministry, education and communication.

A particular feature of comment in the contemporary church in Ireland is the welcome emergence of a more theologically aware lay voice. More lay people are studying theology in the country today than clerics, most of them are women and many of them take their studies to post graduate level. One only has to scan the contents pages of periodicals to see the number of lay people who are writing.

Bearing in mind, however, the leadership role accorded to the ordained ministry in the Catholic Church, it is imperative that priests play their part actively and visibly in the necessary reflection that will contribute to the renewal that everyone who cares about the church hopes for.

Many people want to hear priests reflect at greater length on issues concerning the faith and the church. There is a worrying impression that they have maintained a silence which, while it may appear stoical, is actually debilitating. Thus a particular effort has been made here to engage a wide cross section of priests who are working in different areas of ordained ministry including parish, chaplaincy and education.

While it might have been interesting to confine authorship only to priests, it is clear that the call to leadership in the church is inherent in baptism and that no volume on the church today would be credible without a contribution from the wider church. The experience and expertise of all who are concerned with living their Christian calling are indispensable to discourse, effective planning, administration and ministry.

The authors of the various essays have been engaged actively, in their different ways, in the processes that seek to address the issues that have arisen in the life of the Catholic Church in Ireland in recent years and which confront all Catholics, whether they regard themselves as 'practising', sceptical, estranged or hostile. These writers also reflect something of the diversity of opinion found in the Irish church today.

The Second Vatican Council urged Catholics to explore again the work of the Spirit in the early church and to be conscious of the ongoing presence of that same Spirit in the life of the church today. These themes have been reiterated many times but the pre-eminent sense is that Catholicism in Ireland has been quite theoretical about the type of renewal called for at the Council, while maintaining for all practical purposes a 'business as usual' approach in her general conduct and ministry. There remains a deep sense among many Irish Catholics that their participation in the life of the church is peripheral, while 'full' membership is somehow reserved for the ordained. So it is still common to hear people speak of the 'church' when they are actually referring to the hierarchy, the bishops in particular. The articles in the first part of this book reflect on some quite basic ideas concerning the life of the church. Paul Fleming considers the sacrament of baptism as the 'gateway to the whole Christian life' and the root of all ministry. Martin Tierney wants Catholics to have a deeper appreciation of what baptism calls them to and he is anxious that they do not settle for a minimalist or utilitarian approach to the sacrament: 'The vision of a Christian community is more than functional. It is environmental ... The goal of the church is not to have structures, but to have people who are living as Christians.' Nuala O'Loan reflects on the peculiar character of the Catholic Church in the North of Ireland where religious affiliation still plays an important part in personal and communal identity but where too, as in the South, there is a deep need for an expression of religious identity that is more rooted in the gospel itself. Joseph Briody, drawing on the scriptures, is anxious to reassert a particular vision of the ordained ministry.

Tom Layden discusses the implications of the common baptism which unites all Christians throughout Ireland. Christopher O'Donnell's raising of the issue of love for the church seems to touch upon something even more foundational. 'Love' of the church has an elemental character about it which O'Donnell firmly asserts must be rediscovered, not least through a renewal of the ordained ministry. Michael Router considers the need for a ministry to inactive and alienated Catholics in Ireland and proposes that an adaptation of the Rite of Christian Initiation of Adults (RCIA) may be appropriate.

Education has been at the very core of Catholic life for generations and the nation has benefited in no small measure from the church's commitment to it, especially when the state was not in a position to, or was unwilling to make the necessary provision. Niall Coll, aware of the realities inherent in a much more secular Ireland, reflects on the need to attempt a more convincing catechesis of both children and adults if sacraments are not to become mere rites of passage. In this respect Feidhlimidh Magennis argues for more developed models of involvement by the wider parish community in the catechesis of children at primary level with special concentration on chaplaincy. Concepta Conaty outlines the Home, School, Community Liaison Scheme (HSCL), a programme that strengthens links between schools, parents and the wider community. The programme addresses the needs of children and parents in areas of socio-economic deprivation and, for her, is an expression of the need to integrate gospel and life.

It has been widely accepted that the most focused catechesis in Ireland has traditionally taken place at primary school level but that it is weaker at second and third level. Breda O'Brien, writing on the needs of second level students, suggests that the church appears to have retreated to the upper room, 'hiding out, a bit afraid to be seen outdoors' and that consequently young people's spiritual hunger is not recognised or satisfied. Richard Lyng asks if there is any prospect that theology might emerge as a dynamic force in Irish universities and as part of adult faith formation. Seamus Murphy makes a plea for a courageous Catholic contribution to ethical and philosophical debate in the public square.

The final section of the book examines means by which the church might more effectively organise itself and seek to communicate its message. Paschal Scallon, aware of 'an emerging leadership among the laity' that is 'very determined', argues for a national assembly of the Catholic Church in Ireland in which all the faithful will assume greater responsibility in the life of the Church. Jim Cantwell surveys the history of the Irish Episcopal Conference, one of the oldest in the Catholic Church anywhere in the world. While the Conference is frequently the object of criticisms as an overly conservative, even regressive, institution, he argues that it has often been a perceptive and progressive force in the country. Máire Nic An Airchinnigh recalls her experience of the Women's Forum of the Dublin diocese and anticipates its further development as an even more truly credible body with women in Dublin.

The requirement for true dialogue among Catholics must see us develop the skills that make dialogue real. Dan O'Connell outlines a methodology that enables communities to organise and achieve effectiveness in the projects that they undertake. The skill of 'conversation' and the openness it demands is perhaps an ideal training to overcome a suspicion of the mass media that pervades many large institutions, especially the churches. Simon Rowe argues that the Catholic Church, confident in its own message, must enter the public square and be prepared for the exchange that takes place there.

The volume opens with a memoir written by Paul Andrews in which he recounts what it has been like to spend his life in ministry as the very ground on which he stood seemed to shift. Andrews was ordained in 1958 and while he remembers a 'Catholic' Ireland that has become an object of fascination, he is aware that even at the height of the church's influence, and perhaps because of it, people like his mother knew their own minds but chose to keep their own counsel rather than overtly challenge its heavy handedness. But while that confident and even forceful church has declined, he hopes that a church with a renewed sense of its calling is emerging. Irish Catholics, Andrews says, 'have learned to combine reverence and love for the church with a cool appraisal of its officials.' This is the church that now finds itself in a public square it does not control, but which has, nevertheless, resources in its faith and people to make itself heard. Its future will test the quality of its witness much more than the effectiveness of its work.

A Headier Drink:
Reflections on a Life in Priesthood

Paul Andrews SJ

First Blessing

Priesthood started for me on 31 July 1958. It had been a hot, stressful morning, that feast of Saint Ignatius. We had studied and prepared for this day over fourteen years and were up with the lark. John Charles McQuaid, then Archbishop of Dublin, arrived at Milltown Park punctually and quietly, creating around him an atmosphere of nervous awe. He muttered his way through the Latin ceremony of ordination. For us it was the third such ceremony in four days; in quick succession we had become sub-deacons, then deacons, and today was to be the priesthood. We were dizzy with dressing up, learning how to say the office, and keeping track of new obligations and rituals.

What a relief to escape from it all in the afternoon, and find my way alone to the Forty Foot for a swim. I left my new black suit on the rocks, and lost myself in the deep, crisp, clean sea, glad to leave behind the warm pieties of family and friends, and feel my body come alive. Best moment of all was to step out of the water and towel myself in the July sunshine, feeling the blood course through cold limbs.

The usual scatter of men were there, some friends, some strangers. As I stood there holding my towel, one of them came up quietly. 'Is it true you were ordained a priest this morning?' 'It is.' 'Then, Father, would you give me your blessing?' He knelt on the bare rock in front of me, I placed my hands on his head, closed my eyes and prayed over him.

When I opened my eyes, I saw a sight which, to this day, fills me with amazement. There was a little cluster of men waiting for my blessing. Some I knew, a drummer from a showband, a Dún Laoghaire grocer, a barrister from Cork. The rest were strangers. They knelt one after the other, and I laid my novice hands on them. There was no cameraman to catch the scene: one man standing, half a dozen kneeling on the rocks in the warm sunshine, all naked as fishes.

I still have photographs of the rehearsed and solemn rituals of the morning. But that remembered image on the edge of Dublin Bay is more precious. It was the alternative church of the nineteen-fifties, a group without power or pomp or clothes: six men with a touching innocence seeking the blessing of a new priest, as they might relish the crust of a freshly baked loaf, or the first glass from a bottle of new wine.

What remains from ordination day is not so much John Charles, the muttered Latin, the over-rehearsed rituals – all that was transient. What remains is the faith of those naked men, and the fact that I still live with that body. The day after ordination, at my first Mass in the company of family and friends, I was invited to say a few words. Some of you older readers may remember 1958. It was the year when Sean Lemass, God bless him, started to turn the Irish economy around, but we did not know it then. In the 1950s this was the island of the 'Vanishing Irish', depressed, without much hope of a future. The emigrants' boat to Holyhead was one of the few thriving businesses. And the clergy were powerful.

Clerical anti-clerical

I was joining the clergy, and I remember making two points to the guests at my first Mass: I am joining an unpopular caste and I hope I will not have to dress up in black for the rest of my life. Thanks be to God, the second hope has been fulfilled – priests have the freedom to dress as they did two hundred years ago before the Roman collar became a norm. As for the first remark, I was right – I was indeed joining an unpopular crowd. You may remember the time when on most mornings the front page of the *Irish Independent* reverently featured a bishop or priest making a speech or opening a school. That has changed; now almost any newspaper feels free to attack the majority religion and its repre-

sentatives. Now that Jews are no longer a safe target for journalists' latent indignation, they feel comfortable bashing the clergy.
As Yale professor Peter Viereck commented, 'Catholic-baiting is
the anti-Semitism of the liberals.'

You mature readers are not easily shocked or scandalised.
After all, there is a vein of anti-clericalism in all of us. I knew I
was joining an unpopular crowd because I often disliked the
clergy myself, and resented their power. One thing I liked about
the Jesuits whom I joined was that they vowed never to become
bishops unless the Pope personally commanded them to take
the mitre. St Ignatius wanted to protect his men from the car-
eerism which was corrupting the church of his day.

The household I was born into was reasonably God-fearing,
and I certainly owe a lot to my mother Christina for rearing me
in the faith. She was no church mouse. She had a cool, disen-
chanted view of the clergy, nuns and brothers. She left the
Loreto Convent in Omagh with an excellent Senior Certificate,
and while waiting to be called to the British Civil Service (the
year was 1914) she was invited to help out in a convent school
some forty miles from Omagh. To oblige the nun who asked her,
Christina went to the school and first explained to the 'Reverend
Mother' that she was awaiting a call from London, and might
have to leave at short notice. 'We will look after your keep,' said
the nun, and pay you £1 at the end of four weeks.' Mother was
put teaching German to the sixth year girls. She was accustomed
to the diligence of northern girls, and was appalled to find that
these laid-back students on the western seaboard had forgotten
by Tuesday all she had taught them on Monday. She found the
staff room a nightmare, crusty old harridans full of complaints,
who ignored the young one from Omagh.

During her third week in the school, she received word that
she was to report to Belfast for an interview the following
Monday. It was a huge relief. She approached Reverend Mother
and explained that she would have to leave early. The nun an-
swered briskly: 'Very well, Miss McAleer, so you won't be wanting your pound.'

Mother was not resentful, just intensely relieved that the ordeal was over. In family folklore it was a funny rather than an anti-clerical story; but it does illustrate the power of the institutional church, nuns and priests, in giving jobs and dictating terms. These people were doing a good job in their schools, and (nuns especially) at such personal expense, that one did not protest. Those who did protest, and walked out of the job, would probably find it hard to be employed in another church-run school. Anti-clericalism might run deep in one's blood, but it was dangerous to air it. Today, in an era of greater freedom, that danger is less, and it is not surprising that we wax indignant at the censorship and fear that characterised the church of our grandparents.

There was a strong vein of anti-clericalism in Jesus, and he was not afraid to give utterance. He denounced the Scribes and Pharisees who laid heavy burdens on others but did not move a finger to lift them themselves. He spoke of hypocrites, of blind guides, of teachers who cleaned the outside of the cup but left the inside filthy; who worried more about external observance of the law than about the movements in people's hearts. The clerical establishment of the Jews were furious, and in the end, on Calvary, they had their revenge.

So we have learned to combine reverence and love for the church with a cool appraisal of its officials. We, the people of God, are the church. As the Spanish proverb has it: 'We are the people and wisdom will die with us.' The clergy, religious and the bishops, have their part to play, and we need to keep them up to scratch. We are not astonished when we find traces of the seven deadly sins even in those who profess greater piety. All through the centuries the church has had this job of criticising and reforming itself. But critics today, like the Jews who surrounded the adulterous woman, need to heed Jesus' warning: 'Let the one who is without sin among you cast the first stone.'

A headier drink

Now forty-five years after priesting, I wonder what those years have done: the new wine has become a mixed drink, bitter-sweet. So many of the things I found objectionable in 1958 have changed for the better: for instance control and power. The informal alliance of clergy and state was so pervasive that we did not see it. There was a respect for priests and a holding back from them as being powerful and different, a caste apart. We have been gradually relinquishing non-priestly power. History had put it into our hands. We were educated, leaders in education and active in the national movement, useful in helping to build up an independent Ireland. We became used to exercising power in a way that was not always conscious. Police would be reluctant to bring an action against a priest even for a traffic offence. If people criticised us, we tended to write them off as enemies of the church.

The exercise of power distorted the priestly vocation. We ran practically everything, including football clubs, drama and youth clubs and charitable organisations. The collection-boxes on shop counters were predominantly for Catholic charities. Government committees on educational, health and social issues normally included, and were often chaired by, clergy – I chaired a couple myself. We were dominant in schools. This suited the state – through the religious an excellent education was available for peanuts. The flip side was that when the state moved into these areas, the church was sometimes loath to cede its dominant role. The change has taken a lot of power out of the hands of the clergy, and in the long run that has been a good thing.

The Outcast Caste
When you stop being a separate caste, you have the freedom to be more of a human being. Relationships become warmer. What was taken to be natural in a celibate existence was no longer felt to be natural by many priests. There is a difference here between diocesan priests, who often live an isolated existence, and religious priests for whom their community is an emotional support.

It was when I was away from community, as a doctoral student in England, that the issue became real for me. I fell madly in love with an English (devout Anglican) girl who worked with me and was untouched by the constraints that marked Irish girls in dealing with clerics (the girls in UCD in the 1940s used to say: You never look above a Roman collar). It was a straightforward struggle between my heart, which was singing with joy and poured itself out in poetry to Susan, and my head, which was quite clear that even apart from celibacy we would not be compatible. The memory is still tender and joyful, but after a painful retreat (on my part) we broke it off, remaining good friends.

Celibacy has become more of an issue because of the freeing up of priestly life. Priests are like other men, married or unmarried; they enjoy mixed success, and sometimes make fools of themselves, in living with the challenge of their own sexuality. Their failures draw more public comment than other men's. Though ministers of (any) religion constitute only 1.3% of all abusers of Irish children, the media perception is that they are dominant. The other 98% are hardly mentioned and are seldom sued for compensation.

The best evidence we have, in the IMS and SAVI reports, lists different groups of the population in terms of their danger to children. These are (in descending order, from the most dangerous to the least) strangers, neighbours, other authority figures, friends, acquaintances, uncles, baby-sitters, cousins, brothers and fathers of the victim, teachers, and behind them, in the lowest 1.3%, ministers of religion, which includes clergy of all churches and faiths.

To say this is not to minimise the scandal; it is simply refusing to exaggerate it. The betrayal of trust involved in clerical child abuse is scandalous, but not more so than the betrayal of trust in the majority of abuse cases, which is by members of the victim's family and household.

If people react savagely to clergy who have abused, they are angry in particular with the unspoken assumption that we are above reproach, holier than thou, and must not be accused. Those who have suffered from our power have relished saying to us, as Nathan said to King David: 'You are that man.' It is when we are criticised that we learn, and adjust especially our own image of our virtue.

Things that upset us

Conservative people see the church as a force for stability in society. In the French Revolution, the Italian Risorgimento, the Russian Revolution of 1917, the institutional church was not behind the red flag. Ireland was different; the rebels in 1798 and 1916 tended to be Catholics, often fervently so. The same is true in South America. The prospect of radical change in society pushes us all to the dilemma faced by Jesus.

He destabilised people, but was not a political rebel. He pulled people away from their trade, whether it was fishing, prostitution or tax-collecting. He pulled them from their families. But he was not a king, nor setting up any new hierarchy (as he told the sons of Zebedee). Rather he was dismantling our ego, rocking the comfortable sense of having an unshakable place in an unshakable society. Marriage at its best can do this, invading the other's ego. In marriage, as in teaching, you are regularly reminded of your shortcomings.

That sort of abrasion can be missing from the celibate life. There is no intimate Other to get under my skin, and emotional inertia can easily prevail. Small things can upset me, a strange bed, a blanket instead of a duvet, Little Chip instead of chunky marmalade, unexpected breaks in my routine, new work at which I do not shine, a new boss, losing the prospect of a holiday, being bad-mouthed. They break into my ego, destabilise me, show the limits of my inner freedom and the defences I erect to defend my way of being me. We can be grateful for these destabilisers.

The humbled church

At the time of writing, the church too is experiencing its destabilisers. We live under the Chinese curse: 'May you be born in an age of transition.' It was a fate familiar to the Psalmist and the Old Testament writers who were used to adversity, exile, persecution, irrelevance. St Luke, by contrast, writing of the beginnings of the Christian church, relished the signs of expansion. Forty years ago I lived in USA where the church was in an upbeat mood: forty million Catholics, one of them running for President. Like the man in the gospel with a rich harvest, they built bigger barns to house their riches, the young men with vocations.

In Ireland we have witnessed something analogous, not identical. Our big houses were built to supply educational, health and other services that the state now takes over. We have seen religious houses pass into other hands, and schools handed over (the FIRE committee, which I chaired in 1972, set up a useful blue-print for this handover). We pass them on with sadness, with their legacy of prayer, companionship and high standards. We show our vitality to the extent that we develop real poverty of spirit and can travel light.

It is a gift to be born into an age of dispossessing ourselves, with fewer large establishments and greater readiness to share others' lives. In a society, which changes rapidly, we still need monasteries to offer stability, religious centres that last; we treasure our Mellerays and Glenstals. The rest of us, the light cavalry of the church, should be mobile and carry small packs. We live on campsites. Let us pray for poverty of spirit to match our shedding of buildings and land.

Supervision and hyphenated priests
Priests in any line of responsible work – in parishes, schools, prisons or hospitals – need supervision. I do not mean more lectures and courses, but regular contact with an experienced friend who knows and challenges you. The notion that Father knows best is obviously mistaken. You can grow stale, hardened in your attitudes; and addictions like alcohol or sexual deviations can take hold of a man and blind him to reality. There are times when you must talk to a good friend who can sense what you need.

Much of my life was spent in education, as teacher and principal. Twenty years ago I retrained as a therapist, and moved into one-to-one work with young people and their families. People in training to be psychotherapists, and for years after they are trained, go every week to an experienced person who is called a supervisor, and seek advice about their work. My supervisor was a wise doctor called Michael. One day as I described my work with a 12-year-old boy, Michael interrupted: 'Paul, does this boy see you as his father or as his grandfather?' Once he had asked the question, I realised that the boy was relating to me as to a grandfather. It was an incisive question, not merely for the sake of that boy, but for my own readiness to accept my stage of life. It was the first time I had seen myself in that role, and it felt comfortable.

The new job raised the issue of the hyphenated priest: priest-psychotherapist, priest-administrator, priest-teacher. You have to ask yourself, what am I doing as a priest? Am I taking a job from someone else? Where you settle into a hyphenated existence, you take on the same supervision and professional ethics as your peers.

My job is to listen to people who are bound up and tormented in some way, and help them to the point where love can flow again. Whether they call themselves heathens, Jews, Catholics or whatever, where love is flowing, God is there. Freeing people to love and grow is to open them to God.

We are ordained to be in some sense leaders of people towards God. Most obviously this happens at Mass, the place of the priest's greatest privilege. Here we need to be at home in things spiritual, in reflecting on the scriptures in a thoughtful and careful way, opening the knowledge of Jesus to the people of God. I do not mean just grabbing texts and using them uncritically, but trying to understand what the gospels are saying to us. Reflecting on the scriptures, and translating them into the here-and-now of family life, industrial, political and social life, is central to priesthood.

Central also is the task of sharing work and handing over. A priest's priority is to delegate, to envisage how parishioners can play their part, and then carefully, diplomatically, persistently persuade them to come forward, enabling all the gifts of the parishioners to find a function in the community. If the church is to flourish with fewer priests, it will be through the faithful owning their own parish. Beyond that is the question: who is in the pews? People at the height of their physical and mental powers are often somewhere else. A priest's place is with them wherever they are, not running the show, as fifty years ago, but listening.

Love your enemy

We all know parishioners who look on the clergy as easily seduced into condemnations. I say seduced because there is a part of us that reaches for anger and indignation almost with a sense of relief. People expect us to 'tut tut'. They forget the story of the wheat and cockle: wait till the harvest. 'Your Father in heaven causes his sun to rise on the evil and the good.' It is not our job to eliminate all sin by coercion – that was the sin and illusion of the Spanish Inquisition.

I have been reading Peter Hebblethwaite's life of Pope Paul VI. He was living in an Italy which could easily have been taken over by the communists in 1948 (they had eight million voters). The Cold War was a large reality. When Paul, then Archbishop Montini, was helping John XXIII prepare for the Second Vatican Council, he found the Italian bishops wanted the church to do only one thing with the communists: condemn them. They were afraid that any appearance of softness would lose votes for the Christian Democrats. Paul faced down one such declaration in 1962: 'Throughout this document the communists are made to feel condemned and crushed by excommunications – nowhere are they seen as erring sheep. They experience our harshness, not our charity.' John XXIII remarked: 'There is no need to condemn errors; today people are condemning them of their own accord.' Sure enough, the communist empire showed itself a house of cards.

Jesus shows how to find goodness where others see only bad. The prime example is the father of the prodigal son. Once the boy has turned towards home, the father falls on his neck and throws a party. The party is not for the son or for the rest of the family. It is the father expressing his own joy; it is his party: 'there is more joy among the angels in heaven over one sinner ...' Jesus urges us to be perfect in this way, going the extra mile, generous to a fault. It is a counsel of perfection, rare in this world, but when it happens, God shows himself.

Light of the world

Light remains bright even if nobody is seeing it. There were times when the Irish church needed the metaphor of the light of the world, the city on a hill, for instance in Famine times, when it gave us an identity to survive misery; or in 1932 when we were establishing ourselves as a nation and seized the chance to show that we do exist and can run things (like the Eucharistic Congress) splendidly.

Now two things have changed: the culture of the country has grown more secular; and some bishops have been found to be covering up the crimes of priests. One result: we may be afraid to put our heads above the parapet, or even to preach the gospel, and when we do, we are liable to make fools of ourselves. Perhaps it is time for another image of the church: yeast in the dough, working for good even when unseen.

Yeast is a less attractive image than light. If there is anything of the exhibitionist in us, this image will discover it. Young priests and religious can feel sad that their initial ambition to serve is rebuffed. Jesus showed the same disappointment over Jerusalem, over Nazareth and his own people, over the rich young man. His commitment did not waver, though he offered an option to his disciples: 'Will you also go away?' Few of us could have improved on Peter's reply: 'Lord, to whom should we go? You have the message of eternal life.'

Diminuendo

The other end of life is a *diminuendo*, and it too deserves notice. One Christmas I stopped working in St Declan's, a special school where I had been director for eighteen years. Once the government gave me free travel, and started enquiries about the sort of pension I was due, it was clearly time to look to the future of the school. It is vital in any job to know who is your deputy and who is your successor. I was lucky and thankful that I could hand over to a good person, a younger Jesuit who was enthusiastic for the unpaid berth. (Alas, I buried him five years later.)

Anybody who steps out of a job like that knows that it is more than just a matter of changing your daily timetable. It can be disconcerting to find that the place you sweated for goes on without you as though nothing had happened. It takes a while to accept that if you do not get out of bed in the morning, nobody will be screaming. Wives who see their husbands (or husbands who see their wives) move out of a job, have to make their own adjustments. There are two people around the house all day, bumping into one another too much.

There is a sense of mortality. After the farewell parties, no need to guess what is next down the road. You are struck by the number of friends' funerals you are attending. Daily Mass becomes important, not just as a focus for the morning, but also as a meeting point with the Lord whom we will soon see at closer quarters. The prospect of the Beatific Vision is comforting though mysterious; I relish the goal but not the journey there, all that happens to the body in those last months and days. I would pray for a quick passing.

There is no need to be morbid, however. In the absence of any clear timetable for living and dying, we tend to look at family patterns. In my case they are puzzling. Do I resemble father or mother? My father died nine years below my present age. My mother, not much younger than he, had still one third of her life to live when she was left a widow. She decided to learn how to drive the old Morris Minor daddy had left her, but gave up when all her attempts to move it out of the back yard, shunting forwards, backwards or sideways, seemed to be blocked by walls. Instead she learned how to ride a horse, and be a good grandmother, and later a great-grandmother, and went through four more changes of house. When eventually at the age of ninety-three she went to the place prepared for her by the Lord, it was her thirty-second home since her marriage (all rented, except for a little flat she bought at the very end of her life).

They never felt like temporary campsites. They were secure bases, centres of life. St Paul wrote – and mother illustrated it – that we have not here a lasting city but seek one that is to come. But while we are here, whatever about the Beatific Vision, life is given us to live to the full.

So when I handed over St Declan's that Christmas, I managed to dodge the Irish winter and spend three months in parish work on the South Island of New Zealand. I had often dreamt of it, an empty land with marvellous rivers and lakes. It was better than my dreams. The sun and the people were equally warm and welcoming, and the trout were plentiful and wild, though not easy to catch. I found myself pastor of Twizel, a little (1500 people) town in the mountains, built round an enormous green space which was the playground for both adults and children.

That may seem like the perfect retirement dream come true. But my best-laid plans came unstuck when the old man's sickness, prostate trouble, hit me. It is one of the few bodily matters in which men have it harder than women. There are worse places to convalesce, however, than that sunny land, where life moves at an easy pace, and people have time to talk.

Retirement is a complicated mixture. You find that you are going to your friends' funerals, and the world and your job continue without you. You learn to enjoy the fact that no work is waiting for you. You have time to stand back from the businesses you worried about, and watch the younger generation with affection and sympathy. You grow used to the body's infirmities, which are not going to vanish. You are saved from cynicism by the wonderful communities, different from us in many ways, which flourish in other parts of the church and the world. You find that in spite of retiring from one job, you can still be useful to people. Whether you are closer to the cradle or the grave, the sun can still feel warm on your back, the lilacs still smell sweet, and God still speaks to you in laughter and the love of friends.

Jesus was never seventy

Under the Southern Alps, near the centre of New Zealand's South Island, the river Twizel flows into Lake Benmore across several miles of gravel and rounded river-stones. In this grey waste it links up with two other big rivers. In winter the valley is one raging swollen flood. In summer the three rivers, Tekapo, Twizel and Ohau, separate each into its braided stream, flowing sometimes ankle-deep, sometimes up to the waist.

The Twizel in particular holds big, powerful trout in this stretch, and one glorious mid-summer day I set out to fish it. I walked for the best part of a morning from the nearest road, sweating under the sun in shorts and T-shirt. The big round boulders under my runners tested my sense of balance. When I waded across smaller streams, the moss-covered stones were slippery as ice. As I slipped into water or onto rock, I had to ensure that my precious fishing rod suffered no violence in the falls.

By the time I reached the Twizel, I was hot and weary. The stream was crystal clear. Since the fish face upstream when feeding, I had to approach them from down-stream and cast the fly above them. I saw a large trout lying in the shadow of a bush, and cast a nymph above him. He cruised out, inspected it, but did not take. I tried him with it a second time, and again he came out to have a look, but again turned away. As quietly as I could, I waded to the bank and changed the fly to a green willow-bug, then cast again so that the fly floated down past the trout's shelter. Again he came out to look. I saw the white gape of his mouth as he took, I struck, and had him – not at once, because he struggled, danced and leapt out of the water. But twenty minutes later I had a five-pound trout on the bank.

It was only when I stood up with this extra weight in my bag that I felt the overwhelming fatigue of the day. I was delighted, of course. The march to the river had been worthwhile. But on the long walk back to the car, I stumbled and fell so often on the slippery stones that I began to worry would I make it. This sort of day lends itself to a peculiar sort of prayer. Part of it is possibly unworthy petition. 'Lord send me a fish – not by a miracle like St Peter, but one I can cast to and catch honestly.' My experience of that sort of prayer is not encouraging. But there is another sense of God that is less focused. You are alone in lovely country, conscious of God in nature around you and in your own heart and body.

At that stage I had not seen the Holy Land, but I suspected the Twizel valley resembled it: dry, hot, stony countryside. In that empty land you could imagine Jesus standing in a white robe, preaching and healing, strong and dynamic. At one stumble on slippery under-water boulders, as I tried to hold the fishing rod safe, keep the fat trout from slipping out of my bag, and regain my footing in fast-flowing, thigh-high water, I felt very old and un-Jesus-like. The notion hit me: Jesus was never seventy!

I can tell you, it was a comfort but also a puzzle. One of the attractive things about our picture of the Lord, is that he was, until the passion, at the height of his manhood. He could spend the day talking to the crowds and laying hands on the sick, then spend the night in prayer on the mountain. He walked great distances under hot sun. He could fall sound asleep in an open boat that was so tossed by the storm that his friends feared it would go under. He was alert in face of hostile questioners, always able to give an answer that enlightened both friend and foe. His appearance and touch were such that people longed simply to be near him. This was a man whose health, strength, energy and vitality roused admiration and love, as in the woman who cried: 'Blessed is the womb that bore you and the breasts you sucked!'

But he was never seventy. He never suffered the infirmities of age, stiff limbs, slow apprehension, failing memory, blunting of senses, tottering balance. As I dragged myself back to the car, I tried to remember a paragraph written by the aging John Henry Newman. I have looked it up, and here it is:

The greater part of our devotion in youth, our faith, hope, cheerfulness, perseverance, is natural – or if not natural, it is from an ease of nature which does not resist grace, and requires very little grace to illuminate. The same grace goes much further in youth as encountering less opposition – that is, in the virtues which I have mentioned. Old people are in soul as stiff, as lean, as bloodless as their bodies, except so far as grace penetrates and softens them. And it requires a flooding of grace to do this. I more and more wonder at old saints. St Aloysius or St Francis Xavier or St Carlo are nothing to St Philip.

I do not expect this angling story to comfort young people. But as I staggered back to the car, I slipped into a comforting conversation with the young Lord, apologising that I could not keep up with him. That thought brought me home.

Baptism: An Equal Share
in the Life and Ministry of the Church

Paul Fleming

From the earliest years of Christianity baptism has been an essential element in the Christian Church. Down through the centuries, however, the implications of it became obscured. It became understood as a ritual, which removed original sin and was necessary for membership of the church. Nowadays, however, it is understood to have a much deeper significance in that it is the sacrament which marks the beginning of a life of growth into the way of life offered to us in Christ. In its description of the sacrament of baptism, the *Catechism of the Catholic Church* (par 1213) states: 'Holy baptism is the basis of the whole Christian life, the gateway to life in the Spirit ... and the door which gives access to the other sacraments. Through baptism ... we become members of Christ, are incorporated into the church and made sharers in her mission.' In a subsequent paragraph (par 1268), the *Catechism* elaborates on this statement when it identifies how the baptised share in the mission of the church through participating in Christ's threefold function of priest, prophet and king, and in paragraph 1270 it elaborates further when it states that the baptised 'participate in the apostolic and missionary activity of the People of God'. This article will focus on baptism as the root of ministry. It will begin with a short overview of the biblical evidence found in the New Testament concerning ministry in the early church, and then proceed to look at a selection of church teachings on the topic from the time of the Second Vatican Council up to the present day. In conclusion, some thoughts will be offered on what I see as some of the difficulties which prevent baptism from fulfilling its true potential as the root of all ministry.

Ministry and the life of Jesus

There is no shortage of books on the topic of ministry in the church today. Many of these books contain a section where they present an overview of key aspects concerning ministry as described in the New Testament. In these overviews attention is often drawn to two central issues: firstly, ministry as understood from an analysis of Jesus' own life, and secondly, ministry as it developed in the years immediately after the death and resurrection of Jesus. One of the clearest reflections on ways in which Jesus exercised his ministry is penned by William Rademacher, an American theologian who has written extensively on ministry and pastoral initiatives. He identifies six types of ministry in which Jesus was involved. He prefaces his comments on these six ministries by reminding the reader that Jesus was not a Jewish priest, 'so we have to be careful that we do not view the ministries of Jesus through the image of the Old Testament priesthood or even through that of today's priesthood' (Rademacher, 13). He suggests, rather, that Jesus' ministries can best be understood in the context of Jesus being a prophet (like the Old Testament prophets who challenged the value systems of the religious establishment) and a servant (not just in the context of the Suffering Servant of Deutero-Isaiah but also in the context of the servant who ministered to the needs of others).

The first ministry which he identifies is that of healing. Rademacher sees the healing ministry of Jesus 'as one of the first and most important ministries Jesus undertook'. In his healings Jesus confronts the evil of sickness – and the healings are a dramatic sign of the presence of the kingdom of God.

Another dramatic sign of the presence of the kingdom is the second form of ministry identified by Rademacher – the exorcisms performed by Jesus. Permeating the kingdom message of Jesus is the notion that the coming of the kingdom is a time of salvation from evil; and Jesus' ministry of exorcism was a clear manifestation of good confronting evil.

The third mode of ministry by Jesus which Rademacher identifies is Jesus' teaching ministry. It is clear from the synoptic

gospels that Jesus himself saw teaching as an essential feature of
his ministry – in Luke's gospel it is recorded, 'I must proclaim
the good news of the kingdom of God to the other cities also; for
I was sent for this purpose' (Lk 4:43). Throughout the gospels
there are references to Jesus teaching (cf. Mt 4:23; Mk 6:6; Lk 6:6;
Jn 7:14); he is referred to by others as a teacher (cf. Mt 22:16; Mk
12:14; Lk 20:21); and he instructs his followers to continue his
ministry of teaching (cf. Mt 28:20).

The fourth type of ministry considered by Rademacher is
Jesus' reconciling ministry. This reconciling ministry has a dual
purpose: it is to reconcile people with God and also reconcile
people with each other, and reconciliation comes about through
forgiveness. God's willingness to be reconciled with the sinner,
as seen, for example, in Jesus' parable of the prodigal son in
Luke 15:11-32, must be mirrored in people's relationships as
well, as seen in Jesus' directive, for example, concerning offering
gifts at the altar in Matthew 5:23-24.

Linked with this ministry of reconciliation is Rademacher's
fifth form of ministry, which describes Jesus as peacemaker.
Jesus' desire to offer peace to his followers is made explicit in
John's gospel when, in his final discourse, he says 'Peace I leave
with you; my peace I give to you' (Jn 14:27), and when he appears to them as a group after his resurrection his first words to
them are 'Peace be with you' (Jn 20:19). This peace, which Jesus
offers, embodies the whole biblical notion of *shalom* which indicates a state of perfect harmony between all creation and the cre-
ator, or in New Testament terms the fullness of the kingdom of
God.

The sixth and final form of ministry that Rademacher identifies is Jesus' liberating ministry. The focus of this ministry is
again indicated by Jesus himself when, at the start of his public
ministry in the synagogue in Nazareth, he reads from the text of
the prophet Isaiah which talks about proclaiming liberty to cap-
tives and release to prisoners (Is 61:1), and Jesus then states:
'Today this scripture has been fulfilled in your hearing' (Lk
4:21).

From this overview of the six types of ministry presented by Rademacher one overarching theme can be identified which links them together: the making present of the kingdom message. Rademacher admits that it is not his aim 'to reduce the ministries of Jesus to exactly six' and goes on to say that 'we could understand Jesus' ministries as one ministry with six aspects' (Ibid 19). What Rademacher does provide, though, is a systematic overview of the key elements of ministry as exercised by Jesus – and if we accept these as the key elements of Jesus' ministry, then they must form the basis of ministry for the follower of Jesus.

Ministry and the early church

When we come to consider ministry in the early church, the best descriptions of ministry are offered by St Paul in Romans (12:6-8) and 1 Corinthians (12:4-10). Certain observations can be made about the various types of ministries identified by Paul. In the long list given in 1 Corinthians it is clear that all these varieties of ministry are gifts of the Holy Spirit. To this extent they are dynamic, filled with the power of the Spirit. It is also important to note that in 1 Corinthians 12:7 Paul states 'to each is given' – this implies that ministry is something which all share. Also worthy of special note is the fact that while these lists are extensive, they are most likely conditioned by time and place and the particular situation which Paul is addressing. Consequently, because they are gifts of the Spirit, allowance must be made for development of other gifts.

While it has been stated above, on the basis of 1 Corinthians 12:7, that ministry is something which all share through being gifted by the Spirit, and Paul (1 Cor 12:4) groups these varieties of ministry under the three titles of gifts/charisms, services, and activities, it is also worth noting that in 1 Corinthians 12:28 he prioritises certain ministries. In that text he identifies three specific ministries: those of apostle, prophet and teacher. It is important to note here that Paul's use of the term apostle does not just refer to those who, in the gospels, were specially chosen by

Jesus and known as the Twelve. The term also applies to those sent by their local church communities to preach the gospel message in the early years of the church. As for those described as prophets and teachers, Paul himself states that those who prophesy 'speak to other people for their upbuilding and encouragement and consolation' (1 Cor 14:3). Furthermore the teachers appear to be individuals who were involved in explaining the truths of the Christian faith.

While Paul does identify these three specific ministries, their significance must not be isolated from that of the whole range of ministries identified by him. The need to keep this wider range of ministries in focus is emphasised by Thomas O'Meara, a leading Dominican theologian based in the University of Notre Dame in the United States:

> These three activities – external evangelisation, preaching and assembly leadership, and teaching – formed the core of many communities. New Testament lists, however, show other ministries and they should not be neglected nor shunted aside: ministries of healing, of consoling, of serving those in need. Perhaps Paul implied that these are arranged around the core ministries, but all are charismatic ministries. (O'Meara, 70)

In this context it is also worth noting that while Paul does identify core ministries, he locates his descriptions of ministry side-by-side with his description of the church as the body of Christ. Thus in Romans his description of all as members of the one body (Rom 12:4-5) precedes his description of the different gifts, and in 1 Corinthians (12:12-26) it comes between his description of the wide range of spiritual gifts and his description of those who have particular roles. This juxtaposition of these two aspects of Paul's ecclesiology highlights how interrelated they are. James Dunn, an English author and New Testament scholar, emphasises the essential link between Paul's understanding of the nature of the church as the body of Christ and his understanding of how all share in ministry: 'In short, ministry in the Pauline churches belonged to all, and each depended for his life within the body of Christ not just on some special ministry of a few, but on the diverse ministries of all his fellow members' (Dunn, 111).

In concluding this overview of the understanding of ministry as presented in Paul's writings in Romans and 1 Corinthians it is worth referring to what O'Meara calls the three characteristics of primal ministry ('primal' in that it is the closest we can get to the original ministry exercised in the earliest years of the church). The first of these is that 'Christian ministry is not sacral office' – rather it is something new which is not restricted to a holy place or a holy time, but it is something which takes place among people in the midst of the community. Secondly, 'Christian ministry is action that is service to the kingdom of God' (O'Meara, 74-76). Here O'Meara stresses that the essence of Christian ministry is that it is something active, and involves much more than just being given some title or office. Furthermore, it is based on the example of Jesus whose primary task it was to inaugurate the building of the kingdom. And finally, 'Christian ministry is universal and diverse.' Paul's writings emphasise the diversity of ministries within the local communities, but these individual communities are part of the bigger community of the wider society, and it is this wider society which is also the focus for the spread of the gospel.

This overview of the understanding of ministry as seen in Romans and 1 Corinthians indicates that in the early years of Christianity ministry was viewed as something which was radical and varied. It was radical to the extent that it was based on the example of Jesus himself who placed service at the heart of his ministry, and it was varied in that it was dependent on the power of the Holy Spirit working through individuals to address a whole variety of needs which existed in the early communities. In subsequent years the understanding of ministry was to become more institutionalised – and as the church spread aspects of institutionalisation were necessary. On this development O'Meara comments:

The prominence of some fulltime ministries (their names and

descriptions differed from church to church but a ministry of leader was present) was necessitated by the expansion of the community. As the first century came to a close, central professional ministry, especially that of leadership, was moving (perhaps unconsciously) many *charismata*/services to the edge of the ministerial circle (Ibid 92).

The development of the fulltime ministries, mentioned above by O'Meara, eventually lead to the tripartite structure of *episkopos* (overseer/bishop), *presbyteros* (presbyter/elder) and *diakonos* (deacon). This development took place at different stages and at different speeds in various parts of the ancient world where Christianity was becoming established. In the Acts of the Apostles (Acts 20:17-35) we see the leaders of the church in Ephesus being referred to as elders and overseers. As numbers increased, and more complex structures of administration developed, the focus for leadership became the individual overseer/bishop, with the presbyters/elders and deacons being seen as his assistants.

Along with this institutional development came also the development whereby bishops and presbyters were understood as having a particular priestly function. Because Christians lived in a world surrounded by all sorts of cults with priesthoods, it was believed that they would benefit from having their own priesthood. However, this development of the priestly function as an integral part of the role of bishops and presbyters was not a wholesale adoption of Jewish priestly practices – nor was it based on an understanding of priesthood as found in the various pagan cults of the day. Rather it was centred on the model of Christ as priest, and in particular his actions at the Last Supper. This is borne out by the fact that it was in the celebration of the eucharist that the bishop and presbyter exercised their priestly function in its fullest manner. From the fourth century onwards, the concept of priesthood became centred on individuals who presided at the eucharist. Ministry became intrinsically linked with sacred duties, and the priesthood of the faithful (referred to in 1 Peter 2:9) and the varieties of ministry mentioned by Paul in

Romans and 1 Corinthians, became relegated to biblical terms with no practical significance in the life of believers.

The Second Vatican Council

The Second Vatican Council was the twenty-first general or ecumenical council of the church. The two previous councils – the Council of Trent (held during three phases between 1545 and 1563) and the First Vatican Council (1869-1870) had been called to deal with crises in the church. When Pope John XXIII, on 25 January 1959, announced his intention to convene the Second Vatican Council he made it clear that its aim was not to be defensive or apologetic, but rather to facilitate spiritual renewal, consider the role of the church in the modern age, and to promote the unity of all Christian peoples. One of the most significant issues to be considered by the Council was how all the baptised share in the life of the church.

It is true to say that during the nineteenth century lay associations had been developing in some European countries, especially Germany, France and Italy. These associations aimed to provide support for Catholics who wanted to remain loyal to their faith, but were faced with increasing pressures arising from the growing secularisation of society. Overall, however, the Catholic Church was still very much a clerical church, with a firm emphasis on the church as institution with a clear hierarchical structure. *The Dogmatic Constitution on the Church (Lumen Gentium)*, issued by the Second Vatican Council on 21 November 1964, was a key document from the Council which aimed to move away from this image of church and highlight baptism as the key sacrament which enables all to be seen, equally and fully, as sharers in the mission entrusted to the church by Christ.

From an historical perspective it is interesting to trace the development of *Lumen Gentium*. The early drafts of the document still reflected Counter Reformation ecclesiology which understood the church as primarily institution – and there was still an emphasis on clericalism and juridicalism. No one can dispute the fact that if the church is to function effectively within the world then it must have structures and lines of authority. Yet at the same time one must remember that the church is not just like any other society or group. It consists of people on the way to their final goal which is the completion of the kingdom of God. Under the guidance of the Holy Spirit the community of the faithful moves towards this goal. Too juridical an understanding of the church can leave little room for the dynamic of the Spirit and the flourishing of the charisms which are the gift of the Spirit.

During the debates on Chapter 2 of *Lumen Gentium*, Cardinal Léon Suenens, the Archbishop of Mechlin-Brussels in Belgium and a very prominent contributor to the discussions at the Council, appealed that this idea of the variety of charisms within the People of God be emphasised, and also called for their importance for the life of the church to be recognised (Küng, Congar and O'Hanlon, 29). The Cardinal admitted that, in line with the teaching of scripture, charisms need to be monitored – but such monitoring should not be seen as something which is of its essence negative and obstructive; rather it should facilitate the growth and development of charisms in the church. This positive emphasis was so clearly in line with the theme of renewal which permeated the Council that the main aspects of Cardinal Suenen's submission were to be reflected in the final draft of *Lumen Gentium*: 'Whether these charisms be very remarkable or more simple and widely diffused, they are to be received with thanksgiving and consolation since they are fitting and useful for the spiritual needs of the church' (*Lumen Gentium*, Article 12, par 2).

The final draft of *Lumen Gentium* was to reflect the significance and importance of understanding the role which all the baptised share through being part of the People of God. The Council's teaching on the People of God is contained in Chapter 2 of *Lumen Gentium*. The fact that this chapter comes before any consideration of the roles of the clergy (in Chapter 3) and the laity (in Chapter 4) highlights the importance of baptism, because it is through baptism that all share in the priesthood, the prophetic office, and the kingship of Christ. Article 10 of Chapter 2 is of particular significance in this context: 'The baptised, by regeneration and the anointing of the Holy Spirit, are consecrated as a spiritual house and a holy priesthood, that through all their Christian activities they may offer spiritual sacrifices and proclaim the marvels of him who called them out of darkness into his own wonderful light.' Later in Article 11, when discussing the effects of the various sacraments, *Lumen Gentium* states even more explicitly how baptism is at the root of all Christian activity:

> Incorporated into the church by baptism, the faithful are appointed by their baptismal character to Christian religious worship; reborn as sons and daughters of God, they must profess publicly the faith they have received from God through the church.

It could be argued that the word 'ministry' is not used explicitly in this section of *Lumen Gentium*. Yet, at the same time, it can not be denied that the Council's teaching on the use of charisms and the effects of baptism implies a service to the gospel which is public and focused on the building up of the kingdom of God – the task which was at the core of Jesus' ministry, as highlighted earlier in this article.

The Vatican Instruction (1997)

In August 1997 the Vatican issued, in Italian, an instruction concerning the collaboration of the lay faithful in the ministry of priests. The English translation, entitled 'Instruction on certain questions regarding the collaboration of the non-ordained faithful in the sacred ministry of priests', was issued by the Vatican on 13 November 1997. It is interesting to note that the English title is not a direct translation of the original Italian, with 'non-ordained faithful' being used instead of 'lay faithful', and the word 'sacred' being added to describe the ministry of priests. No explanation is given for these alterations, nor by what authority they were made. The Instruction is of relevance for this

article because, in the second major part of the document entitled 'Practical Provisions', Article 1 deals with the need for appropriate terminology.

In this section the Instruction addresses issues concerning
confusion about the term 'ministry'. It quotes (Article 1, §1) from
Pope John Paul's speech at the symposium on lay participation
in April 1994. The Pope accepts that the term can be used of the
lay faithful because by their work they continue the mission and
ministry of Christ in the church and in the world. He also draws
attention, however, to the fact that the use of the term can cause
some confusion:

> For some time now, it has been customary to use the word
> 'ministries' not only for the *officia* (offices) and *munera* (func-
> tions) exercised by pastors in virtue of the Sacrament of
> Orders, but also for those exercised by the lay faithful in
> virtue of their baptismal priesthood ... It must be admitted
> that the language becomes doubtful, confused and hence not
> helpful for expressing the doctrine of the faith whenever the
> difference 'of essence and not merely of degree' between the
> baptismal priesthood and the ordained priesthood is in any
> way obscured.

It is interesting to note that *Lumen Gentium* itself uses the term
'ministry' to describe how all share in the life of the church (see
par 4 no 1 and par 32 no 3), and in the Apostolic Exhortation
Christifideles Laici (published on 30 December 1988, twenty-three
years after the ending of the Council) that the Pope himself
refers to 'the ministries, offices and roles of the lay faithful' (par
23). In this context it is worth noting that during the Synod,
which preceded the publication of *Christifideles Laici*, there was
actually discussion about the use of the term 'ministry' and its
appropriateness for describing the participation of the laity in
the mission of the church. Commenting on these discussions
Peter Coughlan, an English priest who worked as Under-
Secretary of the Vatican's Pontifical Council for the Laity, and
was involved in worldwide consultation before and after the
1987 Synod on the Vocation and Mission of the Laity, states:

It was evident both from the interventions at the Synod and from the language groups that there was not a full consensus among the bishops as to the way forward in the area of ministries. Some wanted to restrict the word 'ministry', for example, almost entirely to the ordained ministry. Others pointed out that the term had been used in papal documents in relation to the laity, that it is in widespread use in many languages and expresses a good and positive reality, and that an attempt to reverse this usage would at best be misunderstood (Coughlan, 76).

Despite certain reservations as expressed by some bishops, the Pope, as noted above, did use the term. However, as also noted above, six years later he urged caution concerning the use of the term in situations where it could undermine the functions proper to ordained priesthood.

Conclusion

From the above it is clear that, within sections of the magisterium of the church, there is a certain hesitancy about the term 'ministry' being used in an unqualified sense when describing how the laity participate in the life of the church. Some prefer to use the term 'lay apostolate'. But this term also creates difficulties. To participate in an apostolate means to share in the work of the apostles – and this is the role of the bishops in the church today. To talk about a 'lay apostolate' implies that the laity somehow share in the work of bishops, by carrying out tasks assigned to them by bishops. The laity share in the mission of the church in their own right by virtue of their baptism – not by dint of performing tasks delegated to them by bishops or anyone else.

Church authority seems content to use the term ministry when it refers to tasks carried out by laity in a liturgical setting. But even here there is an anomaly. At Mass we can rightly refer to Ministers of the Word, but when we come to describing those who assist with the distribution of the eucharist we find the interesting appendage 'extraordinary' added to their title of Ministers of the Eucharist. According to the 1997 Vatican

Instruction (Article 8, §1 and 2), the 'ordinary' minister for dis-
tributing the eucharist is a bishop, priest or deacon – and extraordinary ministers should only be used when there are not
enough ordained ministers available. One can not but ask the
question as to why lay people can, and rightly do, proclaim the
Word, but can only be 'extraordinary' when it comes to distrib-
uting the eucharist – especially when we believe that it is the
same Christ who is present in the word and the eucharistic
species (see *General Instruction on the Roman Missal*, Chapter 2,
Article 33).

In many parts of the Catholic world more and more pastoral
tasks are being entrusted to the laity. In some, if not many cases,
this is because of the increasing shortage of priests. If this is the
only reason for enabling lay people to become more actively involved in the life of the church, then this is most unfortunate.
There is no doubt that the shortage of priests in parts of the
Catholic Church is something which needs to be addressed. But
the ministry which all the baptised share is theirs by right – and
not just something which can be acknowledged when there is a
need to plug gaps in parishes.

What is facing the church is a great opportunity to build
upon and implement the insights gained, under the guidance of
the Holy Spirit, during the Second Vatican Council concerning
baptism as the sacrament which makes all members of the
church equal sharers in the ministry of the church. The Council
clearly identifies baptism as a sacrament which implies much
more than just the removal of original sin and membership of
the church. As has been seen earlier in this article, baptism in the
early church opened one's life to the influence of the Holy Spirit
who granted a wide variety of gifts and charisms which empow-
ered the early church in its daily life. The workings of the Spirit
at the Second Vatican Council guided the participants to return
to the biblical basis of Christian life. The opportunity presented
to the church at this time involves a twofold challenge. Though
the insights gained at the Council were published in *Lumen
Gentium* in 1964, there is still the challenge to make all the bap-

tised more aware of their responsibilities as equal sharers in the
life and mission of the church. The second challenge is for
church authorities to recognise the gifts given in the sacrament
of baptism and to set in place structures which will facilitate the
baptised in exercising their ministry. The noun ministry comes
from the verb to minister; to minister means to help, to serve, to
look after. This is the task entrusted by Christ to all his followers
as we work together to help build the kingdom of God.

Select bibliography
Coughlan, Peter, *The Hour of the Laity*, EJ Dwyer, Newtown, 1989
Dunn, James, *Unity and Diversity in the New Testament*, SCM
Press, London, 1977
Küng, Hans et al, *Council Speeches of Vatican II*, Paulist Press,
Glen Rock NJ, 1964
O'Meara, Thomas, *Theology of Ministry*, (ed.), Paulist Press,
Mahwah NJ, 1999
Rademacher, William, *Lay Ministry: A Theological, Spiritual and
Pastoral Handbook*, St Paul Publications, Slough, 1991

Some Reflections on the Catholic Church in Northern Ireland today

Nuala O'Loan

Introduction

'The church's task in each country is to make of each country's individual history a history of salvation' (Romero, 21). This was Archbishop Oscar Romero's vision of the work of the church, a vision for which he lived and died. I have been asked to write about the Catholic Church in Northern Ireland today. My primary assumption, therefore, is that membership of the Catholic Church is ultimately about salvation and this is most essentially, and all of the time, about loving God and loving one another; that it is about trying to contribute to a fairer distribution of the world's wealth; about unselfishness. This essay is a reflection on the role and contribution of the church in Northern Ireland in the light of Romero's vision. I will attempt to answer the question: to what extent do we, the church in Northern Ireland, live as Christ called us to live? Is the experience of those who encounter us an experience of love and generosity and caring, of communion? Or is our church merely a place to be visited at intervals in the discharge of some vague social/religious function which is predicated upon the fact that, in the words of James Joyce, 'heaven's my expectation'?

There can be little doubt that the Catholic Church in Northern Ireland is facing one of its most difficult and sensitive periods at the present time. It is above all, however, a moment of purification. It is a grace filled moment of opportunity in which our church is laying aside the pre-occupations with status and worldly things and is coming, painfully, back to a place which will be very different from what has been, but in which we will follow the Way and the Truth and the Life more faithfully. We know that there is no decline in the numbers of people professing to be Catholic at the present time. This is quite clear when one looks at the data. The evidence is clear that the numbers are actually increasing (although there are a number of factors which impact upon census data, not least the hunger strike of 1981 which led to a significant level of people not completing census forms) However the actual figures are as follows:

Census Year	1961	1971	1981	1991	2001
Total Population	1,425,042	1,536,065	1,532,196	1,577,836	1,685,267
Number stated Catholics	497,547	477,921	414,532	605,639	678,462

It is not for me to judge the other 678,461 people who gave their religion as Catholic in the 2001 census, but I think it is clear that there are, among them, those who do not participate to the fullest extent in the church here. That so many people still refer to themselves as members of the Catholic Church is surely significant. They could describe themselves in other ways.

Between 1961 and 1981 the Catholic Church in Northern Ireland was powerful, strong and united; its strength perhaps most publicly stated when hundreds of thousand of people travelled south to see Pope John Paul II when he visited Ireland in 1979. Recent years, however, have seen change on a scale which must have been unimaginable to those who worshipped in the Catholic Church at that time. Change on a similar scale has occurred in society as a whole in Northern Ireland, and it is in the context of that picture that the state of the Catholic Church today must be viewed. Some of the changes are generic – cultural, educational, societal changes which are common to the whole of the Western world.

A traumatised church

There are other changes, however, which have taken place in Northern Ireland, which have not mirrored those which took place in the rest of Ireland. For the past thirty-five years the Catholic Church has operated in the midst of the political and constitutional chaos, the pain and the confusion which have been peculiar to Northern Ireland. During that period over 3,665 people died as a consequence of the Troubles, approximately 50,000 were injured. Many will carry the scars, mental and physical, of their suffering to their graves. The place in which the Catholic Church in the North finds itself today is a different place from that occupied by the Catholic Church in the South of Ireland or in the rest of Europe.

As the rest of the Catholic world was embracing with enthusiasm (in many cases) the teaching and learning of the Second Vatican Council, Northern Ireland was plunged into civil unrest. As priests and people across the rest of the Catholic world sought to apply the principles of Vatican II in their ministry and their worship, Northern Ireland found itself attempting to do so in a maelstrom of death, injury and fear. Death and injury were meted out savagely and terribly by those on both sides of the divided community which comprised Northern Ireland. There was no safe place – churches, schools, hotels, cafes, bus stations – all the normal places in which people live and eat and have their being became the target of the terrorists. Inevitably people retreated into their own communities, becoming divided in a way which has proved to be as damaging as it is inexplicable. Our Christian churches are divided too. Ecumenism is a reality, but it is limited and fragile in the North. We have yet to find real ways to reach out in response to the call 'that they may all be one'.

Between 1969 and 2001 3,665 people died in the Troubles. 1,238 of them were civilian Catholics; many of them died at the hands of other nominal Catholics. Republican paramilitaries were responsible for the deaths of 2,148 people, Loyalist paramilitaries for 1,071 deaths, the police for 50 deaths and the army for 301 (McKittrick et al).

This level of carnage, but particularly the killing by Catholics of Catholics in such a small community, must surely have had an impact on the heart and soul of the church itself. It has been said that 'both political and religious indifference in an inner city context can be a mask that hides the alienation and anger of those who do not perceive themselves to be economic or cultural stakeholders in society' (Cassidy et al). In addition to their economic and cultural isolation, many of the people of Northern Ireland have been wounded and traumatised by the events of the past 35 years. It is most probable that their trauma, with all its inevitable consequences, has impacted negatively on their ability to believe in the God of love, to whom they prayed 'deliver us from evil' and to whom they cried out in their anguish 'My God, my God, why have you forsaken me?'

It is possible also that it is not only the relationship with God which has suffered through these years. The human relationships of love and trust, which lie at the core of Catholicism, have been fractured by terrible violence on so many occasions.

There have been many examples of situations in which Catholics have seen their neighbours beaten, shot and murdered as 'touts' or as 'collaborators'. They have seen thousands of people exiled by their own community. They have been unable, through fear, to console the bereaved or wounded. In 1972 a woman called Jean McConville knelt at the side of a dying British soldier. Within weeks she had been abducted by the IRA in West Belfast and taken away from her ten young children, whose father had only recently died. She was murdered and for over thirty years her children tried to find her body. After the discovery of her remains she was finally laid to rest in 2003. On the day of her funeral doors remained shut in the street, people stayed indoors, children were kept inside, most of her own community was not involved. This fracturing of normality, in all its complexity, goes to the heart of what it is to be a Catholic in Northern Ireland today.

The reality was therefore that there was a traumatised people living in the midst of great violence, whose religion called them

to peace and love, but for whom daily life presented many conflicting experiences and emotions. The call to be a Catholic is not
an easy one; it is not easy to forgive, as we are called to forgive,
those who have inflicted such terrible suffering. It is not easy to
love those who hate. It is easy to reach out in healing and compassion to our brothers and sisters of other Christian faiths who
have suffered also, but it can be difficult to understand the hatred
which leads to sectarianism on all sides of the community. Not
only did Catholics die at the hands of fellow Catholics, but they
also died at the hands of Protestants simply because they were
Catholics. Similarly Protestants died at the hands of Catholics
simply because they were Protestants. The rest of the world was
bewildered, mystified at this conflict in which Christians killed
each other because they were Christians. So, in some ways, were
the people of Northern Ireland. The current position of the
Catholic Church in Northern Ireland must be seen in the context
of all these conflicting and contradictory realities.

There is one other matter in the context of the Troubles which
is, I think, critical to any understanding of the position of the
Catholic Church in Northern Ireland today. The role and contribution of the priest, in terms of ministry, during the Troubles
cannot be overestimated. As the shattered victims of murder,
bomb and bullet sought to deal with their situations they
turned, in their pain, to their church and to their priests for support and solace. That support was there for them. As the various
paramilitary groups fought for supremacy with each other and
with the security forces, priests were called out to inform the bereaved of the death of a loved father, mother, son or daughter; to
anoint the dying; to conciliate between those at war. The acts of
burying the dead and visiting the sick and consoling the bereaved brought people together. Priests risked their lives to
anoint the dead and dying, to negotiate with those involved in
armed struggle to try and secure peace. Day by day they walked
the Way of the Cross with those to whom they ministered. The
toll on the clergy was great – two priests were shot dead in
Belfast, many others carried their own burdens of injury and

mental pain. People recognised and valued the courage and commitment shown by these men.

At this difficult time the church articulated clearly the relationship between violence and poverty. Cardinal Cahal Daly identified succinctly the context in which the violence emerged:

> If one were to place side by side maps illustrating the various indicators of deprivation and poverty on the one hand, and the incidence of acts of political violence and politically motivated street rioting and disorder, on the other, the degree of correspondence between the two would be glaringly evident. It was beyond doubt that no political or security measures to overcome violence could have a hope of succeeding without an attack on the social injustice and inequalities which produced an environment conducive to violence. It is when politics fail to promote justice and equality of opportunity that violence steps in to fill the vacuum (Daly, 244).

Despite recognising the great injustices which the people were suffering, the church in Northern Ireland was vehemently opposed to violence – of that there can be no doubt. The message to the men of violence was clear and unequivocal:

> I appeal to these people in God's name to turn to Christ the Lord and to learn from him the meaning of true justice and the way to a just peace ... to learn from Christ that love is the secret weapon of the only revolution that really works. Violence continues because we, all of us, fail in so many ways to turn our lives towards Jesus Christ, to be converted ... You have every reason, religious, moral, rational and political for calling off your campaign now (Ibid, 414).

There was a period during which people of all denominations clung together with their churches in trying to survive the Troubles. Inexorably, all that has changed.

The church at the beginning of this time was authoritarian and structured. It seems to me that there were more certainties. The local church was the local community. People went to church very regularly. If they did not, their neighbours would note the fact! Sacraments were celebrated, people were born, got married and died within the community of the church. Entertainment in the form of dances and sports were provided by organisations like the GAA and the parish boxing clubs. The movie portrayal of the Catholic priest with the blackthorn stick hunting young couples from the bushes back onto the dance floor is not altogether a caricature. Many will remember the parish priest who did not fear to dictate how his flock should live their lives. People sought guidance and counsel from their priests. They were more content to be led, advised and, on occasion, dictated to by their priests. Priests wielded huge power in the community, and their attitude to their parishioners, in particular their women parishioners, seems to have been learned in seminary. The notion of women as 'an occasion of sin' now seems bizarre, but it did seem part of the thought process of some of those who ministered.

Changing loyalties and conviction
All that has changed beyond recognition. Changing patterns of thought, greater independence, opportunities to travel and to see ways of living across the world have all altered the relationship of people and church. There has been the emergence of new understanding in relation to matters of social justice, environmental responsibilities and human sexuality. The impact of documents such as *Humanae Vitae* was enormous. It was known that the document published by Pope Paul VI was not the document recommended to him by his advisors, both lay and clerical. People began to challenge the teaching church in a way hitherto unknown. The church did not respond in a hearing and reflective way to those challenges. It became split. Priests, the traditional leaders, had different views and the faithful became less blindly faithful. Traditional thinking was no longer universally accepted. The old larger families have virtually disappeared. Traditional church teaching on marriage is observed less. Young people live together in partnership quite happily. The authoritarian rule of the church in these matters, which had been the

experience of previous generations, has quite simply become irrelevant to many of those who had been born and brought up in
the Catholic Church.

So where is the church now? Forty years after Vatican II and
after thirty-five years of troubles, the church in Northern Ireland
is no longer powerful, strong and united. There is clear evidence
that congregations in many urban parishes are decimated.
Where once they believed that they were committing a mortal
sin if they did not go to Mass on Sunday, they no longer, for the
most part, believe in mortal sin. They certainly do not believe
that they are damned because they do not go to church. The importance of the community of the church has been diminished
by new societal structures and people no longer relate out of a
sense of duty to the church. It is also the case that people go to
community workers and advice centres for help, in circumstances in which they would formerly have turned to the
church.

This reduction in the numbers of those engaging with the
community of the church has been experienced across the
Western world. It was probably inevitable, and it could be argued that it derived from the fact that church membership was
often as much a social as a religious process. Where social out-
lets could be found elsewhere, one of the aspects of engagement
between people and church became less important to the people. Social life still occurs in community, but most often it does
not occur in the community of the church. Equally important
however, is the fact that people have learned to challenge those
who sit in authority over them. This applies as much to the
church as to their doctors, dentists and lawyers. Concepts such
as 'openness' and 'transparency' and 'accountability' are part of
the vocabulary of governance wherever governance occurs. We
live in a world in which it is acceptable to challenge those in
authority, and to call them to account for their stewardship of
funds, for the manner in which they exercise their authority, and
even for their pastoral outreach. Priests are seen much more as
another set of professionals doing a job for which they are

responsible. It seems to me, however, that the institutional church does not have the comprehension, the language or the mechanisms to engage in the necessary dialogue. This is, however, but another opportunity.

The next vital question concerns the extent to which the traditionally Catholic people of Northern Ireland are a people who currently acknowledge the particular call to holiness which is inherent in Catholicism. Surveys have shown that people generally still believe in God and religion. Their practice has clearly changed, though not to the extent of the change in practice in England and Wales and in the rest of Ireland. Mass attendance in many rural areas remains high. The journey of the remains of St Thérèse of Lisieux through the North in May 2001 attracted thousands of people. The devotion and fervour were almost palpable. Packed churches are still a reality, particularly at Easter and Christmas. Parents continue to bring their babies for baptism even though many of them are not married within the church. Children are still presented for first confession, first communion and confirmation.

Significant numbers continue to send their children to Catholic schools, although the popularity of integrated schools is increasing. Catholic schools, particularly the Grammar schools are under pressure to achieve the best results. It has been the case that the desire to get the best academic results has led to a few occasions on which the much vaunted Catholic ethos of the school, with all that that means, has been abandoned and they simply admit those children whose academic ability is not hampered by sickness and other medical conditions. Our young people recognise this when they see it, and harm is done. Above all Catholic schools must value children for all their skills and talents, their strengths and their weaknesses. That is what the call to holiness in education is about.

There has been huge change in the number of people marrying and in the way in which they marry. Weddings were once relatively modest affairs. Those who married rarely owned their own home and part of the early experience of marriage was to

build the home together. That has changed. Weddings, according to media reports, now cost an average of £14,231 each in
Northern Ireland. Once the decision to marry is made, the
preparations are lengthy. It is not uncommon for a couple to
spend two years planning a wedding. Getting married is a complex and expensive process. Big business has identified significant money-making opportunities. Couples still want to marry
in church, but the flowers which they bring to the altar and to
adorn the church are, on occasion, removed after the wedding
and taken to the reception. Preoccupations with dresses, photo-
graphers, cars, appear in many cases to be the dominant concerns. What is happening? Is it ritual observance? Have baptism
and first communion and even weddings become merely rites of
passage in which to dress beautifully and take lots of photographs in a wonderful setting?

It is at the time of death that people still relate most strongly
to the church. The process of dying, and of burying the dead and
consoling the bereaved, is still largely conducted within the
church. Other forms of community life have not provided the
answers to the needs of the bereaved.

Despite all this, across Northern Ireland large numbers of
people still attend Mass daily, and large numbers receive communion on a regular basis. City centre churches still attract significant numbers at lunchtime Mass, especially during Lent. The
older generation still holds on to what it knew prior to Vatican
II. Corpus Christi processions still occur. Little girls still scatter
rose petals before the Blessed Sacrament, and Cemetery Sundays
still bring the people of the parish together. Exposition of the
Blessed Sacrament still occurs in many parishes, and even on occasion Benediction. Prayer groups are common, and organisations such as the Apostolic Work and the Society of St Vincent
de Paul still operate effectively across Northern Ireland.

In the context of the other sacraments, there has been great
change too. Confession, once a weekly event for many Catholics,
is no longer part of many people's religious practice. Twice yearly,
however, penitential or reconciliation liturgies attract huge

numbers. Hundreds of individual confessions will be heard in the space of an hour or so by up to a dozen priests, most of whom sit openly in the church to meet those who seek reconciliation. There is music and prayer, candles and even exposition of the Blessed Sacrament. It is a very different experience from the long queues which formed in cold, quiet churches in the past. Parish missions still occur in some churches. Events such as the Clonard Novena continue to attract thousands of people. Pilgrimages to Knock, Lourdes, Fatima and other places form part of many parishes' agenda during the year.

A time to change
The church in Northern Ireland remains a clerically dominated church. Parish structures and practices are for the most part unchanged since Vatican II. The expectation following that Council was that there would be change. I have noted above the absence of the structures necessary to enable communication and dialogue to grow community in the church. Yet the Code of Canon Law provides for the creation of Diocesan Pastoral Councils, which would, if created and allowed to be effective, provide the necessary mechanisms (canon 511-514). The function of such councils would be 'to study and weigh those matters which concern the pastoral works in the diocese and to propose practical conclusions concerning them.' There was an expectation, too, that parish councils would be established, to share responsibility for the spiritual life of the parish. There was an equal expectation that lay people would be involved in more pro-active ways in the life of the church. Over the years there have been repeated calls by both people and priests and religious for the establishment of a synod, first at diocesan level and then at national level, which would bring together the people of God. Little of this has happened, and even where it has there is little communication to the people of what is going on. This is no longer a sustainable position. We need mechanisms through which we can enter into dialogue with each other, learn, explore realities and ensure that the vital reality of the gospel is not lost, and that the church is relevant and engaged with its people where they are.

Something has happened also to the concepts of priesthood and of religious life as vocation. The numbers entering the seminary to train for the priesthood have fallen dramatically over the past ten years. This year, however, has seen an increase as twenty-two young men entered Maynooth to train for the diocesan priesthood in Ireland. Convents are closing across Northern Ireland as the number of sisters declines and their age increases. Where once the figure of a robed nun was a common experience it is now a rare sight. There are very few priests and nuns still at the helm of our schools. Many of our children will never meet a religious sister or brother. Many meet priests only on rare occasions. The potential for loss of vocations is obvious. Priests and religious over the years were role models for those who might follow them. We need people prepared to dedicate their lives to God. Our church will be a poorer, sadder, lonely place without them. It is good, therefore, to see that the North is home to a new monastery, established by Benedictine monks in Rostrevor.

The church will have to address the issue of compulsory celibacy for the clergy. That debate must occur in a wider context which contemplates the role and formation of the priest, his (or her?) lifestyle needs and the understanding of priesthood which lies behind the celibacy requirement. While valuing the courage and commitment of those who answer the call to serve God in celibacy, we need to consider also those who might offer themselves to minister as priests, but would not commit to life-long celibacy. We need priests and religious. They play a special part in our life as church. We need the sacraments. We need people whose love for God is visible. We need people to study and understand the Bible, to communicate the Word of God to us in all its richness. We need leaders who are servants, and we need, each of us, to become servants to one another. We face a future in which it appears that we will no longer have access to priests and to sacraments as we do today. It is not clear whether the people of God have grasped this reality. We must.

Much damage has been done by the clerical sexual abuse

scandal. Although there were very few cases of sexual abuse by priests in the North, the impact of them was massive. The perceived betrayal of trust inherent in the ways in which the church dealt with the early allegations of clerical sexual abuse has alienated many people, especially the young. The authority of the institutional church has been much diminished also by the actions of men like Michael Cleary and Eamon Casey. The reality is that as a church we have had to face the fact that priests are men of clay and not gods, and that much of the theology of the *'alter Christus'* which gave them a status beyond that of ordinary men was a false theology. As a church we had come to see our clergy as *'dominus'* rather than *'Christus'*, master rather than servant. Parochial houses were often the largest houses in an area despite the fact that they did not house a family, but were occupied for the most part by one or two men. Bishops lived in 'palaces'. At one stage we even genuflected and kissed their rings. It is good to see change in these matters and change is occurring.

We currently have a diocesan church which relies for its effectiveness largely on the priests of the diocese and on their individual energy levels. Those energy levels appear to be diminishing at an alarming rate. The reasons for the reducing morale, the diminishing energy levels are many. The people of God still tend to make huge demands on their clergy. We expect them to be available twenty-four hours a day. We expect to be able to call on them at times of sickness and death. We are accustomed to a level of service which is not sustainable. Parishes which used to be run by three or four priests still provide seven or eight Masses over the Saturday night vigil and Sunday. The problem is that there may be a couple of priests now and some of our serving priests are very old, in their late seventies and eighties and still working. This level of service clearly cannot continue. There will not be the priests to do the work.

In Britain, the United States and elsewhere, it is increasingly common to find three or four parishes are now grouped together and served by one priest. This has not happened in Ireland yet. It is surely vital that an audit be done of where the church is in this context. The information is available to the bishops and priests, but it must be shared with the people. The people must come to understand that there must be a reduction in the number of Masses and other religious occasions, and that care must be taken of our priests to avoid, where possible, exhaustion and burn-out. In so doing it is not suggested that we should pray less, merely that we should be prepared to come together in larger numbers with the same frequency. We must face reality and take responsibility for our church. We must pray for, encourage, value and care for those who answer the call to priesthood, to religious life and to other ministries.

Working together in the church
There is great energy in the ordinary people of God if a way could be found to channel that energy for the church. There is a strong core of people who still believe and belong, and want to be part of the church in a way in which membership is currently not possible. There are those who could make significant contributions to the administrative and financial affairs of parishes. There are options available in terms of grouping parishes for administrative purposes, which would allow efficiencies of scale in the employment of staff.

There is also a huge need to reaffirm the value of voluntary work as part of the Christian calling. It is necessary to contradict the modern philosophy that only that which is paid for is of value. It is equally necessary to assert that the contribution to the welfare of others really is a Christian duty, and that we must be prepared to give to others, even when it involves cost to us in terms of time and energy. It is not enough simply to donate to charity and assume that thereby we have discharged our obligations as Catholics.

In simple matters such as membership of the church there are practical difficulties. The church has been slow to come to terms with the level of marital breakdown and its consequences. Its pastoral care has not been adequate. Marriages break down for a thousand different reasons – some of them should never have taken place at all, others fall victim to the pressures of poverty, unemployment, alcoholism and drugs. The laws and processes of the church are inadequate. It is not uncommon for an application for an annulment to take eight years to process in the North. Those caught in this twilight place, waiting for the declaration which will give them the right to full practising membership of the church and to a new partnership (if that is what they seek), will in many cases be wounded by the length of time which they must wait. They will become marginalised by the church itself.

A person who wanted to become a Catholic and wanted to know who to talk to, would probably have a difficulty unless they knew someone who was already a Catholic and who could point them in the right direction. Unlike our Protestant friends, our churches are, for the most part open all day. We can go and pray in God's house. It is one of the great blessings of being a Catholic and it is something we should cherish. We should also make sure that the details of our priests are clearly displayed, together with an indication of reasonable hours during which they can be contacted, or some other indication to those who might wish to know more about the church about what they should do.

There are changes too in the way in which we live and work. People often work in one parish and live in another. They are mobile. They may want to choose in which church they pray. They can do this, but they are not permitted to be formal members of a parish unless they live within its geographical boundaries. They may not participate in the election of the Parish Councils. They may not be members of Parish Councils. They may participate in parish activity, but will find themselves excluded at regular intervals. The reality is that our structures are outdated, and that those who come to pray in our churches should be welcomed and should be encouraged to participate fully – they should never be excluded.

A time of hope

So where lies the strength of the church in Northern Ireland today? How can it be energised and revitalised? To answer this question I believe we must look back into our history, and identify clearly what the role and function of the church is. The buildings are, of course, important – we need a place which is God's place and in which we can 'visit' and pray. As houses of God those places should be as beautiful as possible, warm and full of light, places which are conducive to prayer. They are not, however, the most important thing: what is most important is the individual relationship of each member of the church to God, and their relationship with one another as a community. The two sets of relationships are the key to the life and being of the church. What is happening in Northern Ireland today is not unique. It has happened at many stages throughout the history of the church. We are at a time and in a place where we must set aside the irrelevancies, the materialism, the false gods and re-focus on what is real. It will not be easy but it will happen.

I will conclude this article with an account of an incident which occurred in a small Catholic town in the North a couple of years ago. A young man in that town was accused of having sexually assaulted someone. The local 'community justice' people intervened and he was sent out to walk up and down the main street wearing a sandwich board proclaiming his 'crime'. No-one dared intervene. Eventually someone rang the local curate who got into his car, drove down the street, collected the young man and took him home to his mother. At the moments of greatest darkness there are always those who respond as Christ would have done. This is what that priest did. I recount this event because it shows that the church in Northern Ireland is still a vital part of people's lives, still capable of responding, still courageous. The challenge for us, the church today, is that we should all respond as Christ would respond in all our interactions. We must be as Christ was. Then our history will be the history of our salvation.

Select Bibliography

Cassidy, Eoin G. (et al) *Belfast: Faith in the City,* Veritas, Dublin, 2001

McKittrick, David (et al), *Lost Lives: The Stories of The Men, Women and Children who Died as a Result of the Northern Ireland Troubles,* Mainstream Press, Edinburgh, 1999

Romero, Oscar, *The Violence of Love,* The Plough Publishing House, 1998

Love of the Church

Christopher O'Donnell O Carm

The First Vatican Council (1869-1870) is best remembered for its decrees on the papacy and infallibility. It intended to give a full exposition on the church, but the outbreak of the Franco-Prussian war put paid to that. The Council had to be suspended. Just as well, some would say. The documents on the church that had been prepared were neither exciting nor innovative; indeed they were similar to the preparatory work for Vatican II's document on the church, which was swept away after an assault by bishops such as Alfrink, De Smedt, Lercaro, Montini and Suenens.

But Vatican I did have one remarkable statement on the church. It is found in the document on faith. The council was dealing with the intellectual grounds for belief. Recognising the difficulty of faith, it proposed a solution: the church guarantees revelation.

> To the sole Catholic Church belong all the manifold and wonderful endowments that by divine disposition are meant to put into light the credibility of the Christian faith. Nay more, the church by herself, with her marvellous propagation, eminent holiness and inexhaustible fruitfulness in everything that is good, with her Catholic unity and invincible stability, is a great and perpetual motive of credibility and an irrefutable testimony of her divine mission. Thus, like a standard lifted up among the nations (see Is 11:12), she invites to herself those who do not yet believe, and at the same time gives greater assurance to her children that the faith which they profess rests on solid ground. (*Dei Filius,* chap 3)

This text has surely a bitter-sweet taste today. Things have changed and one might not today be so ready to draw people's attention to the church as a motive for credibility. As the text above has it, 'nay more,' the traditional value of love of the church is not at all easy.

Difficulties

There are many reasons why people today will not easily resonate with an appeal to love the church. There have been many scandals, the most publicised being sexual crimes against minors. There has also been shameful activity of bishops in these islands, in Europe and elsewhere. Priests and religious have contributed even more to the church's dishonour in concealing wrongdoing from fear of scandal. Scandals invoking deviant sexuality and money are more public reasons why many people have lost respect for the church. One might hope that in a new climate of honesty, public confession of crimes and misdeeds, as well as appropriate reparation, the church will emerge purified and a good deal more humble.

But there are deeper problems that may prove to be still more intractable. The mentality of society has changed profoundly. We are now in a postmodern age, with a harsh secular climate, in which institutions, and not only religious ones, no longer command respect. There is widespread cynicism about political and social institutions. When we look at popular perceptions of the Catholic Church we find an anti-Roman feeling. The central bureaucracy of the church, the Vatican, is seen often as repressive, intrusive and unloving. Its declarations are frequently judged as ill-timed, poorly expressed, harsh or irrelevant. The birth of feminism in the 1960s and 1970s has allowed people, especially women to see a new side of the church, a deep-seated and far-reaching patriarchy. The sheer maleness of the church's structures is felt as extremely oppressive.

History may well see 1968 as a decisive moment in the church's history. Before then there were many people who disobeyed church law, sometimes with a sense of guilt, sometimes not. But with the publication of the encyclical on marriage,

Humanae Vitae with its paragraphs on contraception, a huge number of people – priests, theologians and laity – were prepared to say that the Pope was wrong in his teaching. This was a huge breach in the church's authority, a Rubicon was crossed. Papal teaching was henceforth open to widespread criticism; it did not even enjoy a presumption of truth, as many people approached it negatively.

A very serious problem is the attitude of media in Ireland where one encounters contempt and even hatred of the Catholic Church. A result is that whatever pertains to the church tends to be presented in the worst possible light. The media would reply to this charge by claiming that they are objective and truthful, cutting through decades of church obfuscation and authoritarianism.

What church?

In all of this one might ask, what church are we talking about? There are about ten meanings of the term 'church'. It can be a building or a community of believers, local or universal; it is an institution with authority figures; it is a people on pilgrimage; it is the Communion of Saints comprising those on earth, those undergoing purification and the blessed in heaven; it is People of God, the Body of Christ, the Temple of the Holy Spirit; it is the first stage of the kingdom. Love of the church will have a different complexion depending on which of the above is foremost in mind at a particular time. But one can say that difficulties in loving the church are mostly connected with the church as seen in authority figures – pope, Vatican officials and bishops – in clergy and religious. Ordinary believers are generally left alone by media commentators – seen perhaps as simple and misguided with no real future. So for our purposes we look mostly on love of the church especially in its institutions, whilst not neglecting the whole people.

In our time it is appropriate to reiterate the theme of love of the church. It is also necessary to see how such love can again be possible and the role of the church's ministers in the reinstatement of this love.

A traditional theme

Love of the church has been a value that was unquestioned by most Catholic faithful. It is hard to argue one's way out of the implications of the text in Ephesians in which we find teaching on marriage and the spousal nature of the church:

> Husbands, love your wives, just as Christ loved the church and gave himself up for her, in order to make her holy by cleansing her with the washing of water by the word, so as to present the church to himself in splendour, without a spot or wrinkle or anything of the kind – yes, so that she may be holy and without blemish ... For no one ever hates his own body, but he nourishes and tenderly cares for it, just as Christ does for the church, because we are members of his body (5:25-2:29-30).

Here we find an uncompromising demand that there be genuine love within marriage, and the model of such love is Christ's love for his Body, the church. We cannot avoid the realism of the Pauline teaching about the Body of Christ. The church is his Body; he is its head. In human terms we would not see much future for an engaged couple if the man or the woman said to the other, 'I love your head, but your body disgusts me.' Likewise we cannot assert that we love the head of the church and hate the body. No doubt the body is flawed, but it cannot be rejected.

The theme of love of the church can be seen as an extension of the universal theme of mutual love taught by Christ: 'love your neighbour as yourself' and 'a new commandment ... love one another as I have loved you' (Mt 19:19; Jn 13:34). The letter of John develops this further: love of God cannot be authentic unless we love one another (1 Jn 2:10-11; 3:11-19).

In Christian tradition there are many images that imply the duty of loving the church: Mother, People of God, Temple of the Holy Spirit, Queen, Bride, and many others. There is, however, the difficulty that such images may appear vague and remote. The challenge is to love the real church; one cannot really love an abstraction. The real church is at local level: priests and laity in the parish; it is the bishop, clergy and people in the diocese; it is the pope, bishops and laity throughout the world. It is people and it is institutions that operate through people. Love of the church involves loving persons whom we may not like. Prejudice, racism and hostility make love difficult. The very name or the office of an individual may immediately cause hackles to rise. But Christian love, if genuine, cannot exclude anybody, even if they are sinful, unattractive or misguided.

An impasse

The present dilemma is easily stated. One the one hand, there is a Christian obligation to love all, and this includes the church and its members; it is the Body of Christ and we have to love the church, just as Christ himself loved it. On the other hand, there are serious blockages that prevent or hinder people from loving the church. One might speak of an impasse.

It is not enough to snort that people should love the church. This would be further negativity and a repetition of the very attitude that has turned many from the church. There are many important steps that must be taken before people can be at ease with the church.

If we look deeper at the present reality we can judge that love of the church is in decline. But before what we might call an impasse, there has been a loss of respect and trust of the church. These have led to a very negative perception. We are very familiar with the effects of downbeat observations. If I am turned off some person for a particular reason, I will usually not stop there with the annoying feature; everything else about the person can begin to annoy me, and I tend to put a negative construction on anything they do or say. Indeed I can be so negative that I resent somebody else praising a person whom I hold in distain.

So how to get out of the impasse? If a wall blocks our way, we can attempt to demolish it. That would be the equivalent of telling people who find love of the church difficult, that they are wrong and they should straighten out their thinking. It is rarely useful to attempt the demolition of what constitutes an impasse.

It is far better to get around it. In our somewhat tortured image of an impasse, however, it is not just the wall that blocks, it is many other kinds of clutter, some of which we must get rid of before we can successfully negotiate the impasse. There are many things lying around, rubbish of various kinds that can obstruct our progress.

Negative clutter
The church's message for our society is radical and complete. It is one preached for two thousand years: love, forgiveness and conversion. In the memory of us older people the church has indeed taught these values. But the approach was rather paternalist and authoritarian. We were told what to do and often threatened with divine punishment if we disobeyed. But the message was still valid.

There are good arguments for holding that the heart of the church is the eucharist. Here we have the paschal mystery of the death and glorification of the Lord celebrated. At Mass we invoke the Holy Spirit on the gifts and on the community so that the people, along with the bread and wine, may be transformed into the Body of Christ. At Mass there is a union of heaven and earth, with both concerned for any people who need purification after death. At the liturgy the Communion of Saints (holy persons and holy things) is dynamic. Where else should we look for the meaning of the church, the meaning indeed of our lives?

If we take these two assertions of the central values taught by the church and its heart the eucharist, we can see that in many people's minds they evoke negative feelings. Church teaching is demanding. To live a Christian moral life in society, in family, in business dealings and in recreational activities is very challenging. It means that we have to say no to many things superficially attractive. Love and fidelity in marriage at times come at a high price in terms of generosity and sacrifice.

People remember that they were told about the obligation to attend Mass, under pain of serious sin. Today the quality of celebration varies from place to place, at times meaningful and beautiful, at times appalling or inept. If we add to this picture authoritarianism it is easy to see why people are not attracted to Mass or to the teaching of the church.

We have what might be called 'clutter'. By this we mean all the negative features that surround the genuine values and gifts that the church has for society. It is not enough to tell people what to do. The Archbishop of Dublin, Kevin McNamara, who could never have been described as a flaming radical, often said that the church needs to explain its teaching very carefully, so that people are helped to accept it. Instead we were often offered unadorned teaching frequently cast in negative terms. The tone can be rigid, even dictatorial, so that people are immediately turned off.

In liturgy we have similar problems. Some priests take great care of their role in celebrations, so that they give the impression that they really believe and respect the mysteries they hold. But elsewhere, bad liturgy has done untold damage. Here again we have clutter that blocks the way to people entering into, even enjoying liturgy: poor celebration, hectoring and ill-prepared homilies. When one goes around the country and sees what people are exposed to in their parishes, one can sometimes be amazed that there are still people who worship in their local churches at all.

Ministry as removing clutter
Given the structures of the church that exist it is up to those who are involved in ministry at every level to take care to lessen the negative features of the church today. We do not have women priests. It is then surely important that those who are priests be sensitive in their language and avoid everything that might smack of paternalism or male hegemony.

In liturgy we need higher standards. In teaching we need new approaches. Church pronouncements are too often marked by a serene neglect of presentation. One might think of the way that the motor industry sells cars. They are insistent that if we buy their model, it will be good for us; indeed advertising in-

vokes a pseudo-salvation. If you drive the latest, your life will be
changed, and you may have romantic experiences – really, can
you afford not to drive this model? Vatican statements are much
more like communication between car manufactures and car
dealers: unadorned facts. They are not customer orientated.

When we have dealt with clutter, that is a whole collection of
lesser blockages, then we can eye more clearly the impasse of
our times. The church's ministers must continue to seek forgiveness for serious crimes and to ensure greater transparency in
their handling of problems.

Seeing the church anew

One of the difficulties of our time is that the church is not seen as
having relevance in our society. We are in the strange situation
of the church having much to offer our world, but it is not seen
in this way. One of the deepest problems of consumerism is not
excess in possessions, but the mentality, which says simply, 'I
want.' And if something is not attractive or does not seem ad-
vantageous to me at this time I ignore it.

Does our society need the church? Has the church a value for
today? If we survey a week of newspapers, looking only at national news, we can see a fairly bleak picture: about one murder
and one suicide per week; nightly violence in cities and towns,
drink-driving, crime, drugs, binge-drinking at an ever earlier
age, sexual deviance, personal and corporate greed, and con-
stant spinning by politicians, trade and professional groups, not
to talk about deceptive and manipulative advertising. These are
all things that damage our society.

We can sense helplessness in the face of these negative facts
in our society. Some will speak of longer prison sentences; others
of a need for other forms of judicial censure or punishment.
Indeed there are social conditions behind much crime. Though
much has been done, there is further work for statutory and voluntary agencies.

But in the end social and economic solutions will not suffice.
The church has wisdom from Jesus Christ. The only way for-

ward lies in conversion, in a change of understanding, of vision and of behaviour. One might wonder how to help society with the church's message. Many of those engaged in such crimes and evil behaviour may indeed not be regular churchgoers. They may well not be open to advice from the church, especially if they are called to change their values and actions, and turn to ways of generosity and love.

Ministry as confident humility

The church has been through a hard time. But if, as we have said, society desperately needs the church's message of forgiveness, love, healing and the person of Jesus Christ, we cannot go and hide. An image that might make sense is of a child who has been bold, or a dog that has done damage in the owner's absence. Both are very quiet, hoping not to be noticed. Then gradually they get courage. It is now time for the church to emerge and recover morale.

The pride of church ministers has been damaged. Now is the time to speak with a new humility. This humility must be marked by genuine New Testament boldness, such as the apostles had in proclaiming the resurrection. The new means will be an offer of humble service, sharing good news because we are convinced that society needs it. The church cannot again risk arrogance in imposing its view. It must seek to convince by the strength of its arguments and the attractiveness of its teaching.

Such confident humility might go a long way to establishing once again respect for, and trust in the church. In the past we might have presumed on being trusted and respected. Now, however, these have to be earned. If trust and respect can be recovered, then people might again look on the church with compassion. It is the very weakness and sinfulness of the church that can evoke such compassion. It cannot be demanded or presumed.

Still no matter what people in the church will do or say, there will be others who will continue to reject it. People may be cynical and still continue to hate the church, seeking to undermine it, celebrating its failures with *Schadenfreude*. So be it, even if some of those who are most critical are, in their own way, no less arrogant than the churchmen they decry.

Paul: a ministry for love and healing
At this time when respect, trust and love for the church are difficult we can look to the church's ministers for a recovery. It will not be in terms of the pedestal on which the church was placed and was pleased to occupy. It will be more like the ministry of Paul who continued in fidelity against the opposition he encountered in Corinth. We can read chapters two through six of the Second Letter to the Corinthians as a model for Christian ministry. Each element points to vital features for a renewed ministry that will enable the church to recover its proper role in our world. We can outline them:

A triumphant ministry (2:12-17) Christians ministers spread the aroma of Christ: 'we speak as persons of sincerity, as persons sent from God and standing in his presence.'

A commended ministry (3:1-6) Ministers depend on the divine Spirit: 'Not that we are competent of ourselves to claim anything as coming from us; our competence is from God ... the Spirit gives life.'

A ministry of splendour (3:7-18) The ministry is one of glory transforming into Christ: 'The Lord is the Spirit and where the Spirit of the Lord is, there is freedom ... seeing the glory of the Lord are being transformed.'

An honest ministry (4:1-6) Relying on God's mercy, ministers avoid discouragement: 'We have renounced the shameful things that one hides; we refuse to practice cunning or to falsify God's word; but by the open statement of the truth we commend ourselves to the conscience of everyone in the sight of God.'

A tried ministry (4:8-18) Though persecuted ministers do not lose heart: 'Yes, everything is for your sake, so that grace, as it extends to more and more people, may increase thanksgiving, to the glory of God.'

A courageous ministry (5:1-10) Having been given the Spirit ministers look towards heaven whilst being committed to others: 'So we are always confident ... for we walk by faith and not by sight.'

A reconciling ministry (5:11-21) Ministers are urged on by the love of Christ and are a new creation: 'Christ ... has given us a ministry of reconciliation ... we are ambassadors of Christ ... be reconciled to God.'

A suffering ministry (6:1-13) Ministers of Christ put no obstacle in anyone's way: 'As servants of God we have commended our-selves in every way through great endurance, in afflictions, hardships, calamities ... by purity, knowledge, patience, kind-ness, holiness of spirit, genuine love, truthful speech and the power of God.'

It is only then that Paul can say to the Corinthians: 'Open wide your hearts' (2 Cor 6:13).

If we present Paul here as giving as it were a charter for min-istry today, and the way which will allow people to respect, trust and love the church, we are not suggesting something new. At all times there have been ministers working quietly who dis-play this Pauline paradigm for ministry; there have been coura-geous public figures who have died in and for such ministry. But we can say that the perception of the church in past decades has not been of such service. A new style is needed in ministry.

Beauty

In the past the church relied on the truth of its message. Preachers knew that Christian teaching was right and was good for people, so they expected to be heard and obeyed. In our time this approach will not work.

Recent theology has rediscovered the theme of beauty. What is beautiful attracts and pleases. There is so much Catholic teaching that is beautiful, but it must not be enforced solely by authority and in terms of obligation. Let us take the Mass. Yes, Catholics should gather for Mass on Sunday. But why? The wonder of the Mass is the strange beauty of Calvary leading to the triumph of Easter. It is that God became man to reach the deepest human degradation out of love, that he remained loving in spite of torment, that he surrendered his life for those who hated him. It is the mystery of Calvary that can give meaning to our whole lives. We need the values of the Mass, the teaching of the church for the sanity of our society.

If the Mass is seen in its deepest beauty, then questions of the celebrant and his inadequacies will be less damaging. If the supreme religious experience for a Moslem is the *hajj,* the once in a lifetime sacred pilgrimage to Mecca, what should the wonder of the Mass mean to Catholics? Faith in the Mass, and in other Christian truths is not something forced on us, eliminating our sense of inquiry. It is rather allowing ourselves to be drawn by wonder and beauty into life-giving and enriching truth.

In our time people speak of a spiritual hunger. Contemporary spirituality is like a bazaar with many offerings: self-improvement, Wicca, New Age, new movements, Celtic druidism, not to speak of hosts of eastern ways of life. The church meanwhile is sitting on a treasury of mystical experience, which is capable of refreshing the human heart and of giving profound meaning to life. We need to expose the beauty of this heritage and offer it widely to people. The beauty of the church's mystics can draw people into profound transformation of their lives and values.

Vatican I again

Can we return to that tantalising text of Vatican I that might seem so distant from present perceptions of the church? It is still true, and always has been. But we must look more profoundly at the reality. The church has had problems with the heritage of Constantine, which glorified it and allured it with secular values. We can read the Vatican I text and think of worldly splendour and the church radiant with baubles. But where this text is still alive is in the hearts of simple people, in the poor, the struggling, the marginalised, the people who continue to struggle with faith. These are the ones who show 'eminent holiness and inexhaustible fruitfulness in everything that is good.' In the lives of simple believers we find 'a great and perpetual motive of credibility and an irrefutable testimony of her divine mission.' In the past we looked at structures; now we should look at people. It is ordinary people who can convince others who struggle 'that the faith which they profess rests on solid ground'. Many among missioners, voluntary workers, contemplative and other religious show such holiness and fruitfulness.

Love of the church is not an easy virtue. The blockages have to be removed, and we have to get around popular perceptions. The past times of prestige are unlikely to return. The future glory of the church will lie in its weakness (see 2 Cor 12:7-10). Those who have served the church best have known God's power perfect in human weakness.

We can end with some examples of love of the church from those who have served it and have in some cases suffered from it. The late twentieth century has given us some forthright examples of love of the church. For example in the 1950s Yves Congar and Henri de Lubac, among others, suffered much persecution and harassment from church authorities after the encyclical *Humani Generis* (1950). The former afterwards wrote a book entitled, *The Church Which I Love*. The latter developed powerfully both the idea of motherhood and that of the splendour of the church. The chief architect of liturgical reform after Vatican II, the Vincentian, Annibale Bugnini, encountered much opposition; he was eventually consigned to semi-exile as Nuncio in Iran. Before he died he said of himself, 'I have served the church, I have loved the church, I have suffered for the church.' In his *Thoughts of Death* Paul VI exclaimed, 'I could say that I have always loved the church ... and it seems to me that I have lived for her, not for anything else.' John XXIII expressed similar ideas in recalling the day of his priestly ordination. In an interview some time before his death, Henri de Lubac remarked: 'It is not enough that we learn to suffer for the church, we must also learn to suffer from the church'.

Welcoming Back Alienated Catholics in Ireland

Michael Router

The Rite of Christian Initiation of Adults is the process through which non-Christians, and non-Catholic Christians, are brought into the Catholic community. It is a restoration of the ancient practice of Christian initiation and its promulgation in 1972 was seen as one of the major developments of the post-Vatican II church. The RCIA deepened the theology of baptism and re-focused it on the centrality of faith, the community and the word. It requires of adults, who ask for baptism, that they make a profession of faith. Then, over time, it is hoped that this faith will grow and develop, and that the candidates' incorporation into a community of believers will happen on a gradual basis.

Since the introduction of the RCIA the whole community has had a role to play in the process of initiating new members and in forming their faith in the light of the gospel. This process is often the seed for parish renewal: there is the joy of new members in the community, and the community itself is part of the formation team. The positive reaction to the RCIA has led some to believe that it should be the norm in relation to initiation and indeed in the *General Directory for Catechesis* it is presented as the model for all catechesis.

Because the vast majority of Irish Catholics are baptised as infants, the church in this country has had until recently little experience of the RCIA. While the majority of people here, though, may be Catholic (88.4% of the total population of the Republic) many of them have little or no affiliation with the institutional Catholic Church. Moreover, while the average attendance around the country remains reasonably high, there are some urban parishes where less than 10% of the Catholic population are participating in regular celebrations of the eucharist.

This trend provides a serious challenge, particularly in a country that has been Christian for a long time. It demands a new initiative in order to bring the gospel message to those who have become alienated from their faith. Such an initiative may be placed in the context of the church's teaching on evangelisation since Vatican II, with particular reference to the teachings of Paul VI and John Paul II. A number of programmes from North America have based their outreach to the alienated on the structure and process of the RCIA. Some of the elements of these programmes, and of the RCIA, could be useful in establishing a similar outreach in Ireland.

The Rite of Christian Initiation of Adults
The RCIA was the standard format for adult initiation in the early church until the fourth century. The weight of numbers seeking baptism and the growing emphasis on infant baptism brought about its decline. The catechumenate was a lengthy process of discerning and ritualising the stages of conversion. It led ultimately, when the participants were ready, to initiation into the Christian community at an elaborate and symbolically rich ceremony at Easter, when the candidates, know as the elect, received the sacraments of baptism, confirmation and eucharist.

Those preparing for baptism were deemed ready when they had a good understanding of the faith and, more importantly, when it showed in their lives. Those responsible for their preparation and formation looked for signs of conversion that went beyond basic intellectual assent. Such an approach was necessary because the early church community was very small, and various other lifestyles and non-Christian activities were easily available. The participants were only considered suitably prepared to accept the challenge of Christian living when they had demonstrated a distinctive change in lifestyle and a noticeable and verifiable rejection of their old sinful ways.

Reasons why the Catechumenate was restored
The situation faced by many Christians in modern Western society

was one of the major reasons why the church restored the catechumenate in the form of the RCIA. Today's experience has parallels with the situation faced by early Christians. Once again
active Christians are in a minority in many countries. Almost
everywhere in the West they confront a society that has largely
rejected the Christian faith or is indifferent to it. Christian communities do not enjoy the social support they once did and this
can have a corrosive effect because many people need such support if they are to remain Christian. Vatican II recognised this
need in many of its documents and placed much emphasis on
the church as a community and not merely as a collection of individuals sharing similar beliefs.

In the RCIA the church provides this support to those wishing to become members by emphasising the importance and role
of the whole parish in their formation and on their journey of
faith. As they become

> familiar with the Christian way of life and are helped by the
> example and support of sponsors, godparents, and the entire
> Christian community the catechumens learn to turn more
> readily to God in prayer, to bear witness to the faith, in all
> things to keep their hopes set on Christ, to follow supernat-
> ural inspiration in their deeds, and to practice love of neigh-
> bour, even at the cost of self-renunciation (par 75.2).

The community is encouraged by the rite to participate in the
liturgies marking the catechumen's movement through the
process.

Adapting the RCIA as an outreach to alienated and inactive Catholics in Ireland

Evangelisation

The widespread use of the term 'evangelisation' within the
Catholic Church is quite a recent phenomenon. Although
preaching to non-believers has naturally always been part of
Catholic practice, 'evangelisation' was by and large seen as a
Protestant activity and, before Vatican II, most Catholics would
not have considered themselves evangelisers. Since the Council,

however, there has been a gradual movement towards assimilating the concept of evangelisation into general Catholic consciousness.

The document that is regarded as the most influential statement on evangelisation in modern times, Pope Paul VI's apostolic exhortation *Evangelii Nuntiandi* (1975), appeared on the tenth anniversary of the closing of the Council. Evangelisation can be understood in the restricted sense of converting non-believers to the Christian faith, and also in the broad sense as a process of ongoing conversion within the Christian community. This latter sense is reflected in *Evangelii Nuntiandi*, which stresses the importance of Christian witness by all the faithful; witness that is a powerful and effective proclamation of the gospel. Such witness will not only attract non-Christians but also non-practising, nominal Christians (par 21). This witness is supported by preaching, catechesis and by participation in community life, including the sacraments (par 22-23).

The primary proclamation of the gospel is and always has been directed to those who have never heard it. *Evangelii Nuntiandi*, however, recognises that there are many baptised Christians who live outside the Christian life and a considerable number who, while they may have a simple faith, have not been properly catechised. To evangelise, therefore, also involves communicating the vitality of the gospel message in a language suitable to the understanding and circumstances of all.

Special mention is made in *Evangelii Nuntiandi* of the importance and usefulness of basic Christian communities in the task of evangelisation. These small groups are found worldwide and, for the most part, 'they arise because men want to live the life of the church with greater fervour or because they desire to seek a more human way of life which the larger ecclesial communities cannot provide' (par 58). Paul VI acknowledges that there can be problems with some basic Christian communities, particularly if they set themselves up in opposition to the local church and become sources of bitterness and rancour. In the majority of cases, however, these communities are extremely beneficial, and can 'be nurseries of evangelisation and will be of great service to larger communities, especially to individual churches' (Ibid).

New Evangelisation

Evangelisation has also been a recurring theme in the writings and speeches of Pope John Paul II. He often refers to this as a 'new evangelisation'. In *Redemptoris Missio* (1990) he presents the church's teaching on evangelisation in modern times and he declares that the church must commit all its energies to this 'new evangelisation' (par 3). By evangelisation he means the proclamation of salvation through Jesus Christ, a message which never changes from age to age (pars 4-7). There are numerous ways of proclaiming this message, and it is not directed just to unbelievers, but is also addressed to non-practising Christians as well (par 33). In different ways the Pope insists that it should be adapted to the people and circumstances of today. He reiterates the message of *Evangelii Nuntiandi* that all the people of God have a responsibility to evangelise (par 2).

This call applies to lay involvement in the mission to non-Christians, in continuing evangelisation of believing Catholics in communities of faith, and in the outreach to non-practising Catholics who have drifted from the faith. This last form of mission is truly the 'new evangelisation' or 're-evangelisation' that is so urgently required in much of the world today. In *Novo Millennio Ineunte* (2001) Pope John Paul restates the message that evangelisation cannot be left to 'specialists' but should be seen as the responsibility of all the faithful. Therefore, 'a new apostolic outreach is needed, which will be lived as the everyday commitment of Christian communities and groups' (par 40).

There is little doubt that the increasing numbers of non-practising Catholics pose a major challenge to the church throughout most of the Western world. This fall away from active participation in the community and from participation in the liturgy has led church personnel, particularly in the United States, to reflect on the situation and try to find a strategy to reach out to those who feel alienated. The drop in the number of vocations to the priesthood, however, means that an ageing clergy is already under severe pressure in their ministry, leaving them little time or energy to minister to the alienated and the inactive. Where this ministry has been pursued with vigour, it has provided lay people and priests with a worthwhile and rewarding ministry that leads to personal renewal for everyone involved. Among the programmes used in the USA, and also in Britain, based on the structure and process of the RCIA, are *Re-Membering Church*, *Landings*, and *The Reconciling Community: Remember, Return and Rebirth*.

Adapting the RCIA to the Irish context

All of the programmes, briefly noted above, draw heavily from the structure and process of the RCIA in that they advocate a small group setting, usually in the comfort of a participant's home, where active and inactive Catholics share their stories and discuss issues of faith and practice. They strive to provide support for those who are seeking to understand and deepen their faith or who wish to be reconciled with the church. Similarly, any outreach programmes designed to meet the need for a new evangelisation among Irish people, that are suitable to their culture and temperament, could be adapted from the RCIA model. The elements of the RCIA which could prove to be most beneficial in this regard are: 'welcome and listening', 'gradual catechesis' based on shared experience and witness, and the establishment of Basic Christian Communities.

Welcome and listening

The period of evangelisation and pre-catechumenate in the RCIA is a time in which 'faithfully and constantly the living God is proclaimed and Jesus Christ whom he has sent for the salvation of all' (par 36). This proclamation of the gospel, as we have seen in the writings of Popes Paul VI and John Paul II in particular, is the work of the whole church as it attempts to bring about conversion and transform humanity. The fact that there are inquirers in a parish looking to become full members suggests that

that parish community is witnessing to the gospel in the way it lives and the hospitality it extends.

The questions that the inquirers bring to this stage may be many and varied, but it is important that they are listened to and treated with respect in order to build a relationship of trust. This is also essential when communicating with those who are alienated from the church, particularly those who have been hurt in some way.

Ministers who witness

Those who minister at this stage in the RCIA are above all asked to be witnesses. They must be witnesses to Christ, people of faith and of hospitality, and be good listeners. In *Evangelii Nuntiandi* Pope Paul VI wrote that people today 'are more impressed by witnesses than by teachers, and if they listen to them it is because they also bear witness' (par 41).

The American adaptations of the RCIA listed above emphasise how important it is that those involved in outreach and ministry to the alienated dedicate time and effort to ensuring that returning Catholics are met with warmth and friendship. Those chosen to minister in this area should, by nature, be open and friendly people, who are willing to become involved in the lives of those returning as sponsors and spiritual guides.

Initial contact

This first stage of making contact with the alienated and inactive is very important. It can also be quite sensitive. What may appear trivial can often be critical. 'Attention to the appearance of the church, concern about how we welcome people, awareness of what we communicate to our community, are all practical manifestations of Christian love' (Kollar, 60-61). *Landings* emphasises that meetings should be held in the homes of team members, and a full meal should be provided for all because everything that is done in the process, including the refreshment time, is aimed at reflecting the unconditional love, forgiveness, and welcoming spirit of God.

The pre-catechumenate is a critical part of the RCIA and, in itself, provides an almost complete blueprint for the quality of ministry and outreach necessary to respond to the challenge of evangelising those who are alienated or inactive in Ireland. A process of hospitality and welcome, which includes a considerable element of genuine, non-judgemental listening and meaningful response, may often be enough to bring people back. It can provide an experience of genuine reconciliation involving both the community and the alienated members.

Gradual and Ongoing Catechesis

The necessity of ongoing catechesis

Survey results over the past twenty years indicate that Irish Catholics are moving away from traditional church teaching, particularly in relation to sexual morality, and that they have less confidence in the church's ability to give adequate answers to the problems they encounter in life (Cassidy, 17-45). A considerable number of the respondents had a limited and inadequate view of who Jesus was, and as such, had little or no relationship with him. Evidence is also emerging that the specifically Catholic quality of people's beliefs is diminishing. The limited availability of catechesis for adults in Ireland plays no small part in this lack of basic knowledge, and it could be seen as a major factor in the drift away from active involvement in the church.

Most people in Ireland receive their formal religious education in childhood and are subsequently never helped, in any real way, to develop a faith capable of meeting the challenges of the adult world. Many people hold on to a childish faith, or abandon it altogether, and only those who have an interest in learning themselves, or who go on to study theology have an opportunity for faith development.

It is necessary, therefore, that any programme aiming to welcome back alienated Catholics should have a strong element of catechesis and faith development attached. It should also be open to the whole community and be held in a welcoming, non-threatening environment where people are encouraged to share their faith, discuss church teaching and seek answers to their questions. If such a forum does not already exist in a parish, it should be developed with a view to providing faith formation for those who have not been participating in the life of the church community and who have missed out on the catechesis that occurs there, formally and informally, throughout the liturgical year.

Basic Christian Communities
The RCIA depends on small groups of people gathered together for the purpose of forming new members and integrating them into the Christian community. The group usually consists of two or three enquirers along with their sponsors and, if possible, a priest of the parish. This model has proved effective, as it helps to build up trust between enquirers and members of the community, and gives them the support they need in the process of conversion. The group provides a doorway into the liturgical and missionary life of the parish. It forms a basic Christian community that, in itself, mirrors the life of the church.

A more personal experience of church
As noted above, *Evangelii Nuntiandi* makes special mention of Basic Christian Communities and the role they play in providing a more personal experience of church, especially in the larger ecclesial communities found in large towns and cities (par 58). Basic Christian Communities encourage a sense of belonging by presenting, more intensely, the human face of the church, a church that is seen to care for the individual. The methodology of these communities should be a very important component of any programme intending to welcome back inactive Catholics and reintegrate them into the wider church community in Ireland. The anonymity of contemporary living can leave many people not just alienated from the church but also from wider society.

The parish is often seen as the basic model of church, particularly in Ireland, where many accept it as part of the apparatus of organised religion. Because of its large and somewhat rigid structure, the parish has failed to nourish many Catholics and has alienated some of them: 'They see the parish as going about its own programme of activities in a way that does not seem to connect with their own spiritual needs ... a carry over from the past, not adapted to life in the contemporary world.' (Harrington, 58) The difficulties inherent in the structure and organisation of most parishes were recognised by Pope John Paul II in *Christifideles Laici* (1988) when he noted that 'Since the church's task in our day is so great, its accomplishment cannot be left to the parish alone' (par 26). In order to create parishes that will truly be communities of Christians, he recommends two strategies to ecclesial authorities: firstly, that they adapt parish structures, as necessary, to the full flexibility allowed by canon law, particularly in relation to lay participation in pastoral responsibility; and, secondly, that they establish

> small, basic or so called 'living' communities where the faithful can communicate the word of God and express it in service and love to one another; these communities are true expressions of ecclesial communion and centres of evangelisation, in communion with their pastors (Ibid).

An essential component of outreach to the alienated

The American adaptations of the RCIA aimed at inactive and alienated Catholics, mentioned above, use the format of a Basic Christian Community. This serves to provide a comfortable and supportive base for those who want to explore the possibility of returning to active church membership and they also counter the often-alienating effect of the large, impersonal parish.

These Basic Christian Community models could provide invaluable strategies to people in ministry, helping them to respond to the problem of alienation in Irish parishes. The warmth, support, encouragement and respect for the individual's experience that they provide, along with their inbuilt flexibility concerning forms of prayer and reflection, may provide settings for reconciliation, spiritual formation and renewal for many who are now on the fringes of the church community.

Evangelisation

The Basic Christian Community is essentially a small group of people who seek to evangelise and help each other through the relationships that develop in everyday living. Ideally, everyone has the potential to be an evangeliser in their own home, family, workplace and neighbourhood. Opportunities for sharing faith exist all around us, and a Basic Christian Community prepares its members to be alert to these opportunities through prayer, scripture and faith sharing. This is in essence 'oikos evangelisation', making God known through everyday relationships.

A setting for prayer and reconciliation

Small Christian communities also do much to deepen the prayer life and experience of participants: by helping them to reflect on their lives in the light of scripture; by giving members an opportunity for reconciliation; and by deepening their appreciation of the eucharist as the source and summit of Christian life. This last point is important in relation to those who are inactive and alienated. In our affluent and materialistic society, individuals are often encouraged to be self-sufficient and to achieve their own goals in a self-centred way. Such attitudes have led to the belief that each individual can inevitably follow and worship Jesus in their own way. Jesus, however, is not separate from the church: he is inextricably linked to its life and practice. The individual's spirituality, if it is removed from the life of the church, is in serious danger of withering without the support and guidance the church provides. This, of course, also places a huge responsibility on the leaders of the church to ensure that its liturgies and organisation are life-giving and inclusive. The small community can help deepen the participants' appreciation of community and, therefore, their understanding of the importance of the eucharist.

Conclusion

It is clear that the proper implementation of the Rite of Christian Initiation of Adults can have a very positive effect on the life of a parish community. It helps to build a sense of belonging through its stress on the community's involvement in the catechesis and ongoing support of adults entering the church, and also by its focus on the sacraments of initiation, which enable all Catholics to deepen their understanding and appreciation of their faith. It also increases the awareness baptised Catholics have of the depth and richness of the liturgy surrounding initiation, and highlights their need for ongoing and gradual conversion to the gospel.

As the numbers of alienated and inactive Catholics increase in Ireland, it becomes more obvious that committed church members will have to find some means of reaching out to these people. As the church in Ireland faces the challenge of secularisation and growing individualisation, it must find ways that are appropriate to the culture and tradition of the people. Whatever form that outreach takes, it ought to include elements of the RCIA process examined here: 'welcome and listening', 'a commitment to gradual and ongoing catechesis', and 'the establishment of small faith communities in order to improve people's experience of community and sense of belonging'. These elements will be essential if there is to be renewal in the Irish church.

Select Bibliography
Kavanagh, A., *The Shape of Baptism: The Rite of Christian Initiation*, Liturgical Press, Collegeville, 1991
O' Brien, J., *The Seeds of a New Church*, Columba Press, Dublin, 1994
National Conference of Bishops United States of America, *Rite of Christian Initiation of Adults: Study Edition*, Liturgical Training Publications, Chicago, 1988
Harmony, S., *Re-Membering: The Ministry of Welcoming Alienated and Inactive Catholics*, Liturgical Press, Collegeville, 1991
Landings UK, Welcoming Returning Catholics Back to the Church, 'More About Landings', http://www.landings-international. org/

Brennan, P. J., *The Reconciling Parish: A Process for Returning or Alienated Catholics*, Tabor Publishing, Allen 1990

Kollar, J. A., *A User Friendly Parish: Becoming a More Welcoming Community*, Twenty-Third Publications, Mystic, 1998

Cassidy, E. (ed.) *Measuring Ireland*, Veritas, Dublin, 2002

D. Harrington, *Parish Renewal*, vol. 1, Columba Press, Dublin, 1999

M. Hurley, *Transforming Your Parish*, Columba Press, Dublin, 1998

J. O' Halloran, *Small Christian Communities*, Columba Press, Dublin, 1996

Environment, Community, Evangelisation: The Ecology of Parish

Martin Tierney

I well remember my first visit to Africa in 1966. Stepping from the aircraft at Entebbe Airport in Uganda, a wave of warm sultry air hit me full in the face. In the terminal building among the milling crowds I felt ridiculously conspicuous as a white face in a multitude of colour. I was nervous, apprehensive, and excited. That is how I felt on being appointed to parochial ministry after an absence of twenty-two years. I was in a new country. What I had learned in the seminary had fallen away, like an expended rocket. I had to begin again. But I was not beginning where I had left off twenty-two years before. So much had changed that I had to enrol once more in the school of experience and learn quickly and desperately. In 2001, I stood in a huge cavernous church, built in 1972, designed to hold twelve hundred people. I was informed that in the past the crush of people at Sunday Mass provided enough body heat to remain comfortable on the coldest day. How the situation had changed!

A careful count over a number of Sundays indicated that approximately 10% of the parishioners attended weekly Mass in their own parish. Further, of these 10%, the overwhelming majority were like myself, sixty plus years of age. Three large galleries were empty. Like the deserted village, they held memories of a different church in a different age. Now the congregation scattered itself here and there like buttercups in a meadow right throughout this mighty building. I was stunned at the absence of young people, particularly those in the twenty to forty age group. There was little sense of community, of belonging, of connectedness. Nothing I had done heretofore prepared me for this!

Environment

In house buying programmes on television the mantra is location, location, location. I have a sense that when it comes to liturgy the mystical chant needs to be environment, environment, environment. One did not need to be a rocket scientist, or have a doctorate in liturgy, to appreciate the unsuitability of this parish church for the celebration of an effective liturgy. It did not work! Even eye contact was impossible because of the dispersed nature of the congregation. Communication is at the heart of what the church is all about, and here I was in a building unsuitable even for a Dale Carnegie or a Billy Graham! The church exists to bring people into communication with God and thereby open them up to communication with each other. It is very difficult to grapple with the natural reticence of people in church, while at the same time coping with an unsuitable environment for communicating. Many of our churches, particularly in large urban areas, are now fundamentally unsuitable for true community liturgical celebrations.

First century Christians would have wondered about expressions like, 'I'll meet you in front of the church,' or 'is the church fireproof?' The building where these early Christians met was not the primary focus of their concern – the church was the assembly, the people, the community of faith. The community pre-existed the provision of the building. We probably have that first century experience when we celebrate Mass in a private house surrounded by family and friends. It is on occasions like that we have a palpable sense of community and church in the people gathered. At such celebrations we instinctively know the environment to be right. I had a sense from the beginning of my present assignment that community and environment would have to be the twin springboards from which we would start.

How do we build a community so that each recognises him or her self as part of something greater? A congregation of individuals, who happen haphazardly to live in a particular geographic area adjacent to this particular building called church, is hardly a community. The main goal of the pastoral efforts of the church is to build communities which make it possible for a person to live a Christian life. The Letter to the Ephesians talks about the purpose of Christianity when it states that we are 'no longer strangers and sojourners but you are fellow citizens with the saints and members of the household of God' (2:19). Effective worship which is life-giving is enhanced when it is a community that celebrates.

When I last ministered in a parish it was the parish community that gave many individuals a sense of belonging. From their catholicity and their parish they received a clearly defined identity. Their patterns of relationships, outside of the immediate family, were frequently those forged within the parish community. The parish was a significant source of social capital. This may still be the case in rural areas. Apart from people who are no longer churchgoers, more and more people are surfing from congregation to congregation. While they may be still religious they are less committed to a particular community of believers. 'Believers' perhaps, but 'belongers', no. Catholics need to reconnect with each other in an individualistic competitive world.

The average parishioner in the parish comes to Mass only on Sunday. Apart from Mass and perhaps an occasional penitential service, the vast majority has no other contact with the parish. When this parishioner comes to Mass, he finds himself in a church filled with people he does not know for the most part, and are a different group from the last group he went to Mass with the previous Sunday. The Mass he attends is 'standard' for that Sunday. At Mass, this parishioner rarely knows the person sitting next to him unless it is a member of his own family or a near neighbour. There is little interaction among the congregation. Our parishioner knows a number of other people in the parish but he knows them not because they are parishioners but because they are his neighbour, his barber, his doctor, and his postman. In other words they happen to be people he knows from another source and who also happen to go to this parish. The parish then is primarily a service institution providing Mass and the sacrament for those who come. Even the clerical leadership in the parish is transitory. Others who have been through the seminary and have been ordained can replace them. The people who work in various ways in the parish form another group. They are the main source of parish activities. Those who work together may know each other. They are a recognisable environment but not a very strong one. The average parishioner is not one of them

Our first effort must be directed towards the building, once more, of community. The church should be restructured to form basic Christian communities. For most people this community will be the parish. There is a tendency to think that structural renewal and institutional renewal are the same thing. Few people think in terms of environmental (or communal) renewal. It is rare enough for people to ask the basic question: how can a Christian environment (a Christian community) be formed most effectively? The same problem can be looked at from a different point of view. The goal of the church is not to have structures, but to have people who are living as Christians.

In theory the parish is the basic Christian community. It is supposed to be the smallest pastoral unit in the church, the ordinary place in which a person's Christian life can be nourished. Yet it is clear that most parishes as we know them are not such places. This is partly because of their size, partly because of the way they are structured. A major problem in dealing with parish renewal is that we do not tend to think much in environmental or in communal terms. This struck me forcibly on my first Christmas in the parish. The Monday night collectors and the weekly count people were having a little party in the sacristy room. In the very next room members of the choir were having their pre-Christmas celebration. Not only were they apart, but I discovered they hardly knew one another. Apart from a few exceptions they did not know each other by name. What appeared from the outside very much like a community of sorts, was in fact groups of good committed people who saw their primary role as one of service in a particular area.

Frequently the word communion is used in a purely functional way. We could talk about the hospital as a community. Credit Union members are in some loose way a community. So is the Irish Farmers Association. But these are functional communities. People come together to do specific tasks. In such a community, people relate in a task-orientated manner. The vision of a Christian community is more than functional. It is environmental.

A person's beliefs, attitudes, values and behaviour patterns are formed to a great degree by his or her environment and therefore the normal person needs a Christian environment if he or she is going to live Christianity in a vital way. A family is an environment, as is a group of friends. A school provides a place for environment to form, as does a parish or a business. There are usually a number of environments in a person's life: family, work, recreation, the group of friends he or she spends time with. An environment is formed when a group of people interrelate or interact with some measure of continuity and stability. For an environment to be Christian, Christianity has to be a strong influencing factor in the way people in the environment interact. In other words the people share a common belief, place a premium on the common values that underpin their beliefs, and interact out of their faith. A stranger wandering in to a truly Catholic parish environment would immediately sense that there was something different here. In an environment that is truly Christian people will interact out of their common faith, and brother and sisterhood, and only subsequently will they relate functionally. In the present arrangement the Roman rite is designed to help the people who have come together in one place to become a unified assembly, to realise that they are with their brothers and sisters, and that Jesus is present among them. But it places far too heavy a burden on the liturgy itself to imagine that it can effect this on its own.

Practical steps towards building community
I quickly learned as a first principal – assume nothing. For instance, I assumed that the good people who attended the daily

ten o'clock morning Mass knew one another, certainly by sight, but probably also by name. We invited the congregations of the morning Mass to the Parish Resource Centre for tea or coffee after Mass one day. What seemed to me a very homogeneous group of like-minded people was in fact a collection of individuals. One lady told me she had been attending the ten o'clock Mass since the church was opened and had not made friends with anyone. This reinforced my view that the energies of the parish ought to be invested in fostering the growth of community as a first priority. Everything else, including a life-giving liturgy, is very dependent on the health of the parishioners as a community. Despite Vatican II we still have a very privatised type of religion.

One of the first decisions we took was to establish a team to greet people as they arrived for church. From my work with New Religion Movements I knew that many people were attracted to these movements because of their need to belong; a need for a sense of community. Many people need to come to terms with themselves, to feel safe, secure, and be able to overcome complexes. In addition most assumed that 'nothing happens at Mass'. How could we indicate gently that we wanted to be that sort of community? Many years ago a young person said to me that 'nobody would miss me if I didn't go to Mass.' I knew that what she said was true. At two of the principal Masses on a Sunday our team of greeters are available at each door of the church to welcome people and offer them the parish newsletter. It is a small gesture. As many of the parishioners are elderly they do appreciate a word of welcome and a gesture of kindness. The greeters have come to know the congregation and the genuine welcome parishioners and visitors receive is very much appreciated.

Our second decision was to initiate, on the first Sunday of every month, a 'Doughnut Sunday'. After Mass in the large hospitality area at the back of the church the congregation gathers for chat and refreshments. Again, it is a small gesture, an effort to recreate a sense of family, of belonging. Probably only half of the congregation remains behind to fraternise. After more than a year people are still shy of making contact with strangers. In big cities, unfortunately, many of our congregations are just that – strangers to each other. Yet Irish people are known universally for their friendliness.

If I say 'liturgy', what comes into your mind? Perhaps actions, symbols, music and words? But something needs to happen first – the building of community. When a parish team meeting takes place it will regularly concern itself with scheduling Masses, repairing buildings, getting readers and commentators, organising collections. It will consider these important because it is assumed that every parish must have certain activities. The function of those in charge of the parish is to see that these activities happen. It is sometimes assumed, in fact, that the more activities a parish has, the better a parish is. A priest, at least, was given certain skills to perform certain activities well. Our practical training was activity orientated. There is a competitive streak in many priests who multiply activities and thereby generate kudos for themselves and their parish. There may be a buzz among the few who are excited and energised by parochial activities. Our vision of community must be broader, to embrace even the disaffected.

With only 10% of the parish attending Sunday Mass and very few young people in sight, there were adequate reasons to be despondent at times. There were times when we only saw the way things were, not the way they might be. I know this is the ultimate blindness. This kind of blindness has nothing to do with sight; it has to do with lack of vision, and vision is the stuff of dreams, hopes, and possibilities. There is always the temptation to scale down our dreams to the size of our fears until our vision becomes so tunnelled we see darkness everywhere. I read somewhere that a 'visionary is someone who sees in the dark'. There is a continuing temptation to sigh, *cui bono?* – what's the use, nothing seems to work! The temptation is to settle for the service model of parish. People are under more pressure than twenty-two years ago. Two parent working families, daily traffic congestion, child-minding problems and a huge array of options for leisure or 'free' time, means that attracting people to ministry is more difficult. Those who tend to volunteer are invariably from the older age group who have fewer pressures and responsibilities to attend to. Few enough people ask themselves the question: where will our parish be ten or twenty years down the line? When a person tells me, 'we tried that before' as a reason for not trying it again, I am tempted to loose heart.

We decided to organise a Ministry Sunday. Looking at the age profile and numbers of people at Sunday Mass the question had to be faced: will our parish survive? It was not beyond the bounds of possibility that this large building would become a massive carpet sales room, or a spectacular theme pub, in ten or twenty years time. The people were asked – is this what you want? They were invited to take ownership of the parish. All the ministries presently operating in the parish were listed and a few new possibilities added. People were invited, if they wished their parish to survive, to name an area best suited to their talents and to supply their names and addresses. This was completed after the homily of the Mass. Fifty-five people, mainly Irish, but from five different countries, volunteered. We organised a meal for the volunteers. This was both a 'getting-to-know-you' and a community building exercise. Just over half of those who volunteered attended the meal, which was a great success. Most of those who volunteered are now serving the parish in a variety of capacities.

We commissioned specially engraved crystal glasses to present to long serving parishioners. At a parish Christmas party we presented these gifts to eight of the longest serving people in the parish. This small gesture created an enormous amount of goodwill and it provided one more opportunity for parishioners to come into contact with one another. One of our most successful initiatives was when we booked the local cinema and invited parishioners to attend the film, *The Passion of the Christ*. We completely filled the cinema. After the film we returned to the parish for Mass, followed by refreshments and discussion groups on the film. There are signs that people are beginning to relate to one another in a new way. The journey is slow and the road is long.

The establishment of a 'Gospelstorytime' for pre-First Communion children during the mid-day Mass on a Sunday provided an opportunity for very young children to relate to the gospel in a way adapted to their age group and knowledge. A small team, led by our pastoral worker, have developed this initiative over the past year. Do not be fooled by what appears impressive on paper. Everything we have tried to do is nothing more than laying the foundations upon which the community may emerge in the future.

The creation of *communio* is the fundamental task of the church and the parish. The word 'communion' comes from the Latin *communio*, which comes from the Greek *koinonia*. We are most familiar with this word in relation to Holy Communion. Communion designates a way of life, a network of relationships among churches and among individual Christians. Being part of a communion is a way of being – being in relationship with God and others.

Dividing the church building

Having moved some way along the road it was time to look at the building. We had plans drawn up to split the building in two. The plans were posted in the church for a number of weeks and comments and criticisms were invited. The architect made himself available for consultation with parishioners. The result was a 500 seat area for Sunday Masses and a smaller Blessed Sacrament Chapel for weekday Mass, and for other spiritual and liturgical activities. In addition we were left with a large area at the back of the main church which was designated a 'hospitality area'. The small chapel was refurbished comfortably. It is carpeted, with cushioned chairs, and a warm welcoming environment. It holds 140 people. As both churches are relatively small the possibility of interaction between the celebrant and worshippers is greater, as is the interaction of parishioners with each other.

We now have a physical environment much more suited to performing the liturgy with grace and style. In our oratory the Blessed Sacrament is exposed every day from early morning until night-time. This has been a significant blessing on the whole parish and indeed it is not unusual to see non-church goers slipping in for a quick visit to the Blessed Sacrament. Is is also an ideal location for small group Masses.

Evangelisation

Throughout this essay I have been referring only to the 10% of regular churchgoers in the parish. What about the 90% whom we never see, except for funerals, marriages and baptisms? They too are parishioners. In his great apostolic exhortation, *Evangelii Nuntiandi* (1975), Pope Paul VI wrote: 'We wish to affirm once more that the essential mission of the church is to evangelise all men; it is a task and mission which the great and fundamental changes of contemporary society make all the more urgent. Evangelisation is the special grace and vocation of the church.' The church exists to know God and to make him known. It exists in order to evangelise. That is its core mission. In many of our parishes there are more people who seldom attend church, than those who are active once a week Catholics. I have always been impressed by a particularly salient point made by Pope Paul: 'The person who has been evangelised becomes himself an evangeliser. This is the proof, the test of the genuineness of his own conversion. It is inconceivable that a person who has received the word and surrendered himself to the kingdom should not himself become a witness and proclaimer of the truth.'

After much indecision, two projects were initiated in the parish: a 'chill-out' club for young people and an ALPHA course. These were faltering attempts to reach out beyond the narrow confines of the regular churchgoers. Our pastoral worker took responsibility for the club and nearly two years down the line it is relatively successful. She has been able to assemble a team of helpers and much energy and creativity has been devoted to this work. The club produced an excellent Nativity Play at Christmas time that I hope will become a regular feature of our parish.

With help from outside we decided to launch an ALPHA course. We recruited participants by brochure, church notices and visiting hundreds of homes. The response was poor enough. Sixty-one people enrolled, about half of whom stayed the course. Many of those participating in the course were already good committed people. We learned that many people today have made a definite decision in relation to the church. Church attendance or participation in any form of liturgy is not part of their future agendas. We also learned that evangelisation has to move centre stage as a concern for the universal church if it still believes in the mandate of Christ, the great commission, 'to go therefore'. The danger is that our parishes may become holy huddles of the like-minded. Even enthusiastic, dynamic parishes can become narcissistic. Like a healthy family, the parish community must always be seeking ways of being open to the wider world of scepticism, doubt and youth. To be always looking, even in the most unlikely places, for signs of the transcendent, is part of a healthy Christian environment. Young people grow up in a different world and face completely different challenges than most of our elderly congregation. Their lives are more complex than mine ever was. They face a whole range of choices every day. But they do not lack commitment. They do not lack beliefs and values. Rather they face an uncertain and every changing world not easily handled. They have to make choices from a range of alternatives unknown to previous generations. They struggle with church beliefs and practices. It could be that in the minds of many former young Catholics, 'religion is equated with belief and therefore with doctrine, and therefore with authority, and therefore with organisation, and therefore with rewards and punishment, and therefore with guilt and fear. And with boundaries and polarisation.' I am at a complete loss how the gospel can touch the lives of young people.

ALPHA has helped many people. It was established ecumenically with the help of our local Church of Ireland rector. ALPHA is primarily focused towards those who are unbelievers or on the very periphery of faith. I remain to be convinced of its usefulness in the strictly Catholic context. It is our intention to make similar efforts to initiate 'Life in the Spirit Seminars'. The seminars are more conducive to the Catholic environment.

We are now exploring the possibility of establishing a Parish Pastoral Council. Among more elderly people the prevalent attitude on almost every issue is: 'Ask the PP.' The priest is expected to have the final say in all decisions. They cannot yet grasp the fact that there may be no PP in ten or twenty years time! The formation of community demands equipping people who are capable of taking and exercising responsibility. In the parish of the future the laity will have to assume even greater responsibility.

The Ministerial Priesthood in relation to the New Testament

Joseph Briody

The People of God

The model of the church as 'People of God' inspires the church struggling to adapt to changing situations. Israel was chosen by God as his people to be 'a kingdom of priests and a holy nation' (Ex 19:6). The Old Testament makes clear that the ordering of this People was not arbitrary or merely practical, but of divine origin. The People of God was not a shapeless mass but had definite order and leadership. It was hierarchically structured.

The church is the New Israel according to the Spirit, the New People of God, 'a chosen race, a royal priesthood'. The New Testament priesthood is not confined to the priesthood of all the baptised. As the general priesthood of Israel did not exclude a specific priestly ministry, neither does the New Testament. Rather it presumes it. All members of the church enjoy an equality springing from baptism but all do not have the same function (Rom 12:4). The New Testament makes clear that the ordering of the community is from God.

In the undoubted confusion about ministry in Ireland today there is need for a better understanding of diverse roles within the church. This will involve greater clarification of the role of the ordained priest and the manner in which the laity can fruitfully collaborate with him and he with them. Unfortunately we have not avoided the pit falls of the clericalisation of the laity and the secularisation of the clergy. Only a priest convinced of who and what he is, will be able to help the baptised discover and live out their great dignity of discipleship.

Called by the Spirit

To be constituted an apostle involved a special rite, the laying-on of hands and prayer (Acts 13:3). The laying-on of hands signified the transmission of a spiritual power by God. The Holy Spirit is the one who calls: 'The Holy Spirit said: "Set apart for me Barnabas and Saul for the work to which I have called them." Then after fasting and prayers they laid their hands on them and sent them off' (Acts 13:2-3). They were sent out 'by the Holy Spirit' (Acts 13:4).

The Holy Spirit called and continues to call, even today. It is perhaps more difficult to hear his voice in Ireland now. The call may also be ignored, smothered or deferred. Some people have even claimed that the Holy Spirit is deliberately not calling people to be priests so as to give the church back to the laity. This view contradicts the New Testament vision of the priesthood as needed and vital: 'The harvest is rich but the labourers are few. So ask the Lord of the harvest to send labourers into his harvest' (Mt 9:37-38).

Attributing the vocations' crisis to the Holy Spirit is a convenient and cosy way of avoiding the real issues at work here. These issues include the example set by priests, the scandals, infidelity to the teachings of Christ and the church, poor church leadership, betrayal of trust, inadequate catechesis, family disintegration, general lack of direction and hope, consumerism, uninformed faith, aspects of seminary formation, secularism, individualism, materialism.

There is also great reluctance to study dioceses and religious orders where these trends of decline have been reversed, where groups are flourishing and attracting steady numbers, some huge numbers. Nor is it a question of quantity at the expense of quality. Why are we Irish so reluctant to look elsewhere and learn? Is it because many of these thriving groups claiming to be faithful are perceived by us to be 'conservative' or 'traditional'? It is also noticeable that some of those who speak most about unity, reaching out and dialogue with other groups are the first to clam up, react and even explode at the mention of some thriving 'conservative' group within the church. The Irish discussion of the church and the future can be very selectively broadminded! If we are to learn from others we have to be genuinely open.

A chosen priesthood

Jesus chose twelve men as apostles, prefigured by the Twelve Tribes of Israel (Mk 3:13-19; Lk 6:12-16). 'He called to him those whom he desired; and they came to him. And he appointed twelve to be with him and to be sent out to preach ...' (Mk 3:13-19). He entrusted them with his mission. He mandated them to preach the gospel to the ends of the earth (Mt 28:16-20; Mk 16:14-18).

Jesus formally consecrated his apostles for their priestly task in his high priestly prayer. He consecrated them in truth (Jn 17:17). In scriptural terms, this is explicitly a formula of priestly consecration. Jesus consecrated his apostles as priests and sent them into the world just as he was sent by the Father. They were to share in his consecration and his mission (Jn 17:17-19 cf. 20:21).

Christ's words: 'You have not chosen me, I have chosen you,' were directed primarily at his priests. In his priestly prayer in John 17, Jesus did not just pray for the apostles there present. He prayed for all those to come: 'I do not pray for these only, but also for those who believe in me through their word' (Jn 17:20). The Father hears his prayer (Jn 11:41-42). Priests of all times were included in Christ's prayer and so in the Father's favourable response to that prayer. Awareness of this call and choseness brings confidence.

A confident priesthood

Paul is supremely confident in his calling as a minister of the New Covenant: 'Last of all, as to one untimely born, he appeared also to me. For I am the least of the apostles, unfit to be called an apostle ... But by the grace of God I am what I am' (1 Cor 15:5-10). In 2 Cor 3:5-6 he clearly asserts that his apostolic authority comes from God. His ministry is not on his own merit, but from God's mercy (2 Cor 4:1). His ministry is 'from the Lord Jesus, to testify to the gospel of the grace of God' (Acts 20:24). Paul's call is not from the community in general, but from Christ.

His confidence in God is palpable: 'We have such confidence through Christ before God. Not that we are sufficient of our-

selves to claim anything as coming from ourselves. But our sufficiency comes from God who made us also sufficient to be ministers of a New Covenant' (2 Cor 3:4-6). Paul is confident because the apostolic ministry is God's creation (2 Cor 4:6). He is
confident because he is dependant upon Christ. The very weakness of the apostle is his strength because it makes him realise
his total dependence on God. Apostles have the treasure of the
ministry ('the gospel of the glory of Christ' cf. 4:4) in earthen
vessels, so that it be clear that the power is from God and not
from themselves (2 Cor 4:7).

Confidence in God engenders confidence in ourselves and
what God asks of us. It also instils confidence in others and attracts them to the God who does not let us down. The only saying of the Risen Lord in Paul's letters appears in this context of
the apostolate: 'My grace is sufficient for you, for my power is
made perfect in weakness' (2 Cor 12:9) (Lambrecht, 203). The
apostle does not lose heart because he looks to what is unseen
and eternal (2 Cor 4:16-18). His growing intimacy with Christ is
accompanied by the conviction that this relationship cannot be
destroyed even by death.

A sacrificial priesthood

The priest's identity is rooted in Christ. He is a priest only because he shares Christ's priesthood, one of sacrifice. Christ's free
sacrifice on Calvary was the sacrifice of a priest who shed his
blood for the forgiveness of sins (Mk 14:24; Rom 5:6; Eph 1:7,
5:25-27; 1 Jn 2:2; Gal 1:4). Jesus presents his death as the sacrifice
of the New Covenant. He did not abolish worship or sacrifice,
but brought authenticity of worship and interiorisation of sacrifice (Mt 12:7 cf. Hos 6:6). The self is to be offered to God along
with Christ's sacrifice on the cross. All Christians, especially
priests, are to offer their very selves to God through Christ, to be
living instruments in the hands of the Risen Christ. The priest offers himself to God to help others offer themselves back to God.

Paul sees his ministry as sacrificial and linked to the cross of
Christ so that 'the offering of the Gentiles may be sanctified by

the Holy Spirit' (Rom 15:16). Paul urges the Romans to offer their very selves to God: 'to present your bodies as a living sacrifice, holy and acceptable to God, which is your spiritual worship' (Rom 12:1). Speaking of his own imminent death he says his life is about to be poured out on the altar as was Christ's: 'for I am already on the point of being sacrificed' (2 Tim 4:6).

Paul is not referring to the Old Testament cult, but to a dynamic Christian understanding. He is referring to a totally different idea of sacrifice: 'It is no longer a matter of putting the corpse of an animal on the fire of the altar … it is a matter of sanctifying living people by communicating to them the fire of the Holy Spirit, and that is done by means of evangelisation' (Vanhoye, 269).

Paul speaks of apostolic suffering bringing people to God. He tells Timothy (Bishop of Ephesus) to 'share in suffering as a good soldier of Christ Jesus' (2 Tim 2:3). This suffering is bearable because of the single-minded aim of pleasing the Lord (2 Tim 2:4). The priest's life is a spiritual struggle (Eph 6:13-17). Paul sees his apostolic life as 'fighting the good fight' (2 Tim 4:7). He makes it clear that the proper living of the apostolic life is a spiritual struggle that will bring much opposition and suffering. Nevertheless Paul exhorts Timothy to shun compromise and cling to sound teaching (2 Tim 4:2-3). He tells him 'always be steady, endure suffering, do the work of an evangelist, fulfil your ministry.' (2 Tim 4:5-6). In 2 Corinthians Paul makes it clear that apostolic suffering is important because of its value in saving others: 'so death is at work in us (ministers) but life in you' (2 Cor 4:12).

The spiritual value of apostolic suffering is deeply scriptural but something we have lost sight of. To regain that vision is to recapture value and meaning in difficult situations. The need to embrace the cross cannot be avoided. There is no Christian life, and especially no priestly life without the shadow of the cross. The servant should be like his Master (Mt 10:24-25). Hopefully this suffering will come, not from doing what is wrong, but from trying to do what is right. The church has frequently suffered unjust persecution. Yet recent great failures on the part of clergy invite us to reflect on Von Balthasar's challenge: 'How seldom can the church look on herself as being punished unjustly?' (*The Threefold Garland*, 88-89).

A prophetic priesthood

The prophets spoke in God's name against the hypocrisy, greed and lack of conviction of some members of the Old Testament priesthood. Yet it is too simplistic a view to oppose prophecy and priesthood. The great prophets Jeremiah and Ezekiel were priests (Jer 1:1; Ezek 1:3). Isaiah received his vision of the Lord in the temple (Is 6:1-9). Zechariah was a priest. John the Baptist the 'last prophet of the Old Covenant, the great prophet of the New' was also a priest (Ratzinger, 44). Jesus, presented as priest in Hebrews, is also prophet who came to bear witness to the truth (Jn 18:37). Indeed he is the Truth (Jn 14:6). He speaks of his twelve apostles as prophets when he commissions them (Mt 10:40-41).

In contemporary discussion the prophet is often pitted against the priest. The caricatured prophet is the one crying out against injustice, institutions and convention. The caricatured priest is the one buoying up the system and supporting the *status quo*.

Caricatures are of limited value. There should be no tension between prophet and priest. Indeed the priest must be a prophet if he is to be an effective priest. This will involve taking a stand on moral, social and religious issues. This will be a prophetic and perhaps a lonely place to be. Speaking the truth in a spirit of love (Eph 4:15) will be the priest's prophetic duty in a society drifting from the ways of Christ. He will also have the privilege of speaking hope to that society. From the strength of his own reflection, prayer and hope, he will be able to give that society reasons for the hope that is in him (1 Pet 3:15-16),

The prophetic priest may also at times have to challenge within the church. As structures and superstructures, committees and commissions, policies and parish councils, fundraising and financial councils increase and multiply, the priest may find that all these structures, originally designed to assist and free him, actually increasingly enslave him. Instead of serving to free the priest for prayer and the preaching of the word (Acts 6:2) he can be increasingly drawn into committee rivalries and disputes.

As a prophet, the priest of the future should avail of the great help of councils and committees. But he must avoid the dangers and pitfalls of new layers of church bureaucracy. More and more layers added to the 'church photocopying' may well smother the Spirit and tend to drain enthusiasm and stifle conviction. As the Irish church struggles to adapt there is a danger of a new kind of clericalism, a new kind of structural bureaucracy that could be more stifling and controlling than anything that went before.

A male priesthood

In fidelity to the New Testament the priesthood of the future will be a male priesthood. In choosing the apostles Jesus chose twelve men (Mk 3:13-19; Mt 10:1-14; Lk 6:12-16). He was not historically or culturally conditioned in this. Christ freely dispensed with custom and tradition when he chose (Mk 2:23-28; 3:1-6). Jesus shattered Jewish convention by appointing women as the first witnesses of his resurrection (Mt 28:1-10; Jn 20:11-19). His great regard and respect for women is abundantly clear (Lk 7:13; Jn 8:3-11; Mk 5:34). He had women as friends and he challenged unjust and corrupt patriarchy when he forbade men to divorce their wives (Mk 10:1-12). He was not constricted by the prejudices of a male-dominated world. His choice of the twelve men was done deliberately, after much prayer (Lk 6:12-13). Christ chose freely (Jn 15:16).

Even though women are the first witnesses of the resurrection, it is the apostles who are commissioned and blessed by the Risen Jesus as his official witnesses (Lk 24:48, 51; Acts 1:2, 11). Vanhoye makes the point: 'When Judas had to be replaced ... Luke states that Peter expressly limited the choice to men (andres) (Acts 1:21) who had accompanied Jesus during his public life, although some women at the time had stronger claims since they had been more faithful to Jesus than his male disciples, even on Calvary and at the tomb' (Mt 27:55, 61) (Vanhoye, Albert, L'Osservatore Romano, 3/3/'93).

The apostles brought the gospel beyond the Jewish world to the cosmopolitan Greco-Roman world. This was a world where women priests were numerous. Still they did not confer the ministerial priesthood on women. Their guiding principle was to remain faithful to the will and plan of Christ.

A celibate priesthood

In contemporary discussion much is made of the assertion that Peter and perhaps other apostles were married. After Jesus speaks of the difficulties of entering the kingdom of God (Mt 19:24), Peter says: 'We have left everything and followed you. What then shall we have?' (Mt 19:27). Jesus promises a hundred fold and eternal life to those who have left everything: 'houses or brothers or sisters or father or mother or children or land for my name's sake' (Mt 19:29). Matthew does not mention a wife but presumably she is included. Luke clarifies this by adding 'wife' to this list (Lk 18:29). Although Peter denied Jesus before the crucifixion, it is most unlikely that after the resurrection Peter would have gone back on his fundamental declaration: 'We have left everything and followed you' (Mt 19:27). There was no question of Peter's wife or possible children being abandoned.

Peter was not leaving them unsupported in some lonely flat. Such an idea is an anachronism based on the modern nuclear family. His dependants would have been well cared for by the very extended family of 'brothers, sisters, father, mother' (Mt 19:29) that he was leaving behind. This included cousins, aunts, uncles and grandparents. The extended family of that time and culture took great interest and responsibility in raising the next generation. Consequently the boy Jesus could be missing for a full day without his parents worrying. They knew he would be with the caravan the extended family, 'their kinsfolk and acquaintances' (Lk 2:44).

Jesus praises the apostles' leaving everything (including wife) for his sake (Mt 19:27-29). He speaks of 'eunuchs who have made themselves eunuchs for the sake of the kingdom of heaven' (Mt 19:12). Celibacy will always have a cherished place in the priesthood.

The pastoral letters state that the one aspiring to ministry, if married, must be married only once (1 Tim 3:2, 12; Tit 1:6). A man in a second marriage was deemed by Paul to be incapable of living the continence expected of ecclesiastical office holders (cf 1 Cor 7:8ff). Jerome witnesses to this understanding in his refutation of Jovinian in AD 393. Augustine also supports this idea that a married man, once ordained was to embrace perfect continence. The apocryphal writings also support this.

Heid, Cochini, Cholij and others have concluded from New Testament studies that an obligation of lasting sexual continence did exist from apostolic times. Perfect continence was what 'the apostles taught and what antiquity itself observed' (African Council of AD 390). Heid concludes that: 'The prevailing opinion that the New Testament is devoid of any evidence for a discipline of celibacy, and even argues against it, can therefore scarcely withstand in-depth and meticulous scrutiny' (Heid, 57).

The problem with contemporary Irish discussion of this issue is that it is not often deep or meticulous but frequently shallow and emotive. Sometimes it even (unfairly and unjustly) connects celibacy with proneness to moral deviance. Fidelity to the New Testament strongly suggests that celibacy will have an honoured place in the living out of the priesthood of the future.

An exemplary priesthood

Paul addresses Timothy as 'man of God'. The priest is 'holy to the Lord' (Ex 28:36; Ps 106:16) or 'man of God' by virtue of what he is. Paul reminds Timothy: 'Do not neglect the gift you have, which was given you by prophetic utterance when the council of elders laid their hands upon you' (1 Tim 4:14). Pope John Paul reminded priests to appreciate who and what they are as well as what they do: 'The ordained ministry ... may never be reduced to its merely functional aspect since it belongs on the level of "being"' (Letter to Priests, Holy Thursday, 2004).

The priest must be holy also because of how he lives. He must be a trustworthy minister. Speaking of the ministry of the apostles Paul says: 'This is how one should regard us, as servants of Christ and stewards of the mysteries of God. Moreover it is required of stewards that they be found trustworthy' (1 Cor 4:1-2). Paul emphasises this to Timothy and Titus. To Timothy he says: 'Be an example to the faithful in word, in conversation, in charity, in faith and in chastity' (1 Tim 4:12). To Titus he says: 'Show yourself in all respects a model of good deeds, and in your teaching show integrity' (Titus 2:6). For Paul the apostle is someone to be imitated: 'Be imitators of me, as I am of Christ' (1 Cor 11:1).

For Peter too the priest must be an example, a selfless model for the flock. Priests are to tend the flock of God that is in their charge (1 Pet 5:2). The priesthood of the presbyters 'constitutes a special participation in the relationship that Christ himself has with the flock' (Vanhoye, 267). As model and shepherd the priest must lead the way and be exemplary. Peter's words are programmatic for the priestly ministry of the New Testament: 'Tend the flock of God that is in your charge, not by constraint but willingly, not for shameful gain but eagerly, not as domineering over those in your charge but being examples to the flock' (1 Pet 5:2-3).

A healing priesthood

The ordained ministry is a 'ministry of reconciliation' (2 Cor 5:18). It is Christ reconciling the world to himself (2 Cor 5:19) and the apostles are 'ambassadors for Christ, God making his appeal through us' (2 Cor 5:20).

James speaks of the priest in the context of healing of body and of soul. In this he is following the example of Jesus who sometimes cured the body to show that he had God's own authority to forgive sins and heal the soul (Mk 2:1-12). James says that if anyone is sick let him call for the priests of the church to pray over him and anoint him with oil in the Lord's name (Jas 5:14). If the sick person has committed sins they will be forgiven (Jas 5:15). James links the priest with healing and the forgiveness of sins. This interpretation is confirmed when James immediately says: 'Therefore confess your sins to one another ... that you may be healed' (Jas 5:16). James obviously intends this confession of sins to be linked to the healing work of the priest.

John emphasises the link between the apostles and the forgiveness of sins. They are clearly entrusted with what Paul calls 'the ministry of reconciliation'. As the Father sent Jesus for the forgiveness of sins, so he sends his apostles (Jn 20:21). He gave them the Holy Spirit saying: 'If you forgive the sins of any, they are forgiven' (Jn 20:23). He gave them his own power of forgiveness.

A rediscovery and embracing of the sacrament of penance should be a major part of the priestly ministry of healing. There are many good supports for people to help them deal with stress, trauma and the pressures of life. But these can only go so far. They cannot delve into the conscience or bring healing of soul. They cannot reach right into that most sacred place deep within us where we meet God. They cannot deal with sin. God must be involved in resolving these issues because they pertain to our relationship with God. The sacrament of penance is a sacrament of healing and through it God reaches into that place where no merely human analyst can reach, where 'the soul is divided from the spirit' (Heb 4:12).

A rediscovery of the priesthood involves a rediscovery of this amazing sacrament, so needed yet so neglected. Unfortunately the movement towards general absolution has turned the sacrament of reconciliation into yet another liturgical battlefield.

A faithful priesthood
Acts 20:18-34 is the only speech in Acts directed to the clergy and so of particular interest. Paul addressed the elders of Ephesus: 'Take heed to yourselves and to all the flock, in which the Holy Spirit has made you overseers, to care for the church of

God' (Acts 20:28). Paul warns of future heresy. This is the only time in Acts that reference is made to erroneous teachings within the church. It is significant given that this is the only direct address to clergy in Acts. Paul predicts that some priests would deviate from sound teaching, leading people towards themselves and away from Jesus: 'Take heed to yourselves ... after my departure, fierce wolves will come in among you, not sparing the flock; and from among your own selves will arise men speaking perverse things, to draw away the disciples after them. Therefore be alert' (Acts 20:28-31).

What Luke presents here is borne out by the message of the Risen Jesus to the church in Ephesus (Rev 2:1-7). She is praised for her toil and endurance. She has tested and found wanting those who claimed to be apostles and were not. However, unfortunately, she appears to have abandoned the love she first had and is urged to repent. Repentance must be part of the pilgrim church at all times. Enthusiasm will grow only when genuine love of God is rekindled.

Sometime this love has to be tough love. Paul's paternal relationship to the church in Corinth is clear in 1 Cor 4:21 when he asks: 'Shall I come to you with a rod, or with love in a spirit of gentleness?' Paul even speaks of excommunication so that the person may realise the seriousness of his sin and so repent 'that his spirit may be saved in the day of the Lord Jesus' (1 Cor 5:5). If Paul speaks harshly to his people it is out of fear for their sins and unrepentance (2 Cor 12:21). He speaks for their up-building (2 Cor 12:19). He also warns against false teachers and false apostles who proclaim a different gospel (2 Cor 11:13). What emerges most is Paul's pastoral concern: 'not that we [want to] domineer over your faith, but as companions we work for your joy' (2 Cor 1:24).

The priest should seek what is truly good for his people. He should not put his own desire for affirmation or popularity above the task of preaching the gospel fully and uncompromisingly, but always lovingly and sensitively. Unfortunately, to be highly regarded as a theologian in Ireland often means being vocal in deconstructing Catholic teaching. Such theologians are acclaimed as courageous and brave. 'Loyal dissent' is a clever term by which one can pretend to remain a faithful Catholic and simultaneously reject core teachings. One wonders if 'loyal dissent' is not more a meaningless contradiction than a trendy term.

The real risks are taken by those who embark on what Chesterton calls 'the adventure of orthodoxy'. Those who really go against the tide are those who try to remain faithful to Catholic truth, those who try to understand it and make it shine forth for others. C. S. Lewis addresses the dissenting theologian who prided himself on taking every risk: 'What risk? What was at all likely to come of it except what actually came – popularity, sales for your books, invitations, and finally a bishopric' (Lewis, 37). Questioning, dismantling and rebelling are easy – and sometimes profitable. The challenge is fidelity.

Conclusion

Through the laying-on of hands and prayer the priest is consecrated in Christ who is Truth. This establishes him in a specific relationship with Christ and his people. It inserts him into Christ's priestly offering of himself for the church (Eph 5:25-27). The priest is to live this out in a spiritual fatherhood of love and service to God's people.

Jesus still sanctifies and saves through his co-workers (1 Cor 3:9). His power and glory are often hidden under effort, toil and struggle. The New Testament is not silent about the difficulties faced by followers of Christ or even the possible treachery and betrayal amongst priests themselves (Acts 20:28-31).

Yet it is the positive image which shines forth as a challenge to be embraced and lived. The priest is called to be a servant of Christ, a steward of the mysteries of God and crucially, a trustworthy minister (1 Cor 4:1-2). Priesthood is about proclaiming 'Jesus Christ as Lord and ourselves as your servants for Jesus' sake' (2 Cor 4:5). No matter how overwhelming the task seems, human effort still sows the seed and God gives the growth (1 Cor 3:7). What God commands he makes possible by his grace.

When apostolic toil and suffering seem in vain, we have the

assurance that Christ has told us the truth. The ministerial priesthood flows from the will of Christ and the pages of the New Testament. It is not a human invention. This gives us, not arrogance or superiority but joy and conviction. It also gives us the confidence to move forward in faith, to 'put out into the deep,' (Lk 5:4) to try harder and to do better.

Select Bibliography

Cholij, Roman, *Clerical Celibacy in East and West*, Gracewing, Herefordshire, 1989.

Cochini, C., *The Apostolic Origins of Priestly Celibacy*, Ignatius, San Francisco, 1990.

Galot, Jean, *Theology of the Priesthood*, Ignatius, San Francisco, 1985.

George, Augustin, 'Priesthood' in Xavier Leon-Dufour, ed., *Dictionary of Biblical Theology*, (DBT), Chapman, London, 1972, pp. 406-411.

Haffner, Paul, *The Sacramental Mystery*, Gracewing, Herefordshire, 1999.

Hahn, Scott, *The Lamb's Supper*, Doubleday, New York, 1999.

Heid, Stefan, *Celibacy in the Early Church*, Ignatius, San Francisco, 2000.

Lambrecht, Jan, *Second Corinthians*, Liturgical Press, Minnesota, 1999.

Lewis, C. S., *The Great Divorce*, Collins, Glasgow, 1988.

Martin, Francis, '2 John' in Farmer, W.R., ed., *The International Bible Commentary*, Liturgical Press, Minnesota, 1998, pp. 1833-1836.

Mc Govern, Thomas J., *Priestly Identity*, Four Courts Press, Dublin, 2002.

Ratzinger, Joseph, *Ministers of Your Joy*, St Paul's, Slough, 1989.

Vanhoye, Albert, *Old Testament Priests and the New Priest*, St Bede's Publications, Massachusetts, 1980.

Von Balthasar, Hans Urs, *The Threefold Garland*, Ignatius, San Francisco, 1982.

Observations on the Ecumenical Challenge in Ireland today

Thomas Layden SJ

Some forty years after the Second Vatican Council, this article offers ten observations on ecumenism in Ireland, north and south.

1. We do not celebrate sufficiently that which we have in common
In the documents of the Council and in subsequent texts like those emanating from ARCIC (The Anglican Roman Catholic International Commission) and other dialogues, both churches proclaim that they are now at one on certain issues that previously divided them. Mutual recognition of each other's baptisms is one case in point. But how is this reflected in day to day church life? For church teaching to be received by the faithful it must first become known. How can it be known if it is not in some way reflected and expressed in liturgical and sacramental life? This would require imagination and creativity. The people in the pews need some clear signs that developments in ecumenical understanding are for real and are for all church members.

What might this look like in practice? On the feast of the Baptism of the Lord there might be an ecumenical service. The venue would change from year to year. This prayer would in-clude a sermon on baptism and the renewal of the baptismal promises by all present. If the ceremonies associated with bap-tism always take place within the confines of the buildings of one particular denomination, it is hardly surprising that popular awareness of our common and shared heritage in this area is so poorly known and so faintly appreciated. When people have occasion to attend a baptism in another church tradition, they often express surprise at how similar it is to their own. Should this really be such startling new knowledge for them? The churches need to devise ways of communicating to their members the significant agreed theological understanding they already share.

Another area in which we might highlight what we hold in common is in relation to Bible study. For the past three years I have led a Bible study group in a Church of Ireland parish. It has proved to be an enriching experience for all the participants and is an example of how we can appropriate and appreciate the vitality and richness of the scriptures.

2. We have learned to disagree more agreeably
In the past, and certainly in the time before the Second Vatican Council, Catholic-Protestant theological exchanges, where they occurred at all, were often polemical in nature. There has been a marked improvement in the tone of such encounters and they are now most often genuine dialogues. This process has been assisted by the well-established bilateral theological dialogues between the churches. Part of our current reality is the fact that there are often differences between theologians of the same confession apparently just as significant as those between theologians from different denominational backgrounds. There is a greater maturity in inter-church conversation nowadays. Examples that come to mind include how the Church of England and the Church of Ireland responded to the teaching document of the Catholic Bishops of England and Wales, Ireland and Scotland on the eucharist, *One Bread, One Body* (1998). The Anglican response took issue with the document's stance on eucharistic sharing, doing so in a way which was both respectful and non-polemical. The reaction of other Christian churches to the document from the Congregation for the Doctrine of the Faith, *Dominus Jesus* (2001), was in a similar vein.

The ordination of women in the Anglican Church has been problematic in dialogue between Catholics and Anglicans but it has not brought it to an end. Disagreement does not necessarily have to end in the breakdown of the relationship but if handled responsibly can be a moment of growth and opportunity.

A truly Christian attribute is to seek to view a situation from the vantage point of the other. In the past forty years both Catholics and Protestants have enlarged their capacity to appreciate each other's theological and historical perspectives. There is an increased willingness to ask questions and to seek clarification rather than presuming that the answer is already known. Two examples spring to mind: firstly, why did the Reformers opt for two sacraments rather than seven? Secondly, what does Catholic theology intend by use of the term 'tradition'? We have moved from what was in many ways a cold-war between the Catholic and Protestant churches in the years prior to the Council, through a time of initial enthusiasm in the heady fervour of the 1960s, to a time of more sober discussion when there is the confidence to look at difference and discuss it calmly.

There is enough confidence now between the parties to ensure that difficulties can be faced up to rather than swept under the carpet. With Presbyterian friends I have found myself exploring the appropriateness or otherwise of the attendance of Catholic bishops or clergy at the annual General Assembly of the Presbyterian Church in Ireland. With Church of Ireland friends I have had interesting discussions about the propriety of the use of church buildings for services by members of the Loyal Orders. Protestants have asked me whether the Catholic Church is concerned that some northern Protestants feel that Northern Ireland has become 'a cold house' for them.

3. We are insufficiently pained by the reality of disunity and the scandal it represents

We tend to take disunity as a given and are not shocked or discomforted by it. It does not cause any visceral pain. At the 1910 Edinburgh Missionary Conference, which is often hailed as the birthplace of modern Protestant ecumenism, the delegates were possessed of a profound awareness that division, competition and rivalry between various Christian groups was an obstacle to preaching the good news in mission lands. This in turn generated a movement to work against this disunity and towards the

achievement of some form of visible unity. The disunity constituted scandal, an obstacle to faith in Jesus Christ.

Catholic and Protestant ecumenists had something of this
sense in the 1960s but it does not greatly impact upon believers
nowadays. It casts a certain shadow in specific situations. The
reality of disunity, for example, is inescapable for couples con-
templating an inter-church marriage. Problems relating to full
eucharistic sharing become manifestly obvious in certain public
situations. In these moments people experience disunity directly
and it is a painful one. The great prayer of John 17 'that they
might all be one so that the world might believe', could be a
scriptural incentive to quicken our desire for the healing of
divisions going back centuries.

One concrete way of cultivating this sensitivity to the pain of
disunity could be more frequent and judicious use of the Votive
Masses for the Unity of Christians and their accompanying
scriptural readings. These texts are sometimes employed during
the Week of Prayer for Christian Unity, but they can and should
be used at other times. Might not a diocese, a province or an
episcopal conference recommend their more frequent use during the liturgical year, perhaps on a quarterly basis? We often
speak of the need to raise consciousness concerning matters of
social justice. I would argue that the Christian churches and
their ministers have to find more effective ways of raising the
consciousness of Christians about the painful reality of inter-
church divisions.

Friday is traditionally a day on which believers remember
the suffering and passion of the Lord. On certain Fridays of the
year church leaders could encourage prayer for healing of these
ancient divisions. These prayers might be for the grace of a con-
trite spirit, so that we might repent of the ways in which we have
contributed to perpetuating this state of affairs.

4. For many full, organic union seems a far-off prospect, if attainable at all
Substantial change coming rapidly describes one part of church
life in the 1960s. This was especially the case in the area of inter-

church relations. Catholics began to read the Bible, prayed in the vernacular in their official worship and started to sing hymns in church that a previous generation would have labelled Protestant. Growing up in the west of Ireland at the time I well remember a Protestant friend saying to us one evening after coming from a funeral Mass earlier that day: 'You are becoming more like us every day.' Twenty years earlier such an observation would have been most improbable. Such was the apparent pace of change and so stark was the contrast with the experience of previous generations that the attainment of full visible unity between Catholics and Orthodox or Catholics and Anglicans seemed more a matter of time than anything else. Ecumenical activities were coloured with energy, expectancy and enthusiasm.

But the ecumenical train started to slow in the 1970s. Some began to wonder if it had not permanently stalled. Even where there seemed to be progress in bilateral dialogues, the sponsoring churches sometimes seemed slow and hesitant when it came to ratifying and confirming the conclusions. New difficulties appeared on the horizon in the 1980s, which would not have been anticipated in the heady days of the council. Full union was not going to happen in the short term. Would it ever really happen? Was it possible at all? Christian theology summonses us to live in the between-time, that is between the 'already now' and the 'not yet'. We live between all that God has done for us in the life, death and resurrection of Jesus Christ and what God will do for us in the fullness of the kingdom.

The Second Vatican Council was truly a moment of *kairos* for the Catholic and other Christian churches whose delegates attended as observers. It was a moment of grace. But it was not the coming of the kingdom in its fullness. For those of us who wait and labour in the between-time patience and hope are the order of the day. Full unity is not going to occur in the short term. But we can be assured that the work of ecumenism is graced, arising from the call of the gospel and a sign of the Spirit's ongoing activity in the church and in the world in our time. It may be in a slower phase right now but that is no reason to give up or lose heart. If one were to come up with an image to describe this time it might be that of a parent with an adolescent child. The days of playing with the laughing child are now gone and replaced with days of dealing with one who goes through mood changes and seems distant. But development is happening, difficult and all as it can be for the parent to immediately apprehend it.

5. Good practice at local level often remains unreported and under-appreciated
While there may not now be the euphoria of the early days of the ecumenical movement, good things are happening on the ground in many different parts of the country. There are some strong and well-established local ecumenical groups. There is a danger that their contribution can be overlooked or even taken for granted. These groups take many different forms reflecting the area of the country, the gifts of individuals and the histories of those involved.

In north Belfast where I currently live there is a small but committed and energetic ecumenical clergy fellowship. It consists of clergy, Church of Ireland, Presbyterian and Catholic, working in that part of the city. It meets monthly for prayer and reflection on issues of concern in our ministry, and for mutual support. The fellowship helps us to serve better those who live in an area of the city which has known very trying times, and where there is also, however, a strong sense of neighbourly support and pride. In the course of the past year, we have organised various activities: pulpit exchanges during the Week of Prayer for Christian Unity; a meeting with the local police commander; a meetings with Housing Executive officials; a lecture on the traditions of the Russian Orthodox Church and a Lenten breakfast meeting for members of those churches whose clergy attend the fellowship. This last event included some input from the head of the Community Relations Council in Northern Ireland.

A notable feature of the fellowship is that the members look forward to the meetings and that it develops a good sense of

community among the participating clergy. I know that this is
the story of just one group, but it is an instance of good practice
at local level. Such practice needs to be reported so that it can be
a source of encouragement. Variations on the approach of this
group may well prove effective and practicable in other areas.

Another example of helpful practice at local level would be
the course on prayer which a Presbyterian minister and I co-pre-
sented and co-facilitated in the minister's congregation in
Dunmurry, Co Antrim in Lent 2003. It was an introductory
course on prayer inspired largely by the *Spiritual Exercises* of St
Ignatius of Loyola. We took it in turn to introduce the topics for
six successive Tuesdays in Lent, shared in leading the participants in certain spiritual exercises and in reflecting on them in
small groups and in the larger group. The course met a real need
in the congregation and was open to members of other churches,
who, happily, have asked for some kind of follow-up. This format could be adapted and used in other contexts.

It is vital that those involved in this kind of ministry use whatever forms of communication are open to them to inform others
of what they find to be effective and what they have learned. Do
we really make full use of *The Furrow, Doctrine and Life,* diocesan
publications of various kinds, radio, television, and the internet
to pass on stories of good practice to others?

*6. Ecumenism is a different experience in the North to what it is in the
South*
Since ordination in 1991, half of my time in ministry has been
spent in the North and the other half in the South. Having been
involved in ecumenical activities in both parts of the country I
can attest to the differences in both places. The socio-political situation in the North and in particular the enormous sufferings of
the years of the Troubles colours ministry in this area. For someone who has been burned out of house and home by those perceived to be on the other side, or who has had a family member
murdered by those identified with the others, the theological
convergence aimed at in ecumenical dialogue can seem theoreti-

cal and far removed from the realities of daily life. On the other hand, the existence of Nationalist-Unionist polarisation, mirrored in some way in Catholic-Protestant tensions, can be a spur and an incentive to commit to the ecumenical task. The difficult history, the ambiguities and uncertainties of the current stage of the peace process can generate a sense of urgency about the need for ecumenical contacts. We need to be able to talk to others and hear their story and they ours if both communities are going to be able to live here together in mutual peace and respect based on justice.

It is sometimes said that all politics is local and a similar comment can be made about ecumenical ministry. The latter has to take account of the local situation and its peculiar sensitivities. As a southerner working in the North I am aware of how crucial it is to attend to the experience and insight of those who have lived here all their lives and who have been touched by the socio-political realities at first hand. By the same token voices from outside can play a helpful role in encouraging local ecumenical ministry and can point to the experience and practice of the wider universal church.

In the South a different socio-political reality pertains. In recent decades there were some parts of it where it seemed almost impossible to find a Protestant living. With the advent of the Celtic Tiger and the arrival of immigrants in sizeable numbers this has changed somewhat. Ecumenical ministry in Ireland, if it is to be healthy, needs to foster North-South links and contacts between local churches here and local churches in other parts of the world. *Oekumene* refers to the whole-inhabited universe. True ecumenism counters any form of insularity and encourages Christians to take a wider view, while at the same time being in tune with the characteristics of the local situation.

7. Catholics and Protestants need to confront the ugly spectre of sectarianism in the North and the extent to which they might be complicit in it
The groundbreaking work in this area has been done by Joseph Liechty and Cecilia Clegg in their *Moving Beyond Sectarianism*

(2001). If it is sometimes said that ecumenism is ethereal and not very practical, this is one clear instance where its concreteness and practicality come into play. If grace opposes sin, then it is clear that ecumenism must confront sectarianism. To be sure sectarianism is a societal problem larger than its theological component, but there certainly is a role for Christian ministry and theology in tackling it.

One of the key insights which I garnered from *Moving Beyond Sectarianism* is that groups can end up being sectarian in the consequences of what they do, even if their intention was completely to the contrary. As Christians we have the regular custom of examining our lives and our consciences. Those of us who work in the North need to call the groups and the communities whom we serve to reflect on our own practice and to be open to the possibility that we are unwittingly sectarian in some of the things which we do. To give two simple examples. Firstly, I came across a very fine post-primary school which scheduled its open evening for prospective students and their parents on the very evening that the local ecumenical service for Unity Week was taking place in a nearby church. This happened for a number of years. There was no intention to snub the local unity service in any way but those attending the open evening were automatically excluded from participating in the service. Secondly, the words we employ can have meanings other than we intend. The use of the word 'non-Catholic', for example, is hurtful to Protestants. Similarly, it is offensive to Catholics when people question whether they are Christians or claim that they worship Mary.

8. More work remains to be done in relation to inter-church marriages
The work of the Northern Ireland Mixed Marriage Association and the Association of Inter-Church Families in the South, and of sympathetic clergy, has eased the burden of pressure and isolation which had previously affected couples in mixed religious relationships. But more remains to be done in this context, especially in the case of couples in the North where one or both

partners comes from a working class background. Because of the segregated nature of housing in working class districts, real problems can arise when it comes to finding a place to live. There can be practical difficulties in choosing a location for the ceremony in which the families of both parties will feel comfortable and at home. Those involved in ministry with such couples need to show creativity and compassion. For many in ministry a real turning point can come when they have exposure to an inter-church marriage in their own family. With the experience of so many couples over the past generation there is a rich vein of wisdom available for ministers from which to benefit. Often the better teachers are those who have been through the process themselves, both for the younger couples and for the clergy involved. Will those of us in ministry be able to let ourselves be taught by them?

9. The conciliar insight that the Church of Christ 'subsists' in the Catholic Church stands in need of reception and further reflection
When Vatican II's Document on the Church, *Lumen Gentium*, speaks of the Church of Christ 'subsisting' in the Catholic Church (par 8), it opens up a new way for Catholics to look at their own and other Christian churches. It is a movement away from a previous tendency to identify the Body of Christ exclusively with the Catholic Church. It is an acknowledgement that there are elements of the Church of Christ present in the other churches and ecclesial communities. There has been vigorous theological debate about the precise meaning of the word 'subsists', but it remains nevertheless true that the Council has summoned all Catholics to a broader and more comprehensive understanding of the church universal that is inclusive of other churches, be they Anglican, Orthodox or Protestant. Some of this thinking has filtered through on the ground in local churches, but much remains to be done before it becomes part and parcel of the mindset of the average Catholic in the pews. Little reminders to reinforce the point would help, like the simple gesture of praying for the leaders of other churches by name in the prayer

of the faithful and doing the same for the pastors and congregations of local churches of other denominations. One could go a step further and ask a minister from a Reformed church to assist at a day of training for ministers of the word or to help out at a preaching seminar for priests or seminarians. I am familiar with the story of a Catholic priest who trained an Anglican priest in the art of presiding at eucharist.

10. In a more secular society ecumenical concerns can seem irrelevant
A society in which religion is taken seriously and in which regular churchgoing is typical more readily appreciates the function of ecumenical work. In the more secular society of the South today, it evokes less immediate comprehension or support. We are now at a different stage in history, at least in the southern part of the country. There are some signs, too, of secularisation in the North but its pace is much slower there. This has the overall effect of changing the context and the climate in which ecumenists minister. Many readers of Irish newspapers were fascinated at the time by the accounts of the Vatican II debates. Would this be the case now? Hardly.

Those involved in ministry are required to take cognisance of this changed situation. If popular apathy regarding ecumenism is encountered, one ought not be surprised. Again, this can be seen as an opportunity for some creative response. A well written and accessible column in a daily newspaper, outlining the progress in ecumenical understanding and practice in the past forty years, could well summon up previously untapped interest. So could an attractively presented television documentary or an imaginative website. An inter-church group could well provide a forum and a focus for such explorations. One thing to avoid, however, is looking back to an imagined golden age and regretting its demise.

Conclusion
These ten theses will hopefully assist readers in reflecting on the ecumenical dimensions of ministry in the context of the Irish

church. Ecumenism has to be seen as integral to church life and not as some form of optional extra. As Ireland heads into a new moment of history with the possibility of a new political arrangement in the North emerging and a new demographic mix in the South, the churches are being given an opportunity to work together to ensure that Christianity has its due place.

Select Bibliography
The Catholic Bishops Conferences of England and Wales, Ireland and Scotland, *One Bread, One Body: A Teaching Document on the Eucharist in the Life of the Church*, Veritas, Dublin, 1998
Cecilia Clegg and Joseph Liechty, *Moving Beyond Sectarianism*, Columba Press, Dublin, 2001
Interchurch Families Journal Vol 12, Number 2, Summer 2004.
J. P. Mackey and E McDonagh (eds), *Religion and Politics in Ireland at the Turn of the Millennium*, Columba Press, Dublin, 2003

Catechesis:
Bridge from Rite of Passage to Sacrament

Niall Coll

A pastoral situation

Recently I found myself assisting in a quite conventional Irish country parish in the absence of the local priest who was on holiday. My instructions were simple: preside at the three weekend Masses and be prepared to officiate at any funeral that might arise at that time. The Masses were celebrated and, fortunately, no parishioners died. However, one particularly memorable thing did happen. I was approached by the mother of a baby on a Saturday evening and informed that she wanted her child baptised the next day (Sunday). I was somewhat startled by the woman's abruptness and by the short notice she was giving. I sensed that she was not a churchgoer. Wishing to be as welcoming as possible, I congratulated her on the birth of her daughter, her second child; I went on to suggest that it might be better for her to wait a few days until the parish priest returned: she could then discuss the matter with him, do the necessary preparations and have him preside at the christening. The pastor is a conscientious fellow and I knew that he would be keen to meet her and the child's father: he would see the baptism as an excellent opportunity to reach out pastorally to them. It might even prove to be the occasion when they would sense a welcome in the parish and embark on a pattern of regular Mass attendance.

The proposal was met with a withering look. The woman insisted that there was no need for any such meeting or preparation and that she did not have enough time anyway. If this were to be required she would just go to any number of neighbouring parishes where no mention would be made of such things and have her daughter baptised without further delay. I was about to explain that in the United States, Germany, Britain and many other countries this type of process was the norm, when she said that the child was already six weeks old and, moreover, had not been keeping too well. The implication was clear: the old fear (superstition?) that a child does not thrive physically if it has not been baptised has persisted. I had to make a quick decision: do I simply defer the baptism, or agree in the hope that the beauty and meaning of the ritual might strike the right chord? I opted for the latter approach and we duly gathered at the appointed time the next day.

The congregation was small. Only the two parents, the godparents and the baptismal candidate's four-year old brother attended. As the ceremony began it was soon evident that the baptismal party was for the most part at sea with the prayers and rubrics: this was all the more apparent because of the absence of grandparents who normally save the day in such circumstances. We persevered and I tried as best I could, and in the briefest of manners, to help them have a basic grasp of the meaning of the various parts of the rite: anointing with oil, pouring of water, use of the paschal candle and so on. Our progress through the liturgy was punctuated by vigorous acrobatic displays by the four-year-old who found the sanctuary area very inviting for cartwheels. Soon I stumbled on a task for the child to keep him more focused on the baptism: he held the vessels containing the oils of catechumen and chrism, and settled down.

When the ceremony ended, a few photographs were taken and the baptismal party adjourned to a local pub. I was informed that a large group comprising families and friends would be awaiting their arrival there. They had not attended the religious festivities. But the day was yet young and the christening was now to afford an opportunity for celebration and merriment in more secular surroundings. So we said our goodbyes.

Reflecting on that situation

That baptism has given me food for thought. The mother was adamant that the child should be baptised. But there was little evidence that she, her husband or the godparents, saw it as a vital religious or spiritual event through which the child would become a sharer in the death and resurrection of Christ, and a member of his body, the church. To be sure, it was a rite of passage, and it would be ungenerous not to recognise their wish that God, through the ritual, should in someway bless the child – evidence indeed of an enduring sacramental sense. But their grasp of the meaning and consequences of the sacrament fell far short of its deeper reality. As I reflected on the matter and on the downward trend in Mass attendance in recent years, I found little grounds for confidence that the parents would give the child anything other than a nominal rearing in the faith. I hope that I am mistaken. It seems likely that the next three occasions that she, and many others like her, will be in church with her parents will be for first confession, first communion and confirmation. But what about in between and after?

That particular but not untypical experience points to a growing gap between what the church understands by the sacraments and what more and more people in our increasingly secularised Irish society assume about them. For many, the sacraments are little more than individual supernatural commodities to be had on demand. Commitment to nurturing, through regular practice, the faith that is professed at baptism, first confession, first communion and confirmation is often weak, save for Christmas, weddings and funerals. It follows that general levels of Mass attendance and commitment to the parish suffer. The general lack of response from the Irish bishops to this growing trend could hardly be interpreted as implying any ambivalence on their part. It is more likely an indication of an inability to discern an adequate pastoral response. One of their number, however, Dr Bill Murphy of Kerry, did attract media attention recently when he asked if it makes any sense for parents who are themselves lacking in faith, to present their children for sacraments (Chrism Mass homily, 2004). Meanwhile, those on the frontline of the church's pastoral ministry are called upon more and more to preside at sacraments and other liturgies, with substantial numbers of people who have only a tenuous link with their deeper meaning. These events obviously present opportunities for both renewal and conversion, but there seems little expectation of such possibilities. The general thrust of Irish pastoral practice would seem to accommodate all who seek baptism, first communion, confirmation and marriage without delaying long to consider questions regarding disposition and commitment. In such circumstances, there is a danger of demoralisation creeping in for those in ministry if they are over-exposed to indifference and unresponsiveness. Similarly, many of the lay faithful, both committed and searching, can be scandalised by clergy who seem lax and perfunctory in the way that they are prepared to admit people to the sacraments without also attempting at least a minimum level of catechesis. In the current context, to continue unquestioningly celebrating sacraments as before may only serve to secularise the sacraments, rather than sacramentalising or evangelising the secular – grace builds on nature.

There is no doubt that the church is facing a grave cultural and pastoral crisis, which is having profound and far-reaching implications for every aspect of its life and mission. The church is being challenged to renew its pastoral practice. An essential feature of this general process of renewal is the need to breathe fresh life into our appreciation of the sacraments. We must promote among Irish Catholics a more holistic understanding of sacraments as both perceptible signs (which can be seen, heard, tasted, touched and smelled) for the common worship of God, and also as special moments of grace provided by Christ through which we encounter him. Preaching and catechesis must be directed with greater vigour to these ends. Our goal must be to inject greater depth and meaning into both preparation and celebration. To do this, parents and teachers will need much more support from the wider faith community.

Pope John Paul II, aware of the magnitude of the task faced by the church, particularly in Western society today, has called repeatedly on all the faithful to engage in a 'new evangelisation'. Translating this vision into everyday practice will involve transforming the shape of local parishes. The religious educationalist, Thomas Groome, in a compact sentence, reminds us that the ambitious nature and purpose of catechetical education is 'to inform, form and transform Christian persons and communities as apprentices to Jesus Christ for God's reign in the world' (Groome, 6-7). It follows that it is never enough to introduce people to the sacramental richness of Catholicism without also ensuring that it is preceded by a process of evangelisation, which is itself consolidated in the ongoing life of home, school (for children) and parish. As John Paul II puts it in *Catechesi Tradendae*: 'the ecclesial community at all levels has a twofold responsibility with regard to catechesis: it has the responsibility of providing for the training of its members, but it also has the responsibility of welcoming them into an environment where they can live as fully as possible what they have learned' (par 25).

The Irish approach to sacraments

To understand why the Irish church finds itself in the current situation where many people present themselves or their children for sacraments while possessing only marginal commitment, we have to delve briefly into the complexities of Irish history. As the Catholic Church emerged in the nineteenth century from the penal persecutions, it managed, in the memorable phrase of Emmet Larkin, 'to build itself into the very vitals of the nation'. Louise Fuller, in describing Ireland from then until the 1950s, says that the Catholic Church 'exercised a type of cultural hegemony', where Catholic belief, practice and moral order 'provided an all-encompassing definition of reality' (Fuller, 10). Mass attendance and general sacramental practice were at rates unsurpassed in other Catholic countries. The symbolic expressions of Catholicism were everywhere to be seen in the home as well as in public. The church exercised a pre-eminent role in the provision of education and through its network of schools hard won in the nineteenth century, and subsequently jealously guarded, transmitted the Catholic religious and cultural heritage. Generations of children received a religious education and were prepared for admittance to the sacraments of penance, communion and confirmation. This model of sacramental progression constituted an integral part of each pupil's Catholic school experience and was almost universally valued in wider Irish society. As adulthood beckoned each person could expect life's key moments to be similarly marked by the sacramental system at marriage, or in ordination to the priesthood for men, or on one's deathbed in extreme unction (last rites). Meanwhile through the span of a lifetime there would be ongoing recourse to the eucharist and to confession. For most Irish people Catholicism and being Irish seemed inextricably bound.

The secularising trends that have so shaped contemporary Western society have radically altered the church's position in Irish society. The last few decades have seen the collapse of the Catholic Church's cultural ascendancy in the South, and that epoch is now all too often dismissed as one of insularity and intolerance. But there is a curious anomaly. The church, both North and South, still has an important role to play in the provision of schooling at both primary and secondary levels, though its influence on the shape of the general curriculum is peripheral. Catholic primary schools continue to provide religious education and to prepare children for the sacraments of reconciliation, communion and confirmation. They do so with the consent of the great majority of parents who, even though they may vary widely in their commitment to their children's attendance at church, and their own, are nonetheless anxious to have them admitted to the sacraments, and frequently lavish money on ensuring that the trappings are extravagant. Rumours of a total collapse of the Catholic cultural heritage in Ireland are somewhat exaggerated!

The growing non-denominational Gaelscoileanna sectors in both parts of the country, and the integrated schools in the North, sensitive to this parental demand for sacraments, are also anxious to prepare children for first confession, first communion and confirmation. And this in spite of the fact that many of these particular schools have made a definite decision otherwise to

avoid any specifically denominational component in their curriculum; in fact some of the Gaelscoileanna firmly eschew any
other mention of Christian teaching outside of the short periods
of sacramental preparation. One way or another, it is still the
norm in the weeks after Easter Sunday, in Irish cities and towns
as well as rural areas, to see first communion children, particularly the girls, dressed elaborately for the big day. It is very rem-
iniscent of the cultural Catholicism that is such a marked characteristic of the Mediterranean countries.

The enduring popularity of the celebrations of first communion and confirmation, however, does not mean that all is well.
The real work of preparation for these sacraments is left more
often than not to the schools. This places a heavy burden on
them and on individual teachers and many of them make an
outstanding effort to ensure that the children are as well prepared as possible. It cannot always be assumed, however, that
every school or teacher accords the necessary priority to a genuine catechesis. There are competing demands for time and attention in the curriculum, and teachers themselves differ in their
own commitment to the faith. If the support at home both in
terms of catechesis and the example of regular religious practice
– which is vital – falls short, then, in the context of a more secular
Ireland, it is all the more likely that children will lack an adequate appreciation of the faith or of the sacraments.

Similarly, many local parishes abdicate their proper role in
the preparation of children, and confine their involvement to the
actual liturgical ceremony itself. Catholics from other parts of
the world are often amazed at the minimal contribution that the
average Irish parish makes to catechesis. In the interest of fair-
ness, however, it has to be acknowledged that many Irish
parishes might argue that there is little sense in their contribut-
ing to the building costs and management of schools if the work
of catechetical preparation is going to fall back on them anyway.
Whatever the merits of this argument, it is clear that the current
modus operandi is untenable. Happily, there are already some
very positive attempts to model a framework for a real partner-

ship in catechesis between home, school, and parish: one example is the *Do This in Memory* programme for first penance and communion that has been piloted in the dioceses of Kildare and Leighlin and Ossory.

It is increasingly clear that schools need more support from the local faith communities to play their part in handing on the faith. An ageing priesthood with diminishing personnel may feel alarmed at the implication of more work and ensuing financial costs. Nonetheless, as leaders in their parishes, the clergy are well positioned to promote and encourage the development of networks of lay people who, in partnership with the school, will assist in catechesis (though not all teachers may agree to, or feel the need for, such external involvement). Able and committed catechists, working on either a paid or a voluntary basis, could assist the school, as appropriate, in the preparation of the children, and also help strengthen the links with both home and parish. (Of course, due regard for child protection considerations are essential.) More particularly, such groups, drawn from the local parish, or parish cluster, could play a particularly important role in organising courses for parents, something that cannot be supplied by the school. As the pupils are brought through the religious education programmes at primary school, so might their parents undertake a number of evening classes to equip them better to fulfil their vital role with their children. This would also provide an opportunity to help deepen appreciation and knowledge of their own faith: in a curious way the children become the catalysts in the evangelisation of their own parents. Attention could also be given to helping them with prayer, not least because the children's RE programmes lay such stress on it, but also because so many parents in their twenties, thirties and forties, find praying difficult and would benefit from some tutoring on the different approaches to which their children are being introduced. Engaged and well-informed parents who take an active interest in their children's religious education are a tremendous benefit to both school and parish, and above all, to the children.

The urgency of the need to explore and develop new approaches to handing on the faith, both in the school and in a more explicit parish context, is underlined by reports that the Irish National Teachers Organisation has already signalled that in the future many teachers may be unwilling to catechise their pupils and prepare them for the sacraments (Statement by John Carr, General Secretary, 17 February 2004). It would be foolish to ignore such signals. We must begin planning for the future now. With the growth of secularisation and the corresponding decline in the church's influence on government and civil society generally, and in the context of the increasing religious diversity in Ireland in the wake of the Celtic Tiger, it is not inconceivable that schools, in the next two or three decades, will cease entirely to do catechetical preparation. In such circumstances it is likely that whatever time would be available for RE would be given over to a general introduction to world faiths.

Returning to the present, first communion and confirmation are certainly important rites of passage that parents and children cherish. However inappropriate, there are sufficient anecdotes about the purely financial benefits that accrue to children from the wider circle of family and friends to suggest that, if for no other reason, they will remain important features of Irish life for the foreseeable future. But that is no grounds for complacency: it is abundantly clear that the Irish church should do more to help catechise these children and their parents and to help them all appreciate and experience, in an age-appropriate manner, the full richness of the sacraments. Pope John Paul II has spoken more than anyone about the need to ensure that a personal, even intimate relationship with Christ should be the goal of all programmes of catechesis. He writes: 'the definite aim of catechesis is to put people not only in touch but in communion, in intimacy, with Jesus Christ: only he can lead us to the love of the Father in the Spirit and make us share in the life of the Holy Trinity' (*Catechesi Tradendae*, 5). Referring in particular to the catechetical needs of children, John Paul II asserts that their initial catechesis should not be a fragmentary one, 'since it will have to reveal, although in an elementary way, all the principal mysteries of the faith and their effects on the child's moral and religious life'. He goes on to say that it should aim to give 'meaning to the sacraments', while at the same time acknowledging that catechesis itself 'receives from the experience of the sacraments a living dimension that keeps it from remaining merely doctrinal, and it communicates to the child the joy of being a witness to Christ in ordinary life' (Ibid, 37).

Grounding the sacraments in Christ
To draw the threads of the argument here together, it is enough to say that many Irish Catholics have been socialised into expecting an automatic admission to the sacraments and that it is not always clear whether they see an intimate link between them and the person of Christ. The connection may at first seem self-evident; but contemporary experience suggests it certainly is not. Such is the cultural assumption in Ireland that people should be admitted to the sacraments, that there is a real risk that sheer routine results in their spiritual richness being diminished or overlooked in a haze of utilitarian thinking and shallowness.

It has to be insisted then that any good catechesis will underline the intimate connection between Christ, the church and the seven sacraments. The *Catechism of the Catholic Church* asserts that the mysteries of Christ's life which were manifested in his ministry, death and resurrection 'are the foundations of what he would henceforth dispense in the sacraments' (par 1115). And again it teaches that 'The purpose of the sacraments is to sanctify men [and women], to build up the Body of Christ and, finally, to give worship to God' (par 1123). Put simply, the grace that the sacraments extend to us is the grace of our Lord Jesus Christ.

It is imperative that the christological foundations of the sacraments be underlined and that three fundamental points concerning them receive more attention in catechesis and preaching. Firstly, Catholics need a more lively appreciation of the truth that Jesus Christ is the ultimate source of the sacraments and, secondly, that he is also the true minister of every sacrament. The human minister stands in for Christ, but Christ himself remains as the true minister, and the sacraments are his. This is the reason for the church's teaching that the validity of the sacraments does not depend on the worthiness or otherwise of the human minister or recipient. In the language of traditional Catholic theology, sacraments confer grace *ex opere operato*, though it also teaches that right dispositions are necessary on the part of the recipient if grace is to be really effectual. Thirdly, Jesus Christ is also the content of the sacraments. By virtue of each of the sacraments, not just the eucharist, we are encountering Christ, receiving his grace, which means his presence in our lives. The American Franciscan, Kenan Osborne, brings this point out very strikingly when he writes:

> One might hear the word 'baptism', and think immediately of water. One might hear the words 'confirmation', and think immediately of oil. One might hear the word 'eucharist', and think immediately of bread and wine ... [But] when one hears the word 'baptism', one should think of Jesus; when one hears the words 'confirmation', one should think of Jesus; when one hears the word 'eucharist', one should think of Jesus, and so on (Osborne, 76).

To conclude, the Catholic Church in Ireland, in the context of a changing society, is being challenged today to explore new approaches to catechesis and sacramental preparation. Fresh vigour, imagination and a firm rootedness in the faith are qualities essential to the task of helping Irish Catholics bridge the gap between a view of sacraments as mere rites of passage to a full recognition and experience of them as sacred symbols that powerfully mediate, through the power of the Holy Spirit, God's grace in Jesus. A challenge therefore presents itself to us, and calls for a vital response.

Select Bibliography
Fuller, Louis, *Irish Catholicism since 1950: The Undoing of a Culture*, Gill & Macmillan, Dublin, 2002

Groome, Thomas, 'Total Catechesis/Religious Education' in Thomas Groome & Harold Daly (eds), *Horizons and Hopes: The Future of Religious Education*, Paulist Press, Mahwah, NJ, 2003

John Paul II, Apostolic Exhortation *Catechesi Tradendae* (On Catechesis In Our Time), CTS, London, 1979

Osborne, Kenan, *Sacramental Theology: A general Introduction*, Paulist Press, Mahwah, NJ, 1988

Unworthy of their Questions: Tranquillising the Urge towards Transcendence in Young People

Breda O'Brien

'The young are a foreign country; they do things differently there.' With apologies to L. P. Hartley, who spoke of the past as a different country, it is important to realise young people are in many ways inhabiting foreign territory, too. How aware are we of the culture of this 'different country'? How does it impact on the faith needs of young people? To what extent are we meeting the faith needs we presume young people to have, rather than the ones they really have? Are we meeting somewhat hesitantly and ineptly even the needs we presume they have?

A young person's beliefs about religion are formed by eclectic sources, and the media play an important role. When adults discuss 'media', they usually mean broadsheet newspapers and current affairs programmes. Young people may only buy newspapers for sport or the TV guide, and are more likely to be *au fait* with the affairs in *Coronation Street* than current affairs. An American academic, Lynn Schofield Clark, in her book, *From Angels to Aliens,* looks at where religious affiliation, media consumption, and belief in the supernatural intersect. The area of the supernatural intrigues her, because it provides a way of understanding the impact of media consumption on religious beliefs among young people from age eleven to twenty-one. While her book is based on ethnographic research among American young people, and the context in Ireland is very different, there is a large overlap in the kind of media consumed by American and Irish young people. To give some examples, *The X-files, Buffy the Vampire Slayer,* and *Angel* on television; the *Matrix, Minority Report* and *The Sixth Sense* on film; and the phenomenal success of first, *Harry Potter,* and the very different

Lord of the Rings, which span books and films, not to mention
quantities of merchandising. Since so much of the media they
consume is the same in both countries, it is not fanciful to presume that the way in which they construct their religious beliefs
might also be similar. Clark focuses on the supernatural, and
while it is not the intention here to focus on young people's interaction with the paranormal, her work throws light on where
religion and spirituality fit into their lives.

Living in a much more media-dominated world than their
parents, young people to some extent assemble the contents of
their beliefs as they might 'assemble a salad from a salad bar', to
quote Sara Begley in an article on spirituality in an American
edition of *Newsweek*. Yet even that statement is too simple. Many
religious educators will notice that some young people, for example, happily combine a belief in reincarnation with calling
themselves Catholic or Christian. Yet some others choose to assemble something very close to what we would recognise as
conventional religious belief. In spite of that, Clark points out:

> Teens, like their parents and other adults today, do not seem
> to be very interested in learning about ultimate truths from
> authoritative sources like the Bible or religious traditions.
> They consider themselves to be the ultimate authority on
> what it might mean for them to be religious or spiritual
> (Clark, 9).

Clark settles on five categories of young people and their attitudes to religion. First, there are the Resisters. These are young
people who are alienated from conventional religion, who see it
as the province of 'snobs' and therefore unconnected to their
lives. In Clark's study, such teens tended to be from more im-
poverished socio-economic backgrounds. It is not difficult to see
a connection with deprived areas in Ireland, where Mass attendance may be in single figures, but events such as first communion are lavishly extravagant.

Then there are the Mysticals. They are not at all interested in
organised religion, but not as interested in protesting against it
as the Resisters. They 'remain believers of a sort, particularly as

they are intrigued by the realm beyond the material world' (Ibid, 97). They are not interested in whether their ideas are consistent with a particular religious belief system. In fact, they are not particularly concerned with whether their beliefs are consistent at all. They have a fairly conventional moral system and a strong bond with a primary parent. They can also identify themselves as Christian, while their beliefs demonstrate very little knowledge of Christianity. For example, a guardian angel might be portrayed as a witch or a ghost just as easily as a messenger of God.

In short, these teens were in some ways the antithesis of religious seekers, interested in the practicalities of everyday life and only engaged in the considering the possibilities of what lies beyond the material world when such possibilities presented themselves to the teens (Ibid, 113).

Again, this raises a question regarding Irish teens. We tend to think that the 'search for meaning' is to be found in all people. Yet particularly since the advent of the Celtic Tiger, at least some young people are leading quite superficial lives, centred on their social lives, on going out and having a good time. The search for meaning does not intrude too much in their comfortable lives, although they may be briefly intrigued by one or other manifestation, usually bizarre, of the supernatural.

The next category of teens described by Clark has taken this interest a little further. As Experimenters, they have actively participated in some ritual, such as the use of ouija boards or seances. While such experiments have been for a long time common in the experience of young people (Irish college is famous for more than céilis) these teens dabble a bit more. They, like the Mysticals, do not appear to know or be particularly interested in the fact that such experiments are frowned on by the mainstream religion with which they still identify to some extent.

Traditionalists are very different. They have a strong identity based on their beliefs and the beliefs of their parents, although they are not brainwashed but have freely chosen this belief. In Clark's study, these teens tended to come from Evangelical

Protestant, Muslim or Mormon backgrounds. Even allowing for greater cultural diversity in recent years, teens in the Republic of Ireland are more likely to come from staunch Catholic or Protestant families who are probably also involved in their parishes. Some young Catholics will have developed their commitment from involvement in one of the new lay Catholic movements such as Communion and Liberation, or the Neo-catechumenate. Traditionalist teens draw strong distinctions between supernatural or religious experiences as portrayed by the media, and their own beliefs. They are 'respectful of the religious traditions in which they participate, are in fact regular participants, and see themselves as continuing, or conserving that tradition which they hold dear' (Ibid, 140). Certainly in urban Ireland, such teens are becoming rarer, and even in rural areas the degree of adherence may be more based on social convention and the fact that the majority of people still attend Sunday Mass, than on the deep conviction shown by the teens in Clark's research. However, such Irish teens still exist, and may be poorly served in religious education that has to cater for a wide range of beliefs, and often ends up catering for the lowest common denominator.

The final group is the Intrigued, described by Clark as wishing to separate religion and legend, but having difficulty in doing so. These teens have an affiliation to a religious tradition, but 'choose to interpret their religion modally: that is, they talk about their religion when it seems appropriate to the situation, and ignore it or even distance themselves from it when it is not.' They are particularly fascinated by angels. They may come from committed families, and even regularly participate in religious ceremonies, but 'religion, tradition or even belief in God are not central to the way in which they make lifestyle and career choices' (Ibid, 179). Again, it is not hard to identify Irish young people for whom tradition or belief in God are not central to their choices.

Clark's schema is only one way of looking at the various ways in which teens relate to religious belief, but it does highlight the fact that teens and older young people have developed their beliefs in a way very different to their parents. Clark attests to being occasionally annoyed by the deeply individualistic nature of young peoples' religion, and by their failure to commit to a theology of justice or structural change. However, she does acknowledge:

> As noted earlier, they want destiny, a calling, a challenge that is ultimately worthy of their time and energy. They may or may not feel that religion is useful in this quest, and hence some may take a relativistic view towards religion, but most seem committed to justice and equality (Ibid, 235).

Some Irish studies confirm the deeply individualistic approach to faith and belief among young people. Desmond O'Donnell conducted research among educated young adults between the ages of 20 and 35 ('Young educated adults: a survey', *Doctrine and Life*, January, 2000). The good news is that most of the young people surveyed have some experience of, and are influenced by God. They also pray. On the other hand, only 63% are sure of Christ's divinity. Interest in scripture is almost entirely absent, and there is an almost complete rejection of what might be termed 'church morality'. While strongly disapproving of abortion, the young people interviewed rejected church teaching on contraception and cohabitation. Similarly, the failure to attend Mass on Sundays no longer strikes them as a major problem. In terms of social justice, issues such as care for the environment, concern for those on the margins and a desire to secure more equitable division of the world's resources ranked low in their hierarchy of priorities. Nor was there a great involvement in social justice or voluntary service work. All in all, a picture emerges of young people who see themselves, in Clark's words, as 'the ultimate authority on what it might mean for them to be religious or spiritual'. The concern, or lack of it, for the common good, is of particular interest to Michael Breen, in his analysis of a 1999 *European Values Survey*. He wonders whether the erosion of church practice might mean the erosion of religious values, or a transfer of such values from institution to self? He goes on, 'What about issues like care for others, concern for those in poverty, and the challenge of immigration? The data seem to suggest that such care and concern is decreasing'(Breen, 105).

This decline is particularly striking, given the emphasis on social justice in religious education from the 1980s onward. It appears to have had little or no impact on the way in which young people make moral decisions regarding the wider community. David Tuohy conducted extensive research on young people and the way in which they perceive the world in which they live, published as *Youth 2K, Threat or Promise to a religious culture?* Some worrying conclusions emerge. Young people often cling to images of God more suitable to childhood (Tuohy, *Youth 2K*, 49). They feel little or no affiliation to their local church, seeing the parish as a place for adults (Ibid, 78). While many young people pray, their relationship with God often remains at a level of petition, whether personal or more altruistic. Some young people appear to have rejected the idea of God entirely, yet it emerged that sometimes it was the institutional church, or the perceived hypocrisy of religious figures, that was the barrier. Parents and other mentors were often also confused, and dealt with the confusion by 'non-practice, disillusion, critical stance, à la carte acceptance, or commitment to alternative groups within the church' (Ibid, 79). Unsurprisingly, the young people themselves often followed suit.

Religious education classes appeared to have little impact. They were reported to 'focus on more general social issues, and to be rather narrowly focused on a sexual dimension of social relationships'. In contrast, significant experiences were sometimes had during extra-curricular activities, such as 'retreats, prayer and meditation groups and philantrophic activity'. This was also a recurring theme outside the school context. 'Those who expressed religious commitment experienced acceptance and participation in a group involved in meaningful activity' (Ibid, 197). The lack of a 'language' to talk about God or spiritual experiences was highlighted. This was in contrast with their ability to articulate other dimensions of their lives. Tuohy points out that this language does not 'mean an exclusive focus on an academic theological language' but rather developing 'appropriate symbols to speak to the culture and concerns of young people'. He acknowledges that there are great differences among young people, and so concludes that three approaches will have to run concurrently in parishes and schools. The first is pre-evangelisation, aimed at those who are alienated or uninformed about the realm of religious faith. The second is evangelisation, which concentrates on developing the informational and formational aspects of religious experience. The final level is support, which is directed to those young people who have already made a commitment to the world of religion (Ibid, 199). In this writer's view, not only are there few examples of where this work is going on in schools and parishes, there is no central means of disseminating best practice. Communication has long been a problem in the Irish Catholic Church, first and foremost in the area of internal communication. There may be some level of knowledge in a particular diocese, but in many areas a committed layperson or priest wishing to initiate something for young people, would have to do a great deal of searching, or end up re-inventing the wheel. There is an urgent need to look at the area of communication, particularly at how to use the Internet as a way of creating not only clearing-houses for information, but communities of support that are online.

David Tuohy has acknowledged that his research in *Youth 2K* was supposed to be a first step, which identified the needs and concerns of young people. The second, and more important step, was to devise means of coming to terms with those concerns. Let us return to Clark's categories of young people for a moment. How would the Resisters be reached, the ones who feel excluded from a religion for 'snobs'? What about the Experimenters, who mix orthodox beliefs with beliefs in the paranormal with no particular sense of a clash or the need to conform to a traditional pattern? In Ireland, north and south, we have placed a heavy burden on schools to take the primary responsibility for faith formation, particularly in denominational schools. Tuohy's research was conducted prior to the introduction of the state examination syllabus. The Irish Catholic Bishops welcomed the introduction of this syllabus, despite the fact that the Department of Education and Science guidelines clearly state that faith formation is not among its aims.

> The assessment of Religious Education at Junior and Leaving Certificate levels will be based on the objectives relating to knowledge, understanding, skills and attitudes within each section of the course. While students will draw on their own experience in an examination, their personal faith commitment and/or affiliation to a particular religious grouping will not be subject to assessment for national certification (*Junior Certificate Religious Education Syllabus*, 45).

This is to be expected, because one could not possibly assess faith commitment in a state exam. What the Irish bishops did not take fully into account, perhaps, was the degree to which the academic demands of an examination syllabus could squeeze out any faith formation aspects. It is very difficult in a classroom context to reconcile the aims stated in the document produced by the Irish Bishops, *Guidelines for the Faith Formation and Development of Catholic Students*, with the need to prepare students for a wide-ranging examination. To take just one aim, the document suggests that the partners in education will enable the students to 'deepen their sense of belonging to the church: to participate more fully in the church's liturgy and life, prayer, worship and retreats.' As Tuohy's work has shown, where such experiences are made available to students in a systematic and consistent way, it has a positive impact. Yet teachers struggling to reach the end of six sections of a syllabus, five of which are compulsory, may have little energy for such activity. The degree to which there is any real partnership between parish, home and school is also questionable. It varies enormously from place to place, and many parents send their children to Catholic schools because of their desire that their children should be academically successful, and not so that they will receive a deep and meaningful religious education.

In Desmond O'Donnell's study, this dichotomy between

what religious-run or Catholic schools are meant to stand for and the way in which they actually act, is highlighted. Only 10% say the school had a 'great impact' on their relationship with God, while 26% said it had a 'fair impact' (O'Donnell, 44). How are we to square this with the bishops' *Guidelines*, which state that students should be enabled to 'learn by guidance and example how better to express their relationship with God, Jesus Christ, and the Holy Spirit'? Among the educated young adults surveyed by O'Donnell, almost half said that their school had little or no impact on their relationship with God, while 6% said it had a negative impact.

Some authors have cautioned against two extremes, the first being an over-estimation of what schools can achieve, the second being neglect of what schools do well. Patrick M. Devitt, in *Willingly to School,* says that even the best school teaching is unlikely to bring about 'increased Mass attendance among rebellious teenagers or make dishonest pupils honest overnight'. He says, 'Religion teaching in school has real and important aims, but they are quite limited. Religion teaching aims at knowledge, not maturity. Of course, the former may lead to the latter. But equally, it may not' (Devitt, 53). He cautions against the replacement of school teaching with too much 'personal sharing and discussion of experience', saying that it is more appropriate to retreats outside the school. Yet Tuohy has said that more is needed than the development of an academic language, and that 'appropriate symbols to speak to the culture and concerns of young people' are needed. Devitt correctly points out, 'academic' is not a synonym for 'irrelevant'. Devitt may be in danger of underestimating what can be achieved in the classroom, given the right conditions. The right conditions are rare, however, because they include trained and enthusiastic catechists who are supported by their fellow staff and management, in particular by chaplains and counsellors. In these ideal conditions, resources and time-tabling take account of the difficulties in attempting faith formation in the context of a school. Time is given for meeting, planning and reviewing in the teachers' timetables. In a school with this kind of teamwork a great deal can be achieved to build a sense of community which becomes associated with or is a by-product of the religious activity of the school.

Given that there was such an abysmal level of religious knowledge before the introduction of the RE examination in the Republic, it is not surprising that so many hopes were pinned on the new status which RE would have once it joined the ranks of examined subjects. No longer would it languish in the 'doss class' category. It is this writer's experience in the classroom, however, that the breadth and depth of the new examination syllabus at Junior Certificate Level is largely perceived by young people as irrelevant to their experience. They see it as involving much tedious learning of facts for which they have no immediate or long-term use. Much that was creative and stimulating has been squeezed out by the demands of exams. Not that the situation before the exam syllabus was much better, in that RE was a Cinderella subject, despite the best efforts of committed teachers. The set of textbooks authored by Linda Quigley for Veritas made a valiant attempt at integrating both faith formation and the needs of an examination, and yet anecdotally, many teachers report not having time to plan and carry out prayer services or other enriching activities. There is also the issue that many classrooms now have pupils of other faith traditions, which makes teaching from a faith perspective more problematic. While there is much that is valuable in the new examination syllabus, it is this writer's opinion that it cannot be relied upon as a vehicle for faith formation. It is early days yet, so as more teaching resources become available and teachers become familiar with the demands of the new examination, there may be more time for faith formation. The reality may be, however, that faith formation will have to take place primarily outside the school. The implications of the need to provide faith formation outside the school have not even begun to dawn on the institutional church. Since parishes no longer have the significance they once had, new units will have to be found with which young people can identify. It may well be that online communities with regular 'Mass meetings' at a central location might provide a sense of community currently lacking among young people. The 'text' generation are not being reached at the moment.

That is not to dismiss the significance of the wider school community. The importance of school ethos has been recognised in a document issued by the Irish Catholic bishops on the formation of a religious education policy in the school (*Towards a Policy on Religious Education in Post-primary Schools*). It asks many pertinent questions, such as the very practical question of when religion is timetabled and for how many periods a week, and whether the religion department has a budget. It also looks at more philosophical issues, such as the rationale for the 'characteristic spirit of the school'. The issue of school ethos is addressed at more length in David Tuohy's *Beyond Nostalgia – Issues in Trusteeship with regards to the Catholic Ethos of Post-Primary Schools*. Tuohy identifies two models of being a Catholic school. The first is the leaven, where the pastoral care of the students is the primary way in which the Catholic ethos is expressed. This carries the danger of there being no clear link in the students' minds between the person and teachings of Christ and the caring atmosphere of their school. The second image is of a city built on a hill, with a much more explicit Catholic presence. This runs the risk of being seen as intrusive by the teenagers, or even of imposing values on them. As George Boran puts it, the young have 'antibodies which make them react instinctively against anything that they perceive as imposed from above – by parents, teachers, priests or bishops' (Boran, 49).

Tuohy argues cogently that the trustees of schools, particularly since the withdrawal of religious orders from day-to-day involvement in the schools, can have a valuable role in providing practical support. This support could be geared towards the 'development of personnel involved directly in faith development – catechists, chaplains, counsellors and pastoral care teams' (Tuohy, *Beyond Nostalgia*, 79). Many school personnel are unable to avail of in-service or other opportunities for development due to pressure of work. Practical support, including financial assistance, might provide for cover for teachers during such training. He also suggests the development of regional support centres, so that expertise and knowledge can be pooled. While religious orders have varied in the degree to which they have encouraged co-operation between schools, it is fair to say that many schools have operated as islands, with little sense of linkage either to other schools or the wider church.

If trusteeship is to be meaningful, efforts must be re-doubled to address this problem of isolation. There are many 'hot potatoes' which the church has not wanted to face, including how committed many of the lay people who work in Catholic schools are to the overall Catholic ethos. This is a delicate area. People cannot be coerced in any way, because teachers have even more antibodies than young people do to anything being imposed on them. It would also be in contravention of the spirit of respect for human freedom, which has permeated the church since Vatican II. Yet it is fair to say that many religious orders made little coherent attempt to offer spiritual or religious development to staff members, some of whom at least would have been glad to receive it. Some clear ways in which trustees could ensure a vibrant Catholic ethos is to invest in the training and support of full-time school chaplains. Ironically, full-time chaplains, including lay people, are found far more often in the state sector than in voluntary secondary schools. In relation to teaching staff, like their students, they will respond best to initiatives that are relevant and provided locally, either in the school or in an easily-accessed centre. Teachers feel over-burdened and underappreciated. They will be more than grateful to anyone who offers them hope and continuing support.

The other area where the faith needs of young people are addressed is in youth ministry. Gerard Gallagher has written a history of youth ministry in Ireland, both north and south, called *Are We Losing the Young Church?*. In ways it makes for depressing reading. He asks why so few young people make an adult commitment to the church after years of Catholic education, and what that says about the amount of investment in catechetics?

He outlines the heyday of youth ministry in the 1980s, when people were energised by the Pope's visit, and centres such as Teach Bríde in Tullow, Co Carlow, and Baile Mhuire in Limerick were thriving. From that time on, he believes that there has been a gradual withdrawal from youth ministry, though many excellent programmes still exist. He says that two things happened: the church lost confidence in, and withdrew from work with young people. At the same time, increasing prosperity meant that young people had 'more interesting things to do with their time'. He has a number of suggestions to revitalise youth ministry. Among them, he proposes that the Irish Episcopal Conference should re-visit and re-write the pastoral *The Young Church* in time for its twentieth anniversary in 2005. A national plan for youth ministry should be explored, in conjunction with looking at what has worked internationally. Gallagher outlines a number of successful initiatives, including one in the Archdiocese of Chicago. They run a *Theology on Tap* programme for fifty-eight parishes. They stay in contact with a huge number of young people, 28,000 on a quarterly mailing list and over 2,000 receive a regular email. A diocesan youth Mass each year with the Cardinal is followed by a picnic on his lawn. There are many lay people in Ireland who once were active in youth ministry, whose expertise should be harvested. Why did they drift away? Was it because of a lack of an adult community to which they could attach themselves? Can the church afford the luxury of leaving such people out in the wilderness?

Final comments
Meeting faith needs involves identifying them first of all, and many young people will not display the conventional longing for meaning that is assumed to be part of the human spirit. They remain, however, open to being impressed both by individuals and evidence of lived community. This may be the biggest difficulty. The church in Ireland is at a low point of the bell curve of belief. There is an air of depression and demoralisation in the wake of a decade or more of scandals. Nor is there in the Irish

church a great identification with the wider international church, or much creative cross-fertilisation with places that are at a different stage of faith development. This has led to a hesitancy about presenting the message of the gospel in a vibrant way. The Irish church is in many ways again in the Upper Room before Pentecost. It is hiding out, a bit afraid to be seen outdoors for fear of being tortured and killed, not least by a gleeful media. Yet if the adults in the church are not filled with the joy of the gospel, and living it out with serenity and purpose, it is a bit much to expect young people to be on fire. Many people have attested to the fact that there is a great deal of apathy among young people, which is often more difficult to penetrate than actual hostility. Yet that apathy can be pierced in unexpected ways. Ann Walsh, an experienced catechist and author of catechetical texts, writes about an encounter of her students with a stained glass artist, who spoke in quite difficult, yet personal, terms of his work. The students were enthralled, yet found it difficult to articulate why. The nearest one student could come to an explanation was, 'It would remind you of poetry.' The medium of art, and the passion of an artist, moved them. Walsh concluded, 'I felt that in my own teaching I had given the class something unworthy of their questions, unworthy of their dignity, and in fact, of their intelligence. I felt I had trivialised, and indeed tranquillised, the urge towards transcendence which was now clearly in evidence among them, and which I think is latent in everybody (Walsh, 65). Young people are powerfully moved by music, by film, by symbols that are meaningful for them from their own culture. We need both to listen to their symbol making, which is different from our own, and humbly seek to illuminate it with our own lived experience of the gospel and our own ongoing conversion. None of that will happen without vibrant communities, where people are supported throughout the life cycle of family life, and in turn challenged to give to others. Programmes and planning are valuable and necessary, but without openness to the surprise of the Spirit, no attempt at meeting the faith needs of young people will be successful.

Select Bibliography

Boran, George, *Pastoral Challenges of a New Age*, Veritas, Dublin, 1999

Breen, Michael, 'Different from their Elders and Betters: Age Cohort Differences in the Irish Data of the European Values Study (EVS) 1999, in Cassidy, (ed.) *Measuring Ireland: Discerning Values and Beliefs*, Veritas, Dublin, 2002

Cassidy, Eoin G. (ed.) *Measuring Ireland: Discerning Values and Beliefs*, Veritas, Dublin, 2002

Clark, Lynn Schofield, *From Angels to Aliens: Teenagers, the Media, and the Supernatural*, Oxford University Press, New York, 2003

Devitt, Patrick M., *Willingly to School: Religious Education as an Examination Subject*, Veritas, Dublin, 2000

Fulton, John, and Abela, Anthony et al, *Young Catholics At the New Millenium: The Religion and Morality of Young Adults in Western Countries*, University College Dublin Press, Dublin, 2000

Gallagher, Gerard, *Are We Losing the Young Church? A Study of Youth Ministry in Ireland in the years following the Second Vatican Council to 2001*, Columba Press, Dublin, forthcoming.

Gallagher, Michael Paul, *Clashing Symbols: An Introduction to Faith and Culture*, Darton. Longman and Todd, London, 1997

Groome, Thomas, *Educating for Life: A Spiritual Vision for Every Teacher and Parent*, Crossroad, New York, 1998

Hogan, Padraig, and Williams, Kevin, (eds) *The Future of Religion in Irish Education*, Veritas, Dublin, 1997

Irish Catholic Bishops' Conference, *Guidelines for the Faith Formation and Development of Catholic Students,*Veritas, Dublin, 1999

Irish Catholic Bishops' Conference, *Towards a Policy on Religious Education in Post-Primary Schools* http://www.catholiccommunications.ie

O'Donnell, Desmond, 'Young Educated Adults: A Survey', *Doctrine and Life*, 52 (2002), 1-79.

Prendergast, Ned, and Monahan, Luke, (eds) *Re-imagining the Catholic School*, Veritas, Dublin, 2003

Tuohy, David, and Cairns, Penny, *Youth 2K, Threat or Promise to a religious culture?* Marino Institute of Education, Dublin, 2000a

Tuohy, David, *Beyond Nostalgia: Issues in Trusteeship with regard to the Catholic Ethos of Post-Primary Schools,* Presentation Ministries Office, Portlaoise, 2000b

Walsh, Ann, 'The Future of Religion at Post-Primary Level', in Hogan and Williams, (eds) *The Future of Religion in Irish Education,* Veritas, Dublin, 1997

Theology in Ireland:
Background and Prospects

Richard Lyng OSA

Those under forty years of age will find it difficult to fully appreciate the revolutionary nature of the changes that have taken place in Ireland during the last four decades. Those over forty years have found it difficult to absorb these same changes. Christianity is, of course, an incarnational religion, necessarily embedded in the culture of a particular society. Most theologians will agree today that there is no such thing as 'pure theology'. Neither is there 'pure Christianity', only culturally mediated expressions of the manner in which particular communities have interacted with the Christian gospels. Christianity, and of course theology, will bear the unmistakable stamp of the society in which it is taught and practised. So, if we are to understand a particular expression of Christianity, we must first seek to understand its social and political context. If we are to fully appreciate the distance we have travelled here in Ireland, we must seek to get some general sense or flavour of the world from which we have come. I will provide a brief overview of the general context in which Irish theology was practised up to relatively recent times. The overview will contain some unavoidable generalisations. I hope they are not so sweeping as to be misleading!

The late Professor Basil Chubb was one of the more astute political and social observers of twentieth-century Ireland. He regarded the following characteristics as central to any overall understanding of Irish political or cultural life: conservative, authoritarian, loyal and anti-intellectual. These four broad characteristics could also be applied – but with a more specific intensity – to the Irish Catholic Church: 'Traditionally, Irish Catholicism was an austere and puritanical variety, somewhat cold and authoritarian and rather cut off from continental European influences. It was a folk church geared to what it saw as the needs and limitations of a peasant people. Many of its clergy themselves came from that background' (Chubb, 18).

As is well known, Irish writers and artists fled from this repressive atmosphere in large numbers. Draconian censorship laws deprived many of them of a living here. James Kelly's recent study demonstrates the range and depth of this obsession with 'obscene literature' (Kelly, 223-369). Some very innocuous works were banned as obscene. (Julia O'Faolain's *Land of Spices* was banned because of one ambivalent sentence!) But not all who left Ireland emigrated because of censorship! On average, 40,000 a year emigrated from the Free State between the 1920s and the 1960s (Keogh, 215-17). In the main, these emigrants were young and uneducated. And, to an unusual degree, they were female. (European emigration had a two to one male preponderance; but in the case of Ireland it consistently hovered around the fifty-fifty mark [Lee, 376-77]). Those who spoke of the emigration of 'excess population' were flying in the face of reality: throughout the period under investigation, Ireland – with a mere forty-seven people per sq km – was in fact seriously depopulated by European standards. The next least densely populated was France, with ninety-eight people per sq km. The United Kingdom had 229 (Chubb, 341).

By any standards, Ireland was a dysfunctional society. It was a society in denial. Officially, both church and state paid lip service to 'Christian family values'. Emigration was of course consistently condemned. But where did the blame lie? J. J. Lee is in no doubt: 'Emigration was not unique to Ireland. But the type of emigration, the scale of emigration, and the impact of emigration were. In no other European country was emigration so essential a prerequisite for the preservation of the nature of society' (Lee, 374). The more secure farming, business, bureaucratic and professional classes searched around for smokescreens and scapegoats. They rounded up an impressive herd: partition, the cinema, 'featherheaded females succumbing to the glossy image

of foreign lands', English agents enticing girls abroad with offers that it would be impossible to honour, and of course the individual emigrants who 'sold their heritage for a mess of pot-
tage'. Emigration had to be explained in a manner that would
exonerate the possessing classes and the policy makers from all
responsibility for the malady. But, in reality, politician and
prelate must have known that emigration acted as an essential
safety valve. Despite the comparative depopulation referred to
above, the state catered less than adequately for those who remained behind. Even as late as 1980, the Irish GDP per capita
was still less than half the European average (Chubb, 345). Had
emigration not been to hand as a 'solution', how would Ireland
have addressed the needs of an extra 400,000 people every
decade? That uncomfortable question could never be aired publicly. The symptom was mistaken for the problem, and condemned ritually. Irish society was spectacularly dysfunctional.

Yet, some regard the 1940s and 1950s as the high point of
Irish Catholicism. Vocations to the priesthood and the religious
life had reached all-time high. The missionary movement flour-
ished as never before. Sunday observance was little short of universal. If we are to judge the quality of Catholicism by the intensity of its devotional life, or the general level of conformity to
what has often been described as 'the Catholic ethos', then the
period 1930 to 1960 was indeed something of a 'golden age'.
While this Marian enthusiasm had its origins in the nineteenth
century phenomenon described by the historian Emmett Larkin
as the 'Devotional Revolution', it reached its apogee, according
to James S. Donnelly Jr, in the mid-twentieth century. In a well-
researched essay on devotional piety during this period, James
S. Donnelly Jr has presented convincing evidence of this in the
form of new Marian shrines and grottoes springing up throughout the country, a growth in pilgrimages to these new shrines, a
revival of pilgrimages to older ones, and a renewed fascination
with Lourdes and Fatima. There was also a whole new religious
mobilisation achieved by sodalities, confraternities and a proliferation of books, pamphlets, periodicals and films tied to cult of

Our Lady (Donnelly, 252). This was the hey-day of the Marian priests, Patrick Peyton and the Dominican Gabriel Harty.

The degree of compliance, homogeneity and conformity will strike one today as extraordinary. These Marian movements occasionally strayed outside their spiritual remit, to wander at times into the precarious field of female fashion. For example, in 1942, the Mercy Sisters at the women's Mary Immaculate Training College in Limerick established the Modest Dress and Deportment Crusade. The Crusade, apparently, had the formal approval of the Irish hierarchy. The aims of the crusaders, and the means by which these were to be achieved, were outlined in two pamphlets, *The Vice of Today* and *Short Skirts or Slacks*. Skirts should be worn at least four inches below the knee and slacks were frowned upon entirely since they give 'undue prominence' to the female figure. The crusaders were not slow to play the green card! Women were urged to lead Irish society back 'from the anglicising influences which are … degrading it and divesting it of every trait of nationalist characteristic' (Ibid, 281). Of course the real irony was that Victorian prudery and 'respectability' was now doing duty for authentic Catholic morality.

Bruce Francis Biever, an American sociologist, conducted a survey of religious and moral attitudes of Dublin Catholics in the 1960s (Barber, 287 ff). The following 'sample questions', together with their respective responses, will provide us with clear windows onto a very different world:

(1) If there was a conflict between church and state, the state should prevail:

           I agree: 13%   I disagree: 87%

(2) If I had a son I would wish him to be a priest, above and beyond everything else in the world:

           I agree: 84%   I disagree: 16%

(3) The teachings of the church on sexual matters are out of date:

           I agree: 18%   I disagree: 82%

(4) Celibate clergy are not best suited to give advice on marriage problems:

           I agree: 12%   I disagree: 88%

(5) Whatever the church tells me to do, I will do, regardless of whether it makes sense or not:

I agree: 61%   I disagree: 39%

(6) Catholic doctrine on sin in general is too harsh for modern times:

I agree: 12%   I disagree: 88%

The world of the 1960s is now hardly recognisable. But Chubb's principal characteristics of political Ireland are replicated in ecclesial Ireland: it too was conservative, authoritarian, loyal and anti-intellectual. This then is the context in which theology was practised. Is it in fact possible to conduct vigorous theological enquiry in such a stagnant, unquestioning context?

In fact, the Irish Universities Act of 1908 had already banished theology to a ghetto. Through prohibiting the state funding of a theology faculty in any one of the constituent colleges of the National University of Ireland, theology was destined for seminaries. In fact theology ceased to be viewed as a discipline in its own right; it came to be regarded instead as a necessary passport to priesthood. Understandably, this ensured that theology in Ireland was conducted along denominational lines. A more accurate, long-term view will locate denominationalism in the sixteenth century Reformation and the Tridentine reaction. The 1908 Act, however, compounded the situation further. According to Patrick Corish, even the theology taught at Maynooth was 'closed and clerical', and he further states that 'It is indeed arguable that Irish clerical scholarship achieved more in the field of history than theology.' The Maynooth professors were 'worthy labourers rather than original thinkers' (Corish, 231 ff). This was a deliberate choice rather than an intellectual failure. They were charged with the training of pastoral priests rather than the production of speculative theologians. Their source text was John Hagan's *Compendium of Catechetical Instruction*, published in 1911, which was, in turn, based on the *Catechism of the Council of Trent*. Conducted as it was in the shadow of the Reformation, Catholic theology in Ireland was particularly defensive. And its moral branch was based on casuistry and, as Corish remarks, 'it was beginning to show a certain sclerosis of over-refinement' (Ibid, 232).

It is no exaggeration to say that this world was 'blown apart' in the 1960s and 1970s. There is no need to trace this fragmentation in any great detail. A few factors conspired to expose some pre-existing fault-lines. The most obvious catalyst was Vatican II. Obviously, it is outside the scope of an article such as this to trace the full implication of that Council for the Catholic Church in Ireland. It will suffice to reiterate the 'theological landmarks' identified by Dermot Lane: a turn to human experience as a source of revelation; an interfacing of faith and culture; a recognition of historical consciousness; an acknowledgement of pluralism; an affirmation of the existence of a hierarchy of truths in matters ecumenical; a statement that the church of Christ 'subsists' in the Catholic Church; a recognition of other Christian churches as ecclesial realities; the initiation of a new relationship between Catholicism and Judaism; and a recognition of 'elements of truth and grace' as well as 'seeds of the word' in other religions (Lane, 68-69). It is quite impossible, of course, to overestimate the impact of the Council. Heretofore, Catholic theology had concerned itself primarily with providing answers. It will now devote its energies to asking questions.

The second most significant development also had its source in Europe: Ireland's joining the European Community in 1973. This represented the end of industrial and economic isolation. It would have enormous consequences down the line.

But there were domestic factors at work too. The advent of television opened windows (and minds) onto a wider world. Topics which had, up to this, been regarded as the preserve of specialised theologians, were now debated by all interested parties. Moral issues, such as contraception and abortion, are obvious examples. Everyone now had his or her say. People began to speak out of the authority of personal experience rather than professional expertise. As Michael Paul Gallagher remarked, we were moving from 'the experience of authority to the authority of experience'.

The introduction of 'free' education facilitated this development greatly, with enormous repercussions for the Irish church, repercussions that are still ongoing. 'Free' education, however, and industrialisation changed all that (Fuller, 167-77). Within a generation, Ireland had been utterly transformed. It now had a highly educated and a technologically sophisticated population, the envy of many European counterparts. Its young people had, for generations, fled the stagnant economic depression of the Republic; by the beginning of the third millennium, the Celtic Tiger was buoyant and, for some, immigration rather then emigration was now the problem. The transformation has been truly extraordinary. And this is the context in which Irish theology must now be conducted. Today's theologian is painting on a new canvas.

I have worked as a priest for the last twenty years in Galway city. I divide my time, almost equally, between pastoral activity and academic teaching. Galway is regarded as the prime example of the new, educated, urbanised Ireland. It has a population of 70,000, of whom 20,000 are students. I work in a small inner city parish with a *de facto* population of less than 300! The area has experienced physical regeneration in recent years with the construction of a large number of apartments buildings. The three thousand or so occupants of these new apartments have no affinity with the parish as such. Over 90% of those who attend church in the parish come from outside the canonical boundaries of the parish itself. In many ways the parish is twenty-first century Catholic Ireland in microcosm: young, mobile, eclectic, urban, unattached and, increasingly, extremely wary of commitment. Yet, this is the Ireland in which theology must now be conducted. It is the questions and longings of this constituency that must now be addressed.

What are the questions and longings of this 'New Ireland'? Has the institutional church the intellectual and spiritual resources to identify and address these questions? Religious commentators have noted the persistence of a spiritual hunger among people today. They point to the proliferation of 'New

Age' material as evidence of this hunger. And we have ample evidence of this phenomenon locally in our own parish. Charlie Byrne runs a very popular bookshop beside our church. According to him, 'New Age' spirituality is by far the fastest growing sector. He claims that women, and young women in particular, are the most regular devotees of this genre. It would appear that the institutional church, including its theologians, has failed to engage in any significant way with their concerns and issues. They just do not seem to swing on the same gate! So how is the church and its minister to engage effectively with the concerns of today?

This engagement will require a vigorous development in two directions: first, at an academic level and, second, at a pastoral level, in the local parishes. I have referred earlier in this article to the manner in which theology was banished from the 'real' academic world to the ghetto that was the Irish seminary. Theology, for reasons extrinsic to itself, was entirely clericalised. Theology must now break out of that ghetto for two very obvious reasons: first, the ghetto itself (seminaries) is fast disappearing; second, if theology is to achieve full 'academic respectability', it must, on a daily basis, rub shoulders with the other sciences. There is one conundrum in Irish life that never ceases to raise the eyebrows of academics from continental Europe or the United States: over 90% of Irish people claim to practice their religion still; yet the National University of Ireland has no full Faculty of Theology. Enda McDonagh has often pointed out this glaring lacuna:

> Vatican II itself and its theological impetus made some impact in Ireland but not nearly enough to keep pace with the rapid social changes already under way here, still less with accelerating change affecting the wider world into which Ireland was being more closely integrated ... The most powerful retarding force was the lack of conviction among church and academic leaders and perhaps among some theologians themselves of the need or value of a theology really open to the challenge of the social and university world around it (McDonagh, 16).

One of the more serious consequences of this anomaly is that theology has failed to engage significantly in either academic or public discourse. One commentator has observed perceptively that 'religion is probably the only subject about which academics have no problem parading their ignorance!' Michael Drumm has outlined some of the negative consequences of this failure to escape from the 'ghetto':

> The failure to engage fully in public discourse in the academy or in society in general has seriously impoverished both theology as an academic discipline and the quality of public debate on sensitive social issues. Such debates tend to be characterised on the one hand by Catholic fundamentalism ... and on the other by an insufferable dismissal by the liberal intelligentsia of religious sensibilities, as amounting to nothing more than personal sentimentality. The task of theology is not to mediate between these extremes but to provide a public language which would enable all of us to engage in a public discourse, laying bare the various presuppositions at work and demonstrating that there is no presuppositionless perspective. Engaging in such public discourse is the key role of the theologian; failure to do so leaves the theologian open to the charge of being involved in a privatised gnosticism. This is the classic failure of theology – it becomes opaque and quaint, indeed downright boring and irrelevant (Drumm, 40-41).

It would be churlish, however, not to acknowledge the giant strides that theology has made since Vatican II. In our frustrations we can often overlook this real progress. In an article to which I have already referred, Dermot Lane offers a brief evaluation of the impact of Vatican II on the Irish church (Lane, 67-81). He sees much that is positive: the setting up of various institutional bodies charged with implementing the work of the Council on a local level, like the various episcopal commissions, the third level theological and liturgical institutions, and various theological bodies like the Irish Theological Association and the Irish Biblical Association. Lane observes that the Irish church's response to the Vatican Council was both impressive and genuine.

Lane identifies the church's failure to 'activate the priesthood of the laity' as its Achilles' Heel. While he concedes that there have never been more lay people involved in the life of the church, or in the study of theology and religion, the absence of a coherent pastoral plan deprives the laity of a 'vocational pathway' towards participation in pastoral ministry. This is the major serious defect and, because of this defect, adult faith in Ireland is in serious trouble, according to Lane.

My own personal experience supports Lane's contention. Perhaps lessons learned in the local parish may have a broader application. Two years ago, some members of our Parish Council requested some 'theological preparation' for Easter. We agreed to meet for four nights during Lent, for two hours each night. The members were asked to take soundings among their families and neighbours regarding the issues that should be addressed. The two primary concerns to emerge were sin and sacraments. We agreed to explore two sacraments over the four nights: baptism and eucharist. We devised a very 'tight' format: small group discussions (no more than four people); feedback in plenary session; brief presentation by priest – no more than five minutes; individual reading of one-page position paper on topic; discussion on content of paper in small groups; a summarising of the plenary discussion.

Over thirty people attended, ranging in age from eighteen to eighty-nine. It was an amazing experience. Those in the upper age range spent the first night struggling to unlearn, while those in the lower age struggled with what they regarded as very strange concepts. But what they had in common was a desire to nurture their faith. Eighty per cent of the work was done in groups. There they articulated as best they could their spiritual needs and hungers. They explored together how these needs were being addressed or neglected. In other words, they were 'doing theology' together. Throughout the four nights, our numbers never dipped below thirty. Moreover, they insisted on a similar format for the following year, and followed through with undiminished enthusiasm. Then we addressed moral issue with the guidance of Fr Seán Fagan's *Does Morality Change?* (1997). The experience was equally uplifting the second time around.

I have already referred to the dismissal of theology as 'irrelevant' by academics. Unfortunately, this dismissive attitude is not confined to the groves. To the ordinary 'person in the pew' the word 'theological' is a synonym for 'irrelevance'. It is regarded by most ordinary people as a sort of 'holy hobby' indulged in by those who have nothing better to do. I suppose we should concede that this 'bad name' was not entirely unmerited. If Catholicism is to be sustained in today's Ireland, however, it must secure its intellectual struts. The academic and the pastoral worlds must find common ground. The present Professor of Theology and Religious Education at Boston College has attempted to undermine this elitist or esoteric perception of theology. He calls for 'a new paradigm' for doing theology that will enhance the faith of the people:

> To respond to people's spiritual hungers and to empower their responsibility in faith, theology must be taught in ways that engage people's lives and the social reality of their time and place. It must represent itself in the context of what matters to people living in today's world, addressing its themes to the questions of the human condition, communicating, as Aquinas advised, 'according to the mode of the receiver'. To address theology to people's interests would not mean a reductionism of teaching only what people are interested in. As Dewey cautioned on this point, the educator must maintain a dialectic between the personal interests of learners and arousing interest in what they need to know. Theological educators must both teach according to people's interests and get people interested in what they have to teach (Groome, 1999, 298).

Groome calls for revolution in the way 'doing theology' is perceived. We must move away from the notion of theology as 'a lecture delivered by experts' to a model of 'an inclusive community of conversation'.

The conversation should enable participants to speak their own word out of their life context and to listen to each other, lend them ready access to scriptures and traditions, and encourage participants to see for themselves what the wisdom of their faith might mean for their lives. The conversation would be between and among participants, of teacher with participants, of all with their own lives in the world and with traditions of faith' (Ibid, 300).

Throughout this essay, I have stressed the cultural context of faith and theology. While we still have a lot to learn, we have quite a lot more to unlearn. Our ecclesial and cultural history has bred passivity in Irish Catholicism. I have pointed also to an anti-intellectual strand in Irish life generally which will militate against the emergence of a vital theology. I have already referred to the aphorism coined by the Jesuit scholar Michael Paul Gallagher that Catholic Ireland 'has moved from the experience of authority to the authority of experience'. A faith and theology that does not speak to – and out of – contemporary experience will fall on deaf ears. However, it has been my own experience that there are still a considerable number of people who are anxious to deepen and nourish their faith. But has the church still got the resources, spiritually and intellectually, to respond to that hunger? Time alone will tell.

Select Bibliography
Barber, Noel, 'Religion in Ireland: Its state and prospects', in *Christianity in Ireland: Revisiting the Story*, Brendan Bradshaw & Dáire Keogh (eds), The Columba Press , Dublin, 2002.
Chubb, Basil, *The Government and Politics of Ireland*, Longman, London & New York, second edition 1982
Corish, Patrick, *The Irish Catholic Experience*, Gill & Macmillan, Dublin, 1985
Donnelly, James S. (JR) 'The Peak of Marianism in Ireland, 1930-1960' in *Piety and Power in Ireland, 1760-1960* (Essays in honour of

Emmet Larkin), Stewart J. Brown and David W. Miller (eds), Institute of Irish Studies, Belfast, 2000

Drumm, Michael. 'The Place of Theology and Religion in Higher Education' in Pádraig Hogan & Kevin Williams (eds), *The Future of Religion in Irish Education*, Veritas, Dublin, 1997

Fuller, Louise, *Irish Catholicism since 1950: The Undoing of a Culture*, Gill & Macmillan, Dublin, 2002

Groome, Thomas, 'Teaching a life-giving Theology' in *Priests & People*, August-September, 1999

Groome, Thomas, *Educating for Life: A Spiritual Vision for Every Teacher and Parent*, Thomas Moore Press, Allen, 1998

Kelly, James, 'The Operations of the Censorship of Publications Board: The Notebooks of C. J. O'Reilly, 1951-1955' in *Analeca Hibernica*, No 38 Irish Manuscripts Commission, 2004, 223-369

Keogh, Dermot, *Twentieth-Century Ireland: Nation and State*, Gill & Macmillan, Dublin, 1994

Lane, Dermot A. 'Vatican II: The Irish Experience' in *The Furrow*, 55 (2004), 68-69

Lee, J. J., *Ireland 1912-1985: Politics and Society*, Cambridge University Press, 1989

McDonagh, Enda. "Beyond 'Pure' Theology" in *The Furrow*, 50 (1999) 579-86

Ethical and Philosophical Challenges to Evangelisation

Séamus Murphy

It is safe to say that many of the current challenges to the church's evangelising mission will continue to be such, long into the future.[1] While ethical issues arising from new technology (e.g. IVF, genetic manipulation) do require formulation of new moral norms, the principles on which such norms are to be based are not new.

An exhaustive list of the future ethical challenges to evangelisation would be impossible in an article this size, and any ranking would be controversial since it would be based on little more than the author's own moral intuitions.

I propose then, not a ranking, but a qualifying of the issues. There are framework issues, defining the context within which evangelisation is carried out, and specifying the parameters within which more important issues may be recognised, understood, formulated, and debated. There are foundational matters, directly determining the range of possible stances on ethical issues. There are core-issues, indicating appropriate norms for other issues. I shall briefly consider each, before selecting a few practical issues for comment.

The framework: pluralism

The fact that there is a plurality of religions, worldviews and cultures is not new. What is relatively new is the Western cultural framework holding pluralism as a central value. Pluralism is the value that views religious plurality as good and exerts a pressure upon any religion with a defined moral teaching, challenging the idea that there could be one objectively correct position on any moral view. It is in that context that the church seeks to evangelise.

In this matter, the church's position in the Western world today is not unlike its position under the Roman Empire, prior to its becoming the state religion in the fourth century. Outright persecution was the exception rather the rule, being usually local and sporadic. Systematic empire-wide persecution occurred only briefly in the middle of the third century under Decius and Valerian, and again at the turn of the century under Diocletian and Maximian.

As regards religion, the empire was quite pluralist. The republic had earlier adopted the Greek pantheon wholesale, and the empire was tolerant of the deities of its subject peoples. The Roman attitude could be summed up as: 'Give us a statue of your god and we'll put it up in the Forum to venerate along with other deities.' In contrast to modern pluralism, which in certain forms seeks to have the public square stripped of all religion, imperial pluralism was more inclusive: there was room for all religions in the public square.

The Jewish and Christian belief that there was only one god would have struck the imperial officials as intolerant (and unpluralistic by modern standards) and intellectually arrogant. But while Judaism remained a small ethnic religion, Christianity had universal aspirations and was spreading. Popular hostility was aroused because Christians' strict monotheism, expressed in their attitude to other religions, was interpreted as atheistic. Officialdom became concerned by the refusal of an ever-expanding group to accept the civil religion, i.e. to acknowledge the divine sanction inherent in the empire and the order represented by Rome. One pagan author remarked perceptively: 'The Christians are in non-violent revolt against the empire.'

There is a limited historical parallel between the attitude of the Roman Empire to the church then and the attitude of the contemporary Western pluralist polity to the church today. How is the church to define itself relative to that pluralist polity?

On the one hand, pluralism need not in principle exclude religion. At its best, expressed in John Rawls' later work, it recognises that religion cannot be excluded:

A modern democratic society is characterised not simply by a pluralism of comprehensive religious, philosophical, and moral doctrines but by a pluralism of incompatible yet reasonable comprehensive doctrines ... political liberalism takes for granted not simply pluralism but the fact of reasonable pluralism; and beyond this, it supposes that of the main existing reasonable comprehensive doctrines, some are religious. (Rawls, xvi, xviii)

Rawls is not the only liberal theorist who would accept that a religious worldview could be reasonable, but it is not clear that most would agree with him. Few liberal thinkers accept that it could be reasonable to take public policy stances on the basis of religious motivation.

More generally, while wider society sees itself as liberal and tolerant towards religion, it objects to any religion claiming that its doctrines are true or, to be more precise, that doctrines irreconcilable with its own teachings are false. Secular society, then as now, has no problem with religion being meaningful; it has a problem with a religion making itself out to be true. A religion that stands by its truth-claims is refusing to burn incense at the emperor's statue. A religion that presumes to sit in judgement on the liberal pluralist and capitalist Western polity is a subversive force that must be combated. It does not matter whether the religion fundamentally rejects that polity (as certain forms of Islam do) or whether it accepts many elements of that polity, while rejecting others (as the Catholic Church does). The fundamental issue is: is pluralism to be understood within a framework of some set of truths, are compassion and tolerance to be defined and delimited within a specific vision of the good – or are truth and goodness subordinate to the civic religion of pluralism and tolerance?

The problem has been with us for some time, and it will probably become acute. One church document, *Centesimus Annus*, noted:

Nowadays there is a tendency to claim that agnosticism and skeptical relativism are the philosophy and the basic attitude that correspond to democratic forms of political life. Those who are convinced that they know the truth and firmly adhere to it are considered unreliable from a democratic point of view, since they do not accept that truth is determined by the majority, or that it is subject to variation according to different political trends. ... A democracy without values easily turns into open or thinly disguised totalitarianism (par 46).

By way of example, consider the following. Recently, Canadian courts have ruled that the common law definition of marriage as between a man and a woman must be amended to include homosexuals. In subsequent legislation, the Canadian government exempted clergy from being obliged to marry same-sex couples, and then submitted that exemption to the Supreme Court for ruling on its constitutionality. Regardless of the issue or the outcome, it is an ominous sign that a democratic state and its courts should feel competent to determine when the law may compel the celebration of the sacraments.[2]

No more than could the early church under the Roman Empire, the church today cannot accept an understanding of itself as just one religion among many more or less equally true (i.e. equally false) religions. That the state might have such a view of the church or religion is not the problem: it is that the state should require that the church accept such a view of itself with respect to its public life. The church cannot, without betraying its Lord, accept that its teaching is subordinate to the civic religion or relative to the intellectual framework defined by liberal pluralism.

The pressure on the church is evidenced by the fact that a considerable number of Christians (including clergy) have shifted (usually without realising it) into subscribing to the civic religion's tenets, with little awareness of the implications.

One can see it in those who are outspoken about social injustices such as homelessness or racism yet feel that they should be silent on abortion or sexual morality since speaking out on those issues would be 'unpluralistic' and 'imposing our values on others'. The inconsistency is rarely noted.

It is observable in Christian teachers, clerics or laity, who are uncomfortable with the word 'truth', and who think (although usually in denial about it) that the value of any religion lies solely in the meaning it brings to the individual or the community and hardly at all in its being true. It is expressed in the idea, disturbingly common in some religious circles, that for a proposition to be true is no more than for it to be 'true-for-me'. Underlying this is the notion that truth is either unknowable or not really important: this masks scepticism.

The framework challenge: secularism

Secularism is now dominant in Western public culture. I define secularism as a culture or mindset based on the proposition that God's existence need make no difference to the individual and ought make no difference to how society is run. Secularism holds that the public square should be religion-free. This is justified by claiming that religion is inherently divisive, and the Catholic Church in particular is anti-democratic and intolerant, even evil.[3] Religious believers are not excluded from the public square, but they can be there only as 'religion-less' citizens.

Secularism projects itself as tolerant and inclusive through readiness to accept people's religion as a personal (i.e. private) lifestyle choice. The decline of organised religion and the rise of the civic religion of public secularism leads not so much to atheism as to privatised religiosity, oriented to a range of ersatz spiritualities of an often narcissistic nature, focused on a vague notion of personal growth.[4]

In the USA, the concept of church-state separation, originally understood as guaranteeing freedom of religion and non-interference by the state, has been reinterpreted in a secularist direction as mandating the exclusion of religion from the public square. The secularist interpretation of the principle is taken to the point of virtual discrimination against religious believers, as in cases where public funds must be withheld from any project (e.g. schools, drug-rehabilitation programmes), no matter how beneficial, for the sole reason that the providers of the project are explicitly tied to some religion. In France, the secularism is quite open, and explicitly different from the liberal pluralism referred to in the previous section.

Secularism's dominance is overwhelming in Western academia. It is expressed in the following generally accepted assumptions:

a) Since all knowledge-claims require justification, no claim to religious knowledge can have even a *prima facie* plausibility without strong justification.

b) Since atheism is the default position, no such requirement applies to the atheist's claims.[5]

c) Religious experience cannot be used to justify knowledge claims, since that would necessarily beg the question. This applies even if the religious believer in question was an atheist or agnostic prior to the experience.

d) Sufficient justification for religious belief cannot be provided. Even if true, Christian beliefs are simply not the sort of thing that could be objective, rational, or justifiable.[6]

All four are wide open to critique. The first two actually clash, and the great bulk of contemporary scientific knowledge would violate the first and third. The fourth is a piece of unsupported secularist Enlightenment dogma.

At the level of law and politics, secularism leads to the view that moral positions derived, even in part, from revelation or other religious thought can have no validity, and may not be deployed as grounds on which to argue in public policy debates. In this area, intolerance of argument on religious grounds is far stronger in Europe (including Ireland) than in the USA.[7]

Secularism sets the context within which the church's moral and social mission is exercised. The points just listed are academic, but they affect the thinking of Christians, even blocking certain elements of that ongoing formation every Christian needs. Christians are familiar with the forms in which militant Islam or communism might confront Christian faith, but have much to learn about how secularism subverts Christian faith. We are used to ideologies presenting themselves explicitly as rival truths or superior doctrines, but confused by one preaching tolerance and pluralism, apparently asking only that we accept minimal restrictions necessary for a pluralist society. If Christians do not practise intellectual discernment and fight secularism, they may well find themselves accepting it. If they accept it, it undercuts their commitment to promoting justice in society.

Foundational issue: are justice and goodness real or invented?
Contemporary Western secularism presents itself negatively as a denial of the relevance of God and (as Nietzsche prophesied) by implication a denial of the validity of any notion of the good. Here we turn to a foundational issue. As secular and Christian culture diverge, the differences become more fundamental, and we need a little metaphysics to name them.[8]

The dominant cultures of today typically involve either modernity's assumption of metaphysical naturalism or post-modernity's assumption of creative anti-realism.[9] Naturalism is the doctrine that reality is purely physical. It is connected to a kind of scientistic worship of technology. Creative anti-realism (or idealism) is based on the idea that the world has no intelligibility of its own. We create concepts, and so we 'create' the world's intelligibility or meaning. The alternative, metaphysical realism, can be put crudely as the doctrine that the world has its own intelligibility independently of the observer, and that the real includes more than the physical (e.g. meanings, beauty, persons, goodness, universals).

Naturalism and anti-realism each lead to moral anti-realism, which holds that (i) there are no moral facts or objective goods, so that (ii) moral norms are like positive laws, determined by society or the state. So rape is wrong because society says so. Moral realism is the view that there are moral facts to discover: rape is wrong because of the nature of that type of act, regardless of whether any society acknowledges that. It implies that human beings are not deluded in experiencing themselves as morally free, or in raising questions about what is good (values, moral goals) and what is right (norms, moral means). Traditional natural law theory is one type of moral realism.

Moral anti-realism implies that Christian teaching on justice and morality cannot be true or false. Propositions about what is just or unjust, good or bad, are just not capable of having truth-values, since there are no objective moral facts for them to name. Moral anti-realism is now widespread in contemporary Western society, and is promoted by the secular media in the name of promoting tolerance and freedom from religious domination.

The presentation of Christian teaching can no longer rely on generally shared moral assumptions. The claim that 'such-and-such is wrong because it is against the natural law' carries no weight with the moral anti-realist. The claim that the content of Christian ethics is essentially that which unaided reason at its best would arrive at seems less tenable than ever. The church will have to spend more time and ingenuity seeking ways to explain its teaching, not just in the hope of converting non-Christians to its way, but also to continue the ongoing evangelisation of its own members.

Core issues: dignity and solidarity

The major ethical and social issues that the church faces revolve around two core values: human dignity and social solidarity.[10]

The classic era of Catholic social thought roughly coincided with the twentieth century, from Leo XIII's *Rerum Novarum* (1891) to John Paul II's *Centesimus Annus* (1991) just after the final abandonment of the communist model. Much of it focused on specific social issues like work, third world poverty, and rights to shelter, health-care and education. Under John Paul II, the focus shifted to the nature and value of the person and the social solidarity grounded in the person.

While the importance of work, shelter, education, health-care and human rights in general is unlikely to be challenged in the near future, the notion of social solidarity has begun to look endangered. The decline of such socially cohesive ideologies as socialism and nationalism has left the field to an increasingly individualist liberalism. While liberalism is good in its commitment to the individual's rights and in its opposition to racism and extreme nationalism, it has difficulty with the concept of a common good. This will in turn undermine social solidarity, insofar as solidarity is something deeper and larger than feelings of pity and compassion aroused by TV images of the victims of war or famine.

Accordingly, the church must develop and promote its vision of the common good. For the framework considerations discussed above, the post-modern world neither understands nor, even where it understands, accepts the notion of the common good. A number of considerations apply to the Christian vision:

- The good must be presented as a concept that captures something fundamental about a civilised society that cannot be reduced to something else, such as the aggregate goods of the individuals making up that society.[11]
- It must be based on a well-developed notion of the nature of the person, specifying the good for the person,[12] and showing the basis for holding that human rights are antecedent to positive law.
- It must be presented as prior to the notion of the right. In any case, it is something more fundamental than a list of the individual's rights. The good for the person cannot be fully or adequately expressed in terms of rights only. Likewise, it is mistaken to treat equality as though it is self-evidently a trump card with respect to the good in the social sphere.
- It will also involve developing a moral notion of citizenship, as distinct from the ethnic or cultural notion of citizenship that is operative in much public thinking with respect to migrants and refugees. The good is more than well-being and entitlements: it also involves the acting person's empowerment and character-formation in action. A just society requires a virtuous citizenry as well as just social structures.

I should clarify some of these points, in particular the notions of the good and the right, fundamental in normative ethics.

The good is, as Aristotle said, 'what all seek'; and that applies regardless of whether one takes the good as objective (independent of subjective desires and beliefs), or just as what an individual desires. The good has to do with the goals that are worth pursuing, the values we ought hold or actually hold. The right has to do with action, i.e. the permissions and restrictions governing behaviour in pursuing the good.

In contemporary liberalism's political theory, the role of the state cannot be (as Christians and others would hold) to pursue the common good, since that would mean the state committing itself to a particular vision of the good, thereby marginalising and even oppressing groups who do not hold that vision. Liberalism's view is that the state's role is merely to be society's referee, protecting the rights of individuals (and groups) to pursue the good as they see it, but not showing preference for any one theory of the good.

In consequence, liberalism and Catholicism have different understandings of human rights. While liberalism is strong in its support for social and political rights, it is fundamentally (though not overtly) ambivalent about natural or human rights since, unlike social and political rights, they are not created but only recognised by positive law, being held to be inherent in human persons. That points towards a particular view of the good, which is awkward for liberals. While liberalism favours maximal individual liberty, consistent with a like liberty for others, and entailing an overriding equality, the Christian view holds that (a) no coherent view of human rights can be formulated except within a theory of the good for the human person, and (b) that freedom must be understood within the bounds of a reason that seeks truth.[13] The justice that Christian faith does is not the same as secular justice.

Other issues: important but unpopular instances
The core-values of personal dignity and social solidarity are central to more particular issues, a five of which I will now discuss.

Firstly, Ireland should accept increased numbers of immigrants, on a planned and generous basis, for the good both of the newcomers and of the native populations. This will involve ethical reflection on the relevant conditions of citizenship. It will be the task of the Christian community to seek to cast the issue in moral terms, rather than in national, ethnic, or race-oriented categories.

Secondly, the sexual revolution that began forty years ago has moved Western societies far away from the Judeo-Christian ethic as regards sex and marriage. As regards poverty-related issues, that ethic's influence is still widely accepted. The success of the major changes initiated by Margaret Thatcher, however, and the discrediting of non-market socialism eroded the ethic of social solidarity. In the sixties, the left supported sexual individualism and a sweeping right to choose what to do with one's body and one's unborn. In the eighties, the right opted for economic individualism and a larger 'right to choose' as regards one's property. In each case, individual liberty was increased at the expense of social solidarity and human dignity.

Christians should be able to see the parallel and the linkage. Since the 1960s, the philosophical formation of Catholic moralists has been overly influenced by a pragmatic utilitarianism focused exclusively on social structural change. Yet social justice requires just persons as well as just structures, so we need a normative ethic giving full weight to the personal act. In addition, the teaching of ethics and moral theology is often far too focused on dilemma ethics, thereby excluding the ethics of character. Yet solidarity, like charity, begins at home. Those who do not see the importance of commitment with respect to spouse and children are not going to see it with respect to the poor. If Christians do not confront liberal individualism in the sexual area, they will not be able to challenge it in the area of property and social justice.

Thirdly, the Christian sexual ethic is under heavy fire at present. It is no longer a matter of people not living up to Christian ideals. There are new secular ideals in those areas, and the Christian ideals are not merely rejected, but often not even understood anymore. The new secular sexual ethic holds that:

- My body is my own, to do with as I please.

- Any sexual activity between two consenting adults must be

assumed to be morally acceptable, unless it demonstrably injures the interests of a third party.

- Chastity or sexual self-discipline has no intrinsic value: it is not a virtue. It has at most an instrumental value, in supporting marital fidelity or helping one avoid HIV-infection.

The Christian sexual ethic (see, for example, 1 Corinthians 6:13-21 and *Humanae Vitae*) rejects all three: the sexual body is not merely property or instrument, sex is immoral outside of procreative and unitive commitment, and chastity is a virtue.

The fact that the Christian sexual ethic is widely rejected is indicative of a crisis, not merely as regards our understanding of sex and the body, but also as regards the church's authority to teach. While many do not accept parts of Catholic teaching on sexuality, it is also true that no new paradigm, no new coherent teaching enjoying wide support has emerged as an alternative model of Catholic sexual ethics. That alone is a significant reason for holding to the current teaching's basic principles.

Homosexuality and chastity are the current flashpoints. With homosexual marriage moving towards legal recognition and active homosexuality being accepted even in senior Christian clergy in other denominations, Catholics will have to make the effort to comprehend the nature and extent of the challenge and the intellectual rationale behind the Christian tradition.

Rather more has to be said about chastity. The sexual misbehaviour of Catholic clerics with minors has been identified as a failure in fidelity to personal vows, to the Catholic faith, to the people of God, and to Christ. Its medicalisation is also a kind of infidelity, treating it as if it were a blame-free disease. Yet addictions to alcohol and drugs, while involving progressive loss of moral freedom, are seen as involving responsibility for that loss and for doing the little one can to regain it. The Twelve-Step AA programme is a good illustration of a moral phenomenology recognising both the relative powerlessness and the sufficiency, however small, of moral ability and grace to fight it.

The sexual revolution of the 1960s spread the idea that abstinence, chastity, and sexual self-discipline were repressive

and bad, while sexual acceptance and self-expression were un-
qualifiedly good. That view came to grief in the paedophile
scandals, for their sexual self-expression simply could not be
acceptable. Attempting to medicalise it is an evasion, for to talk
about curing paedophilia is about as sensible as talk about curing heterosexuality. There is no getting away from the need for
sexual self-control and chastity for paedophiles. And that will
not work, unless sexual self-control is seen as good for all.

To paraphrase Aristotle on courage: the chaste are found
where chastity is honoured. Those who are sexually attracted to
children must practise chastity, with respect not just to actions
that are criminal, but also to solitary actions and fantasies.[14] So
must those attracted to others to whom they are not married. So
ought those who are at risk of transmitting fatal illnesses
through sexual intercourse. These can be hard things to ask, and
those who give them need a supportive culture to do so.
Chastity must be honoured.

Fourthly, the church teaches that private property is a kind of
stewardship. The wealth and produce of the earth is to be used
for the good of all. Religion's decline weakens that sense, and
strengthens the cultural drift to seeing the right to private property as something absolute. The discrediting of the socialist
model of running an economy has reinforced that trend, manifested in the spreading opposition to tax increases for social programmes. The task of educating people in their duties as holders
of property is increasingly being left to religions.

Finally, there are the ethical issues touching the person: IVF,
gene manipulation to suit parental specification, embryo freez-
ing, euthanasia and abortion. As with the issues surrounding
sexuality, it is ironic that they should be seen as 'conservative'
and 'old-fashioned' issues, since they are new in a way that
poverty, homelessness and inequality are not. Their novelty
makes them important since in some ways theory follows practice. In other words, one's understanding of the nature of the
person and of the dignity and value of the human being will be
affected by the social practices in these areas. As in the area of

sexual ethics, here too is a world of difference between secular and Christian views. The century ahead will be interesting.

Notes

1. I mean the term 'church' in a broad sense.

2. See de Souza, *Thinly Disguised Totalitarianism* and Chopko, *Religious Institutions Serving in the Public Arena: Pressures to Conform*. Mark Chopko, general counsel to the US Conference of Catholic Bishops, draws attention to the increasing legislative and regulatory pressures on religions in areas that have traditionally been beyond the remit of the state, seeking to compel Church bodies to behave in ways that violate their ethos.

3. See Jenkins, *The New Anti-Catholicism*.

4. See Murphy, 'Two challenges for social spirituality'.

5. See Archer, 'Models of man' which begins: 'Throughout their history the social sciences have privileged atheism. They are an extended example of the general asymmetry between the need to justify faith, and the assumption that faith supposedly requires no such justification. Indeed, social science bears much responsibility for enabling atheism to be presented as an epistemologically neutral position, instead of what it is, a commitment to a belief in the absence of religious phenomena.'

6. See Plantinga, *Warranted Christian Belief* for illuminating discussion of this point.

7. See Carter, *The Culture of Disbelief* and Greenawalt, *Private Consciences and Public Reasons*.

8. John Paul II, *Veritatis Splendor*, focusing not on moral issues but on moral theory, illustrates the point.

9. The references to naturalism and creative anti-realism come in this instance from Alvin Plantinga, although he is not the only one to identify them as such. See Plantinga, 'Christian philosophy at the end of the twentieth century'.

10. For an easily accessible and up-to-date treatment, see Massaro, *Living Justice*.

11. See Riordan, *A Politics of the Common Good* for a rigorous presentation of the issues involved in talk about the common good in a pluralist society, including its ineliminability.

12. See for instance the account of the good in Finnis, Natural Law and Natural Rights and in Adams, *Finite and Infinite Goods.*
13. To a liberal, equality for homosexuals implies that they too should be able to marry. A Catholic might disagree, since it ignores the nature of marriage, men and women.
14. In this respect, it is illuminating to look at the 'therapy' for sex offenders.

Select Bibliography
Adams, Robert M., *Finite and Infinite Goods: A Framework for Ethics,* Oxford University Press, 1999
Archer, Margaret S., 'Models of Man: Transcendence and Being in the World,' in Cassidy, ed., 2002
Carter, Stephen, *The Culture of Disbelief: How American Law and Politics Trivialize Religious Devotion,* Basic Books, New York, 1993
Cassidy, Eoin G. (ed), *Measuring Ireland: Discerning Values and Beliefs,* Veritas, Dublin, 2002
Chopko, Mark, 'Religious Institutions Serving in the Public Arena: Pressures to Conform', *Origins* Vol 33, No 25 (27 November 2003)
De Souza, Raymond, 'Thinly Disguised Totalitarianism', *First Things* 142 (April 2004)
Finnis, John, *Natural Law and Natural Rights,* Clarendon Press, Oxford, 1980
Greenawalt, Kent, *Private Consciences and Public Reasons,* Oxford University Press, 1995
Jenkins, Philip, *The New Anti-Catholicism: the Last Acceptable Prejudice,* Oxford University Press, 2003
John Paul II, *Centesimus Annus,* United States Catholic Conference, Washington DC, 1991
John Paul II, *Veritatis Splendor,* United States Catholic Conference, Washington DC, 1993
Massaro, Thomas, *Living Justice: Catholic Social Teaching in Action,* Sheed and Ward, Franklin, 2000

Murphy, Séamus, 'Two challenges for social spirituality', in Jesuit Centre for Faith and Justice, *Windows on Social Spirituality*, Columba Press, Dublin, 2003

Plantinga, Alvin, 'Christian philosophy at the end of the twentieth century' in James F. Sennett, ed., *The Analytic Theist: an Alvin Plantinga reader*, Cambridge University Press, 1999

Plantinga, Alvin, *Warranted Christian Belief*, Oxford University Press, 2000

Rawls, John, *Political Liberalism*, Columbia University Press, New York, 1993

Riordan, Patrick, *A Politics of the Common Good*, IPA, Dublin. 1996

A Renewed Chaplaincy to the Primary School

Feidhlimidh Magennis

A significant feature in the life of the Catholic community is the parish-based school. The church has developed a strong educational presence as a pastoral manifestation of its response to the command of Jesus to 'teach all nations' (cf. Mt 28:19-20) and to build up a civilisation of the kingdom of God. The parish school becomes a focal point in the dialogue between faith and culture, a dialogue which seeks to establish a truly human society, reflecting the divine intention for humanity as revealed in the person of Jesus Christ. While in many countries the separation of church and state means that church schools operate outside or in parallel to a state (or public) school system, the historical development of the Irish educational systems (north and south) has produced a situation where the Catholic school system is part and parcel of state provision. Funded by the state and subject to government regulation, Irish Catholic schools are in a privileged position to further the dialogue between faith and culture, and so inculturate gospel values in our society with the hope of bringing in the kingdom.

This privileged position offers the church an excellent opportunity for evangelisation in the service of the gospel and of the kingdom of God. Rightly, members of the church have seized this opportunity and devoted energy and personnel to the development of Catholic schools over the past two centuries. The creation of religious orders for the educational apostolate, the establishment of schools, the formation of generations of lay teachers – all these and more have been motivated by the call to build the kingdom and thus to improve the condition of Irish society. But, as we are often painfully aware, the reality often fails to live up to the vision. There is work still to be done both to establish a Catholic ethos in these schools and to contribute to a more just and equitable society. And there are new challenges ahead.

Challenged by this vision, we need to ensure that our schools are fully integrated into the church's wider mission of evangelisation as the servant of God's kingdom. Therefore in this essay I will reflect on the link between the parish and the local primary school as a concrete manifestation of the church's mission in education. I will focus on one existing form of linkage, school chaplaincy, and consider how it may be developed to meet new challenges. How might future parish ministers and the parish school work together to harness the energies of the wider community in the task of evangelisation and so support the conversion of society towards the kingdom? What developments are needed in parish ministry to support the school's contribution to evangelisation and catechesis? How should the role of the school chaplain evolve in answer to these questions?

The priests' perspective

In such a short space, I cannot present a fully developed argument so I will proceed by way of various experiences which map out trajectories towards a future, school-related ministry. In making use of such a methodology, I offer a hopeful reading of some signs of our times which allow us to hear what the Spirit is saying to the churches (cf. Rev 2:7).

At a conference in 2004, the priests of the diocese of Dromore considered the changing circumstances of priestly ministry: what present activities, worthy as they are, may need to be surrendered? What indications can be detected of new ways to minister in the future? Many priests spoke highly of parish schools, the commitment of their staff, and their contribution to parish life. They spoke of the increasing burden of administrative work placed on the board of management of the school, and in particular on the chair-person (who is often a priest of the parish). They expressed concern that they were seen more and more as managers invoking and administering the authority of government, rather than as a priestly voice. If the term 'ministerial' were to be used, it may invoke the wrong ministry – state rather than ecclesial! While for some, this was a demoralising situation, others saw it as an opportunity to put into effect the changing understanding of priestly ministry coming from Vatican II. Such priests prized their visits to the classroom and the staff room, their involvement with children and teachers in moments of prayer, and the wider pastoral aspects of school chaplaincy. They sought development and training to be more effective in these areas. In view of the declining numbers of parish clergy and of the virtual disappearance of religious from schools, they hoped to share this new ministry with lay people.

The chaplains' perspective
A second experience links well with this aspiration for a greater emphasis on chaplaincy. I have been involved with a flourishing Masters' programme in Chaplaincy Studies offered by Mater Dei Institute. Based in Dublin but with outreach centres in Munster and Connacht, the programme offers professional training for those seeking to be second-level school chaplains. This training has developed to meet the needs and activities of such chaplains. The degree programme consists of a menu of modules. There are important courses on theological reflection and educational studies. These are balanced with practical units on counselling and liturgical skills, and on other related pastoral issues. The majority of students taking the programme are lay people, and most are qualified teachers. These students are re-sponding to the call to serve the faith community in a school context, and to meet society's wish that schools cater for a holistic education, including the spiritual, moral and emotional dimen-sions of the child. It should be noted that provision exists to em-ploy full-time chaplains in some types of second-level schools in the South of Ireland. The Masters' programme has identified a need and is flourishing in such a supportive environment.

The teachers' perspective

A third experience that I wish to draw upon relates to my work in teacher education in the North of Ireland. This enables me to experience at first-hand the enthusiasm and commitment of teachers and student teachers. They are a highly skilled and dedicated group of people, among whom one finds commitment to the ideals of the teaching vocation as a service for the betterment of society. There are high levels of openness to the gospel vision and a willingness to engage with that vision through the teaching of religious education, pastoral care and the development of a school ethos that expresses gospel values. But students and teachers are acutely aware of the changing circumstances in which they seek to promote that vision. Many teachers speak of the difficulties they face in today's primary schools. While the vast majority of children and parents in a Catholic school are at least nominally Catholic, many are not actively so. Levels of explicit formation in faith in the home – prayer, attendance at church, knowledge of the gospel and of Catholic tradition – are falling. It has become a commonplace observation that the classroom may be the child's first and only exposure to faith practice. Teachers find themselves exposed and isolated as the sole faith presence in the children's lives. Many teachers do not feel sufficiently confident in their own faith to carry the perceived burden of solitary witness. Such teachers are anxiously requesting support.

The second-level school chaplain – a possible model?

These experiences set out a context for a reflection on the parish's commitment to the local primary school. They are both worrying and hopeful. We live in a time of change. That transition needs to be embraced in a positive manner that can both mourn a lost past and celebrate a dawning future. Running through all the experiences is a continuing commitment to the positive value of the parish school as a focal point for the engagement of faith with culture. They are significant institutions through which the faith community can interact with the wider society and contribute to shaping the future of humanity. But while the school is a significant institution, old models for pastoral involvement in the school community are fading away. This is partly a reaction to decline – in faith practice generally and in clerical numbers in particular. But for change to be positive and fruitful, it must be driven by a vision. It must actively read the signs of the times and be open to the creativity of the Spirit. Within these experiences, one can detect lines of development, signs of hopeful growth. While the trends do not coincide, they do indicate opportunities for new ministry. Both priests and teachers are seeking a more collaborative approach to a ministry of service within the school.

From the perspective of priests, one hears a desire for a more collegial approach to replace the perception of the priest as manager. While this may in part be a reaction against the increasing administrative burden on a decreasing number of priests, it does reflect a positive desire to actualise visions of priesthood centred on service, prophetic witness and communion that have developed since Vatican II. From the teachers' perspective, the fragmentation of a Catholic monoculture leaves them less sure of their role as propagators of the faith. They may react to a more multi-cultural environment by teaching about faith, as distinct from teaching the faith. While they are willing to be involved in this ministry common to all the baptised, they do not wish to be left holding the baby! They need help and support. Finally, the experiences gained from the training and deployment of chaplains in second-level schools suggests a positive model for the future. But its present form is shaped specifically for the second-level school sector and cannot be transferred intact to the primary school. To progress in this direction will require some further reflection and comment.

In recent years, research into the practices of second-level school chaplains has led to a broader understanding of their role. Instead of a narrow focus on the celebration of the sacraments and provision of religious instruction, the chaplain is party to a wider concern for the holistic development of the student. The chaplain contributes to the spiritual and personal aspects of that concern as a person of faith who, on behalf of the school and the church community, accompanies and supports each person on the journey through life (cf. Monahan and Renahan, 10). This description reflects the second-level school chaplain's dual mandate: on the one hand, the chaplain is a full-time member of the school staff with specific responsibility for spiritual and personal development, and on the other, the chaplain is nominated by the church community to be a living witness of faith to the school community. Research carried out by Norman (2002) has identified the types of activity that predominate in the work of the chaplain. The results suggest that counselling – the broad range of 'one-on-one' meetings with pupils, staff and parents – is the predominant activity of the chaplain. Following behind counselling were liturgical celebration and providing support for other school staff. It is noteworthy that only 30% of respondents in this survey were priests and the rest were non-ordained. It would seem that even for priests, the counselling aspects have come to dominate. This work has many similarities to the work of a guidance counsellor, providing support and guidance at moments of psychological and emotional crisis in the life of the individual student and of the wider school community. The chaplain undertakes professional training to meet this role but critically adds a faith dimension to it.

Chaplaincy is a healing ministry after the pattern of Christ the healer. It is also a pastoral ministry which reveals the love of the Good Shepherd for his flock. A further image serves to illuminate the potential of chaplaincy in an Irish setting: the chaplain lives in and serves the school community in a manner similar to the *anam-chara* of the Celtic Christian monastic community. The *anam-chara*, or soul-mate, was a member of the community who accompanied the young person on his or her life-journey, in a manner similar to Christ travelling with the disciples on the road to Emmaus. This last image would be a fruitful one for modelling contemporary chaplaincy work. It highlights the embedded nature of the soul-mate within the community, and it underscores that the soul-mate need not be someone in sacramental ministry or a position of authority.

At present, however, some second-level school chaplains serve as a full-time staff member, sharing in the school's pastoral mission as a specialised member of the team. There are no similar arrangements for the employment of a chaplain in a primary school, and given the expectation that this role is one of several functions carried out as part of parish ministry, the aims and functions of a primary school chaplain will be different to those of a second-level chaplain. The primary school chaplain will be a visitor who comes into the school to represent the wider faith community. The purpose of such visits will be to manifest the involvement of that community in the faith-development of the children. The chaplain will embody and promote parish-school links and assist the school in the catechetical dimension of its mission.

A model for primary school chaplaincy

In contrast to the work of the second-level school chaplain, there will be less emphasis on the counselling aspect of the chaplain's work at primary school level. When seeking help and support, younger children will naturally approach an adult who is familiar and regularly present, such as the class teacher. Conversely, given their young age and undeveloped ability to articulate feelings and emotions, it requires regular observation of mood and behaviour to determine the child's emotional state. The teacher is better placed to discern the child's needs and to offer regular support and a reassuring presence. The teacher therefore will be on the front-line in the provision of pastoral care, while the chaplain would serve as a second-line resource person.

The primary school chaplain will probably devote the greater proportion of time and energy to explicitly faith-based activities. In contrast to being available for students in times of need, the primary school chaplain will work with staff to be pro-active in meeting the children and providing a witness to faith practice. The chaplain is present in the school to represent the faith community and to assist the members of the school community in sharing that faith. Thus catechetical concerns will be more predominant than counselling requirements and spiritual and liturgical exercises will play a central part in the routine of the chaplain.

Sacramental preparation is an obvious example that will help to illustrate the work of such a chaplain. Significant thought and energy has gone into the design of teaching resources for sacramental preparation, and these form a central element of the *Alive-O* catechetical series. By means of these resources, the teacher is equipped and guided in the task of instructing and forming the children for initiation into, and subsequent participation in, the liturgical life of the church. The *Alive-O* programme actively seeks to link classroom preparation with parish life by providing guidelines, suggesting parish-based activities, and offering further resources for parish liturgy. But, as many teachers will admit, it is very difficult to put this parish dimension into practice from within the school. It requires the active engagement of the parish community and its ministers. It is the parish, clergy and people, who must take the lead and move beyond the assumption that the school will and can do all the work of sacramental preparation on its own. Here is a great opportunity for a chaplain to become active as the link person between parish and school. As the representative of the parish, the chaplain would work alongside the teacher in delivering this aspect of the catechetical programme so that the children may understand that preparation for the sacraments is a shared task of both teacher and chaplain, school and parish. Further, the chaplain is readily placed to engage the parents in a parish-based programme which equips them to carry out their role as 'primary educators in the faith' in conjunction with the school-based religious education programme. In broad outline, this does not sound very radical or new: in fact, many priests have established excellent examples of such co-operation to bring together the three partners – parents, parish, school – in the shared task of sacramental preparation. In doing so, they are already living out this ministry of chaplaincy. The aim of this reflection is to offer a more cohesive model within which they can develop and extend the effectiveness of their existing work. The way forward is to extend the involvement of the chaplain beyond provision of the sacraments and organisation of meetings, to an active sharing of the catechetical work of the teacher within the school. By working together in a supportive and collaborative mode they will make visible to the children the faith community and its commitment to their faith development.

If sacramental preparation offers a useful example of the chaplain's role in the primary school, it is simply a matter of extending the principles to embrace other forms of spiritual activity. Again, the aim is to provide a visible example of the faith practice of the parish community and thus to initiate the children into that practice. Prayer is a central element of the religious education programme and many teachers offer the children frequent and varied experiences of prayer. It would be the role of the chaplain to relate those experiences to the wider life of the community and so overcome a potential weakness of the religious education programme as presently designed. Many teachers express the concern that children experience prayer only in school; it is not a feature of home life and the children have little contact with worship in the parish. Other teachers go further: the prayer experiences offered by the programme have no counterpoint in the life of the parish. A chaplain who becomes involved in classroom prayer is better situated to overcome this gap by ensuring a continuity between the spirituality developed in the school and the spirituality of the parish. In the past, many priests established this continuity by celebrating Masses in the school or by encouraging the teachers to bring the children to a parish Mass, on the supposition that Catholic spirituality is centred on the eucharist. While acknowledging the centrality of the eucharist, one would hope that our spiritual life is wider and more varied than celebrations of the Mass. As a minister of the parish and of the school, the chaplain is well placed to develop a richer spiritual life for both communities.

The identity of the primary school chaplain

This last point leads to the question of the identity of the primary school chaplain. Traditionally, the role has been filled by a priest of the parish or a member of the religious order with responsibility for the school. Obviously, the decline in clerical and religious numbers has had a negative impact on the provision of school chaplains: in second-level schools the majority of chaplains are now lay people. But there has also been a positive trend within parishes to facilitate the baptismal ministry of the lay faithful in the life of the parish. Chaplaincy to the primary school is one fruitful area where a lay parish ministry could develop. Since the role of the chaplain, in the model proposed here, is to be a visible representation of the faith-life of the parish community, it is all the more appropriate that the chaplain be a typical member of that community. With due considerations for the priorities of child protection, it would be an admirable development if lay members of the parish were to engage with the school community to support the school's catechetical mission. It might help to overcome the mistake made by many young children that the priest alone is holy, prayerful and attempts to live the gospel. The witness given by a lay person would help the child to incarnate their grasp of the Christian message in the ordinary lives of their neighbours.

The parish primary school is a valuable institution in the life of the parish. It is frequently staffed by teachers who are dedicated to their task of providing a holistic educational experience to the children in their care, including an education in the faith of the parish community. The school is only one partner in faith formation. It needs clear and visible support from the parish community. Traditionally this has been provided by the local clergy who serve the school at management level and as chaplains. Both priests and teachers express the wish for a more active involvement by the parish. This essay suggests that a modified model of chaplaincy offers a way forward. This model of chaplaincy differs from that found in second-level schools in that it focuses on catechesis more than on counselling. It also differs from the traditional priestly emphasis on sacramental provision. According to this model, the chaplain would work alongside the teachers to support the catechetical aspects of the religious education programme (sacramental worship and prayer). The chaplain would be present in the school as a visible sign of the local faith community actively engaged in the faith formation of the children. While the priest could fulfil this role, there is a strong argument for lay involvement and participation. Such faith development work would be an important opportunity for the future development of lay parish ministry.

Select bibliography
Monahan, L. & Renehan, C ., *The Chaplain: A Faith Presence in the School Community*, Columba Press, Dublin, 1998
Norman, J., *Pastoral Care in Second Level Schools: The Chaplain*, A Research Report, Mater Dei Institute of Education, Dublin, 2002
Norman, J., (ed), *At The Heart of Education*, Veritas, Dublin, 2004
Sullivan, J., *Catholic Schools in Contention*, Veritas, Dublin, 2000

Home, School, Community Liaison: Supporting the Parent as Prime Educator

Concepta Conaty

This chapter examines how the role of the parent as prime educator can be supported and enhanced in the education of children within a family and community context and within the framework of the Home, School, Community Liaison Scheme. It takes cognisance of the role of the school acting in partnership with the family-community. The theory relates to all families but the experience has been gleaned with marginalised parents living in communities of socio-economic and hence educational disadvantage and has aroused much interest within the European Union and beyond since 1990.

An American educator, R. Putnam, addressed the OECD ministers for education in Dublin Castle last year. He claimed that statistical evidence which he and his colleagues had compiled

> strongly suggests that attitudes and behaviour which parents and students bring to the educational process are more deeply and directly affected by the strength of community and family bonds ... than by measures of teacher quality or class size or spending per pupil.

He proceeded to speak of the potential value to the school of fostering a more active community connection and the desirability of linking parents and community members more immediately to schools.

However, parents who did not benefit much from schooling themselves, who are either unemployed or in low paid work, who are suffering from poor health, and are living in estates with a meagre infrastructure, will find it extremely difficult to sunder the vicious circle through which the legacy of disadvantage is passed from generation to generation. Where there is a dependency culture, where the television is on all day and perhaps there is no book in the home apart from the child's school books, where the only paper bought is likely to be an English redtop which is studied for its photographs and headlines, it is exceptionally difficult to progress an education agenda. In addition, the formal education system cannot compensate for a deprived home life, nor offset the effects of inadequate parental ability. This inadequacy is often sparked by the fact that some parents are too closely engaged in the struggle for existence to devote time to their children. The basic task of programmes seeking to develop the whole-child is the prevention of educational disadvantage. This often calls for respectful intervention within the home. The healthy development of young children can best be achieved by fortifying the families and the community. When parents have the opportunity to acquire knowledge, develop skills and deepen their understanding of child development, they are enabled to make informed choices and decisions in relation to their own lives and those of their children. This empowerment process encourages interdependence at home and community levels.

If we are to truly empower those we meet in the educative process, 'especially those who are poor or in any way afflicted', then we must know them, we must unite ourselves existentially to their life experiences, joys, hopes, fears and sufferings, for 'these too are the joys, and hopes, the griefs and the anxieties of the followers of Christ' (Vatican II, *Gaudium et Spes* 1). In Christ we find the perfect synthesis of zeal for the glory of God and compassion for people, of zeal for justice and peace, and for that justice 'which makes us compassionate as our Father is compassionate' (Lk 6: 36). The presence of Jesus is inherent in every true expression of justice, compassion, love, support, peace and reconciliation.

While charitable work and social help will always be necessary, because we will never have a perfect social and political system, it is not what is in mind in this chapter. The choice for the marginalised parents and communities, in the mind of the author, is an option in favour of the kingdom. Charitable work, while necessary, is peripheral because real generosity lies in striving 'so that those hands – whether of individuals or entire peoples – need to be extended less and less in supplication, so that more and more they become human hands which work and, by working, transform the world' (Freire, 1-22).

This chapter is not a treatise on church ministry nor is it an exposition of the Home, School, Community Liaison Scheme in Ireland. It is intended as a reflection on how the daily activities of family, community and school can be experienced through an integrated approach brought about under the inspiration and strength of the gospel. Authentic evangelisation is education for justice, peace and inclusion. For the followers of Christ this presupposes a faith which translates itself into justice and equality for the disadvantaged, the non nationals and refugees in our society. It is impossible to follow Jesus to the Father in the unity of the Spirit without conversion to a close affinity with the marginalised. At the same time it is also important to witness to the poor the justice and compassion of Jesus so that they too may pursue the admonition of the gospel 'blessed are the poor'. It is necessary to state at this point that the realities of church ministry and kingdom values were not expressed either overtly or covertly by the Department of Education and Science. However, this belief might well be the private view of department personnel. The view on ministry is the personal expression of the author who is privileged to believe in the integration of gospel and life, of allowing prayer to support work and work to enrich prayer. It is within this duality, yet unity, of work and prayer that the discussion on Home, School, Community Liaison takes place.

The Home, School, Community Liaison Scheme (HSCL) in Ireland
The last twenty years have been both exciting and demanding years in education in Ireland. One reason has been the acceptance of the central part parents play as the primary educator of

their children and secondly, through the ever increasing emphasis on the role of the community in education. In Ireland there have been important developments in the interrelationships between home, school and community because of the perception that education was failing pupils in some areas of socio-economic disadvantage (Conaty, 1999). It is a widely held fact that, while the education system has a vital role to play, schools cannot address the multi-faceted nature of disadvantage alone. Marginalised pupils may be described as frequently presenting in school with complex social, emotional, health and developmental needs that are barriers to learning. In addition marginalised pupils generally come from homes where poverty issues preoccupy the family. They are generally the children of the unskilled and unemployed working-class, with a history of educational failure. In marginalised areas there is often a reduced ability to cope within the family and the community. In this way the cycle of poverty, oppression, disadvantage, early school leaving and educationl failure is perpetuated. Families with these characteristics generally live in densely populated urban areas. They are also found, but to a lesser degree, in dispersed rural communities. In situations where equality of opportunity is lacking and social exclusion is prolonged there is a serious loss of talent to society. Inability often finds expression in apathy, voicelessness, vandalism, substance misuse, joy-riding, demotivation, low self-image and alienation from family, friends and school (Conaty, 2002, 19-20).

Since 1990 the Department of Education and Science has been characterised by positive discrimination in favour of the most marginalised. The HSCL Scheme heralded this change in 1990. HSCL is recognised as the cornerstone and integrating factor of the Department's initiatives serving marginalised areas and of current programmes that address educational disadvantage and early school leaving. HSCL is a targeted, focused and purposeful resource serving the most marginalised families in designated areas of disadvantage. It is built on the theory and practice of partnership and promotes parents, teachers and community agents as partners in the learning of young people. HSCL is unified and integrated at primary and post-primary levels. Core to the Scheme is the fact that it is a preventative measure and that it centres on the significant adults in the young person's life.

The activities of the HSCL local co-ordinator

In keeping with the aims and principles of HSCL the local co-ordinator, an experienced teacher from the school staff, is deployed to full time work with parents and community. The theory and practice of partnership is central to the work of the co-ordinator. Partnership presupposes equality and implies that the relationship has been formed on the basis that each has an important contribution to make. It also implies that people will work together, explore possibilities, plan, make decisions, and evaluate outcomes collaboratively. It calls for a consistent commitment to the demanding and difficult work of human relating. Partnership invites power sharing and welcomes mutual vulnerability. It implies that there is an ability to listen and that there is clarity in thinking. A level of self-understanding is called for which leads one to acknowledge feelings, to be compassionate. P. Block, who has been at the centre of changing organisations, including schools, for almost thirty years, admonishes that partnership does not do away with hierarchy because 'people at higher levels do have specialised responsibility, but it is not so much for control as it is for clarity ... of requirements ... of value-added ways of attending to a specific market' (Block, 32). Partnership and service are mutually connected. It is interesting to note that Block selected, 'choosing service over self-interest', as the sub-title to one of his books. J. Whitehead and E. Whitehead draw parallels between partnership, authority and power. They believe that genuine authority expands life and makes power more abundant. They see parents as 'our first authority figures. Good parents encourage their children's first steps and support their later leaps. They learn to correct without stunting ... inviting the child into adulthood' (Whitehead and Whitehead, 27).

In short, partnership identifies, releases and shares mutual yet, perhaps, different gifts, gifts of personality, of experience and of expertise. A new form of listening and leadership emerged in the Catholic Church after the Second Vatican Council and is referred to as 'collegiality' and is viewed from the standpoint of a leader in a community of leaders. At a practical level this collegiality is translated into a commitment to share responsibility at parish council level which, as we will note later in the chapter, has similarities to the Local Committee of the HSCL Scheme. The movement towards partnership in schools and collegiality in the church meets with resistance because not all leaders believe in shared responsibility. Instead of the church being from the priest down and ideas coming only from the pulpit and not from the pews there is a growing awareness, still at an initial stage, that the living out of the faith of the church will be found in its laity as well as in its clergy. There is a need to listen to this living faith. There is a move away from a mere external observance as liberation theology calls us to a different stance on human rights and democracy. It reminds us 'that before the church is for the poor or with the poor, it is first of all a church from the poor' – a compelling agenda for all schools serving the disadvantaged (Ferder and Heagle, 119).

Needs identification

HSCL initiatives are focused on adults but impinge over time on children's lives. The programmes are concerned with promoting the education, development, growth and involvement of parents and with the participation of parents in their children's education. The Second Vatican Council reminds us that 'the family is the first school of those social values which every society needs', hence the obligation on all Christian educators to support families, particularly the marginalised (Declaration on Education, par 3). HSCL initiatives provide a parent room and child care facilities for parents who attend programmes. These facilities enable parents to feel comfortable and welcome in the school. One cannot but notice the light in the eyes of a parent who has found a new sense of pride and an increased confidence in child rearing as they are included and involved in their child's learning and development. The level of hospitality, offered by the school to parents, can be a sharing of the peace, forgiveness, community and table friendship – albeit in a very simple form – experienced in the early church. Almost all initiatives including courses and classes for parents are organised as a direct result of a needs identification process held by the co-ordinators. To really touch the lives of others one requires this ability to listen at a deep level. To listen in this way is to affirm the other. It enables the person to feel heard and accepted. It is to love with the compassion of Jesus.

HSCL activities for parents can be categorised on four broad levels. Some parents progress through a sequence, while others enter at a particular stage. The progression is as follows. Firstly, leisure time activities prove to be a non-threatening starting point for marginalised parents. Secondly, curricular activities enable parents to come closer to their children's learning. Thirdly, parents become involved in personal development courses, parenting courses and leadership skills development. Lastly, parents support and become a resource to their own children, to co-ordinators and to teachers. These parents pass on their skills to children by acting as teacher aides in the classroom and as support persons in the community. Surely this is a response to the invitation addressed to all Christians: 'you go into my vineyard too' (Mt 20: 3-4). This invitation is reflected in the Second Vatican Council's emphasis on the nature, dignity, spirituality, mission, and responsibility of the lay faithful, and has also been issued by Pope John Paul II when he says that the parish should be 'the place where the very "mystery" of the church is present and at work' (Pope John Paul II, par 26).

Parents as a resource
Some examples of how parents are a resource to their own children and also to the wider school community are as follows. At primary level parents work with children in the classroom in

such areas as reading, paired reading, art and craft activities, drama, library organisation, mathematics, computers and cookery. At post-primary level parents work with young people in the classroom on topics such as peer pressure, the prevention of substance misuse and teenage pregnancy. A number of parents deliver modules to pupils doing the Leaving Certificate Applied in areas such as interviewing technique and relationships in the workplace. According to 53% of principals and 49% of HSCL co-ordinators this type of activity takes place 'to a great extent/ some extent' in the HSCL Scheme (Educational Research Centre, 81). In addition to helping their own children with homework many parents are involved in community run 'homework clubs' where children who have personal or home difficulties are supported. In some situations teenage mothers come to the school on Saturday morning, with their babies who are cared for in the crèche, while their mothers are involved in personal development, parenting programmes and Leaving Certificate classes. All these activities are intended to support the young mother in parenting and to enable her to remain on in school. In this way parents share their unique gifts with others and seek to build up the local community. Efforts to assist the full development of the human person, to fashion a more human world, to develop the capacity for right judgement, to promote a value system which is based on the gospel and to enhance family and community life are a direct response to the baptismal and confirmation call. Evangelisation remains the urgent and vital mission of all Christians.

Home visitation by the HSCL co-ordinator
The role of the co-ordinator also includes a systematic approach to home visitation. Home visitation is a purposeful outreach dimension of HSCL to parents and shows the parent and co-ordinator at great ease in each other's company. During the visits, co-ordinators support parents in the education of their children and seek to establish a rapport with the parents. They offer information about the services available in the community and en-

courage parents to become involved with the community, to work with community needs and to harness community energy thereby enabling the community to solve its own problems. Co-ordinators endeavour to show the welcoming, hopeful and human face of the school in the context and circumstances of daily life. The seeking of potential parent leaders who are willing to participate in HSCL activities and to share their talents is another objective of home visitation. Many parents take part in training to enhance their skills following a visit from the co-ordinator. HSCL co-ordinators aim at helping parents to express their fears around approaching school and seek to break down negative attitudes among parents towards schools and schooling. In the gospel we note that when Jesus was present to a group barriers were broken down – 'bring the poor, the maimed, the blind and the lame' (Lk 14: 12) and again 'go out into the highways ... that my house may be filled' (Lk 14:23). People felt accepted by him and they were able to accept themselves. Jesus valued the marginalised and called into question the value system of the time and those whose interest the system served.

Co-ordinators are expected to be sensitive to the needs of the person. They aim to be non-threatening and friendly and they work with the family agenda during home visitation. Encouragement is the key word. There is a deep awareness that one is there for the good of the family and co-ordinators offer support and gently encourage parents into the school. While there is much evidence to show that co-ordinators are very well accepted in the homes of marginalised parents it is also a fact that 65% of co-ordinators claim, due to workload, that 'they had visited more than half of the homes that they wished to' (Educational Research Centre, 65). Since 28% of families are placed by co-ordinators in the 'most severely disadvantaged' group of parents, and of these 60% in the 'not involved' category, a renewed concentration on home visitation, by some co-ordinators, seems fundamental. Home visitation is both a symbolic and a real expression of interest in families, many of which have been alienated from the educational system in the past.

Within this real expression of interest in families it is easier to imagine what the early Christian communities of faith might have been like. The communities of faith, which emerged following the resurrection, emanated from people in relationship and were based in the homes. It was in these environments that the prayer and table-fellowship, initiated by Jesus, were celebrated. It was in the home that the vision of Jesus relating to inclusivity and equality were translated into everyday living.

Parents as community leaders and as educational home visitors
Experience on the ground and outcomes from evaluation point to the fact that the HSCL Scheme 'continues to generate a great deal of co-operation and collaboration between schools, families and communities' (Educational Research Centre, 74). Some parents with basic training volunteer to participate in advanced training. Parents then become deeply involved in the community. The outcomes from advanced training include parent-to-parent contact and the availability of a trained pool of parents providing local leadership and more efficient and effective work at local community level. There is more time for creative work on the part of co-ordinators, due to the process of delegation to parents. There is an increased focus on the school in the community, on the forging of local links and the development of the partnership process. A group of parents and co-ordinators monitor this training process at local level. Parents facilitate parenting and personal development programmes for other parents. The Education Research Centre in Dublin recommends the examination of a 'particular focus on improving literacy and numeracy skills in schemes for the disadvantaged' and holds that HSCL coordinators 'could be very important in facilitating the implementation of family literacy programmes' (Ibid, 60, 62 and 113).

A further and exciting development is the training of parents as educational home visitors. In this exercise there is parent-to-parent visitation within the home so that the understanding of the school and of children's learning can be shared and so that there can be mutual encouragement and support between parents. 'The human person has an inherent social dimension which calls him/her to communion with others, to a community of persons' (John Paul II, par 40). Each parent as home visitor is equipped with a relevant information pack for each primary and post-primary school. Further development of the parents as home visitors initiative would help to stimulate children's learning in the home. The visiting parent listens to the expectations and concerns of parents. Whether the gifts or charisms of parents as community leaders are 'exceptional and great or simple and ordinary, the charisms are graces of the Holy Spirit that have ... a usefulness to the ... building of the church, to the well being of humanity and to the needs of the world' (Ibid, par 24).

The Local Committee

The HSCL co-ordinators are responsible for the setting up and the maintenance of the Local Committee. The purpose of the Local Committee is to identify school related issues at community level that impinge on learning and to seek to address these issues by working collaboratively with other interest groups. Examples of such topics are: school attendance; substance misuse issues; anti-bullying; transfer programmes; homework support; self-image programmes and health and environmental issues. It is important to note, throughout this chapter, the central and integrated nature of three elements of the HSCL Scheme: the Local Committee, policy formation and parents as home visitors. The issues identified at Local Committee level become part of the policy making process between parents, teachers, pupils and community personnel and part of the material brought to the homes and explained through parents as home visitors. Local Committee membership is divided equally between school personnel, representatives of voluntary and statutory bodies on the one hand, and marginalised but developed parents on the other. Many of the Local Committees include primary and post-primary pupils who have, in some instances, chaired meetings, have taken minutes and have been active at sub committee level between meetings.

The Local Committee provides for local ownership of strengths, difficulties, joys and needs of the local community. The Local Committee is indeed an example of partnership in action. Many Local Committee members have done training together on the development of teams, committee work, partnership, and community development. The current climate which accepts the mutually interacting roles of community and school, has opened up possibilities for the further development of Local Committees.

The integrated delivery of service to marginalised children and families-communities

The HSCL Scheme has, from its inception, emphasised the responsibility of co-ordinators in the area of networking. Networking is a consequence of a series of relationships and the dovetailing of activities within the community. It challenges previously held assumptions about job demarcation. It also challenges people's best thinking. It can be said that an understanding of networking, in theory and in fact, is an initial step towards an integrated delivery of service to the marginalised. However, it cannot be denied that networking-integration is a complex process and chiefly because of personal limitation. It calls for the ability to allow others to share success.

HSCL co-ordinators liaise with various voluntary and statutory bodies within the community and encourage a cohesive delivery of service. Just as the school is a significant resource to the community it serves, there are also many advantages for the school in drawing from the strengths of the community. The school, working collaboratively with other interest groups, can ameliorate the effects of the problems associated with educational disadvantage. The links are very obvious in relation to the prevention of early school leaving. An emerging focus in HSCL, since 1996, is that of parents, teachers, pupils and community personnel working together in policy formation. When parents, teachers, pupils and community personnel work together in this manner there is much more chance of the policy being implemented.

Pupils are not only members of families and schools; they are also part of community groups, churches, teams, clubs and gangs. An integrated approach means recognising all the influences at work, aiming to bring coherence to the multiple messages young people receive. Acceptance of the value of the community dimension of HSCL has been growing from the mid 1990s. This growth has been accelerated with the development of Local Committees.

The kingdom of God, preached by Jesus, is about more than the integration of marginalised people in order to initiate social change. It concerns also the active presence of God in the world reaching out in a spirit of peace and inclusion to all those on the fringes of life. Working for the kingdom requires a new way of living in service and commitment to the neighbour. The HSCL Scheme can provide these possibilities and can turn world values upside down where the poor in spirit are rich, the peacemakers are called children of God and those who serve are the greatest.

Additional ways in which teachers support parents
Teachers support parents at transfer time, when the child is starting school or moving from primary to the post-primary sector, by working with co-ordinators to help parents become part of and understand the system which the child is entering. There are possibilities: to identify parent hopes and fears for the child; to explain aspects of the curriculum; to highlight problematic areas such as homework and behaviour; to display explanatory leaflets, while respecting language ability and to facilitate other parents in addressing the group. This process has proved to be highly successful in easing the stress associated with a new school.

However, it must be noted that principals and co-ordinators 'believe that the HSCL has had a greater impact on teacher's awareness of and attitude to parents' role and contribution at home than it had on teachers' awareness of and attitude to parents' role and contribution in school' (Educational Research

Centre, 83). In an earlier evaluation of HSCL teachers were more likely than principals or co-ordinators to have the perception that there was little or no consultation with parents. This finding could portray a lack of communication at staff level, a withholding of information, an unclear view of the system as it is, or a desire for the system that could be or should be. It was noted at the time that 54% of teachers had no understanding of partnership (Conaty, 2002, 182-183).

Conclusion

Following an evaluation of HSCL by the OECD it was reported that

> Ireland's HSCL Scheme ... is a good example of innovative central government initiatives based in schools ... parental involvement, especially in areas of socio-economic deprivation, does not just benefit the children and the school – it is a crucial aspect of lifelong learning (OECD, 38).

School personnel, and HSCL co-ordinators in particular, constantly express the wish that more parents would attend school activities and be further enabled to support their children. Yet they are keenly aware that parents really want the best for their children but often do not know how to exploit the education system in the real sense of the term. Maybe we can take courage from the simple question of Jesus 'What are you looking for?' and more importantly from his invitation 'Come and see' (Jn 1: 38). Are we ready in our schools to pose the penetrating question to parents – what are you looking for? Are we ready for the parent response if they appear to ask for too much? Are we available, in the ordinary places and circumstances of daily life in schools, to give that simple invitation to parents – come and see? Are we willing to give this invitation? Whether partnership is a desired and feasible end-state, an attainable aspiration or whether it turns out to be unrealistic, a responsibility still rests on educators 'to become more responsive to the needs, wishes and experience of parents and children ... the development of an honest partnership that recognises important differences as well as common concerns' (Seeley, 67). The same demands apply to the church – to each one of us. Our teaching, activities, message and ministry are inseparable and must be directed at those who are poor, captive, blind and oppressed (Lk 4 :18-19).

Select bibliography

Block, Peter, *Stewardship: Choosing Service Over Self-Interest*, Barrett-Koehler Publishers Inc., San Francisco, 1993

Conaty, C., 'Partnership in Education, Through Whole School Development with Parent and Community Involvement: A Study of a National Initiative to Combat Educational Disadvantage – the Home, School, Community Liaison Scheme', (2 vols), Ph D thesis, National University of Ireland, Maynooth, 1999

Conaty, Concepta, *Including All: Home, School and Community United in Education*, Veritas, Dublin, 2002

Educational Research Centre: *Review of the Home, School, Community Liaison Scheme*, Drumcondra, 2003

Ferder, F, and Heagle, J, *Partnership: Women and Men in Ministry*, Ave Maria Press, Notre Dame, 1989

Freire, Paulo, *Pedagogy of the Oppressed*, Penguin, London, 1972

OECD, *Parents as Partners in Schooling*, Paris, 1997

Pope John Paul II, Apostolic Exhortation, *The Vocation Mission of the Laity*, Veritas, Dublin, 1989

Pugh, Gillian, and De'Ath, E, *Working Towards Partnership in the Early Years*, National Children's Bureau, London, 1989

Putnam, Robert, 'Education, Diversity, Social Cohesion and Social Capital', Paper in Dublin Castle, OECD, 2004

Vatican Council II, *Pastoral Constitution on the Church in the Modern World*, Rome, 1965

Vatican Council II, *Declaration on Christian Education*, Rome, 1965

Seeley, D, *Education through Partnership: Mediating Structures and Education*, Ballinger Publishing Company, Massachusetts, 1981

Whitehead, J, and Eaton Whitehead, E, *Promise of Partnership: Leadership and Ministry In An Adult Church*, Harper, San Francisco, 1991

Modelling a National Assembly of the Catholic Church in Ireland

Paschal Scallon CM

Scrutiny

When the enormity that has been the crisis of sexual abuse of children by priests broke upon the diocese of Boston in the United States, the scrutiny of the leadership of the diocese subsequently was so extensive that Cardinal Law, then Archbishop of Boston, was compelled to resign. Another view would go further, perhaps, and suggest that the scrutiny was such that the Holy See itself was compelled to accept Cardinal Law's resignation. In other words, the scrutiny forced not only a clerical elite in Boston to give way; it forced the clerical leadership of the Catholic Church to pay attention and to respond to external investigation and to an emerging leadership among the laity of the church that is increasingly well schooled theologically and very determined.

Scrutiny has become ubiquitous. One's every move, it often seems, is accessible by those who need to know and by those who would like to know. Whether for security purposes or commercial reasons we live, for the most part, with the activities of musketeers and marketeers without too much stress, aware perhaps that while scrutiny is invariably intrusive and can often be irritating, it has thankfully brought to light much that in the past would have remained concealed.

The sort of scrutiny that uncovers the discreet activities of those who prefer their business to remain secret has become highly celebrated. Investigative journalism has a certain cachet, complete with heroes and martyrs. But it must seem that this kind of scrutiny is, in the ordinary run of things, too extreme and almost always too late. At another level there must exist a continuing process of examination and assessment that will never make the front page, and indeed can ensure that there is no need for such exposure. Scrutiny must move from espionage to dialogue.

This is most especially true in the life of the church. In his apostolic letter, *Novo millennio ineunte* (par 42), Pope John Paul writes: 'If we have truly contemplated the face of Christ ... our pastoral planning will necessarily be inspired by the "new commandment" which he gave us: "Love one another, as I have loved you" (Jn 13:34).' To love one another as Jesus loves us is a challenging prospect especially in light of his words: 'I shall not call you servants any longer, because the servant does not know what the master is doing; but I have called you friends, because I have made known to you everything that I have heard from my Father' (Jn 15:15). Dialogue or, in the ordinary course of things, conversation has always been the basis of trust between people. Words confirmed by action establish and strengthen relationships and allow them to endure. In the more formal setting of the public community, 'dialogue' has become the indispensable word in reflecting upon the effective resolution of the community's affairs. In the public forum, no less than in private, trust is critical and cannot emerge without dialogue. One might say that trust and dialogue form a double helix – the DNA of faith as it were. A paradox of Christian discipleship is that while it calls everyone to service, it is a renunciation of servitude. When Jesus calls us friends and sets aside any notion that we are his servants because that implies a relationship in which we cannot know him, it seems that the relationship of discipleship must be conducted in a way that allows for a more direct communication.

Momentum

I believe that the only way this can take place so as to ensure dialogue at the widest possible extent is for the Catholic community in Ireland to convene a national assembly in which the whole Catholic faithful will discuss and order the life of their church. It is crucially important too that such a gathering would become a regular event in the life of the church. I have argued elsewhere

that it should take place annually and even though a less frequent gathering, say every second or third year (certainly no
longer or any momentum will be lost) may appear to facilitate
organisational issues with the various dioceses in the country, I
still feel an annual assembly will provide a lead and serve to co-
ordinate a continuing dialogue at national level (Scallon, 4-19).

The most frequently heard reservation to this proposal is that
it cannot happen until there are pastoral councils in every parish
in the country. In response to this caveat I have to point out that
parishes in Ireland have been waiting for such a development
for most of the forty years since the Vatican Council and it remains a fiction. There are, of course, pastoral councils in some
parishes but they must be the exception rather than the rule if
Archbishop Martin has had to call for their establishment in
each parish of the Dublin diocese by Lent 2005. On a positive
note, parishes in Ireland have perfected the *ad hoc* committee. If
a particular task presents, Irish Catholics show real genius in ac-
complishing whatever needs to be done. But, while this model
has served very well on its own terms, it is not going to be
enough in future. Rather than wait the better part of another
forty years, perhaps, before parish pastoral councils do set up
across the country as a matter of course, it could be that a national
assembly will stimulate the emergence of local groups, account-
able at parish and diocesan level, that accept and discharge responsibility for the pastoral care of the parish community with
or without the service of a resident priest. The process by which
the Catholic Church in Ireland takes wider responsibility for
itself can work locally and nationally and can be mutually
supportive.

Local church
In his book *The End of Irish Catholicism?* Dr Vincent Twomey
highlights a bizarre set of statistics. He compares Ireland and
Austria, two predominantly Catholic countries that are about
the same size in area and shows that where Austria has roughly
six million Catholics in twelve dioceses, Ireland has four million

Catholics living in twenty-six dioceses. In a 'perfect world' this might not mean anything very significant but in a situation where many things are not as they could be, these statistics could start one thinking (Twomey, 103-4).

A glance at an ecclesiastical map of Ireland shows that many dioceses are 'trans-regional'. Dating from the twelfth century, and influenced by dynastic issues and concerns in the medieval period that each diocese should have its own access to navigable water, the shape of many Irish dioceses seem rather tortured and make little sense today. Some dioceses such as Kerry may make sense in modern Ireland but Armagh, Clogher, Elphin, Killaloe, Ardagh and Clonmacnoise and others seem to defy logic. For example, the diocese of Elphin stretches from Sligo to Athlone and Armagh includes Magherafelt and Drogheda. In the diocese of Clogher one wonders how much Iniskeen, which is only five miles from Dundalk on the eastern seaboard, has in common with Bundoran, which looks out on Donegal bay. As things stand, the term 'local church', which has a certain meaning in Catholic ecclesiology, loses significance. Of course, were there to be a redrawing of the boundaries of fewer dioceses in the country, the new dioceses would be even bigger than the present ones but they would hopefully reflect a more coherent sense of 'place'.

Until the redrawing of diocesan boundaries occurs, however, and this is unlikely for some time, there is something to be said for inter-diocesan initiative that would allow the faithful from the several dioceses of north Connacht, for example, to gather and address the business of the church in that area. Meeting at inter-diocesan level in this way would provide an invaluable experience of the church beyond the boundaries to which we have been accustomed. It would be an important step, albeit only one, that would bring us into new relationships and new structures.

Inter-diocesan initiatives are not new in Ireland. The bishops whose dioceses are located wholly or partly in Northern Ireland met during the 'Troubles' and the bishops of the western dioceses have also sponsored specific initiatives dealing with the particular needs of the west of Ireland. Building on these experiences and widening participation would go a long way towards modelling an assembly of the Catholic community at national level.

Working models
It is to the dioceses as they actually stand, however, that one must look at present to see if anything is happening that could find expression in a national assembly. There is room here to examine one or two of these and concentrating on them does not in any way imply that nothing is happening anywhere else. In 2000 the diocese of Kilmore, which is located mostly in Cavan and north Leitrim, held a 'Diocesan Congress'. The idea for a congress was first mooted in 1997 but a decision to proceed only came two years later after some one hundred meetings that were part of a listening process and from which it emerged that the people of the diocese were 'overwhelmingly in favour' of holding a congress. The process was repeated and the concerns of the laity of the diocese emerged from this phase. They wanted a congress to reflect on prayer, youth, liturgy, the role of the laity, vocations, adult religious education, family and parish as a caring community. In addition, there were four aims for the congress: to provide a forum for discussion for all sections of the people of the diocese, to give the clergy the opportunity to listen to the laity, to name priorities for the next five years, to set up a Diocesan Pastoral Council (Kelly, 484-9).

Each of the thirty-six parishes in the diocese sent six lay delegates and the priests of the parish to the congress. There were more than three hundred participants who met over three days at the end of October 2000. The event was judged a tremendous success, as much, one feels, because of an unaffected spirit of courage and humility. During the congress there was some verbal 'jostling' for the floor as a lay voice protested the number of interventions from the clergy present, which seem to have been 'unintentionally forceful and obtrusive' (Brady, 683ff). Details such as these are more exciting, in many ways, than what decisions were made or resolutions were passed. The sheer humanity of the moment records that it is possible for lay and ordained to share ideas in an open and robust way without the sky falling in.

If the process, as successful as it appears to have been, had one flaw, however, it could be that there was no subsequent congress. It is not enough only to produce a report, however comprehensive, because unless a body reconvenes to evaluate what progress there has been on whatever decisions were made and work undertaken then there is every chance that the initiative will peter out or worse, it will not be taken up. The church is a dynamic community by any definition. It does not stay still. Theologically, we believe ourselves to be a pilgrim people of God, which means that year on year *we move on.* Perhaps some of those present were aware of a lacuna. One delegate is recorded as saying that she came to the congress with a hunger but was going away with nothing to get her teeth into (Ibid). Without something to aim at: a task with measurable objectives, a deadline and the giving of an account, what can possibly be done? The Kilmore Congress did set itself a programme of action. A report on the congress was circulated within a short period and a Diocesan Pastoral Council was established. Even if the programme has been successful, however, at the very least a decision to meet again in full session the following year or even within two years would have concentrated the attention of those responsible for particular tasks in a significant way. Accountability within smaller, more intimate, groups functions in a particular way. Focus groups and committees, reporting to a management group by document or in person or both, do not experience accountability in such an environment in the same way one does before a plenary session where the chances of receiving an 'understanding' hearing diminish in proportion to the number of people entitled to query one's stewardship.

In April 2004 the diocese of Ossory announced the establishment of a 'Diocesan Forum'. The idea emerged from a consultation with the priests of the diocese as far back as 1999 and 2000. A series of parish cluster meetings in May and October 2004 brought the preparation stages to a close enabling the forum to meet before Christmas 2004. The forum has a three year term of office and is composed of the bishop, forty-two lay people (one from each parish in the diocese), six priests (two from each deanery) and three religious from the communities working in the diocese. There is scope to include others as required.

The members of the forum are elected, each parish nominating three people, a man, a woman and someone under thirty-five years of age. The three nominees from a parish then meet other lay nominees from their parish cluster and choose the single representative from each parish to attend the forum. The nominees are to ensure a gender and age balance among the representatives to the forum. The priests in each of the three deaneries of the diocese are to send two priests from their own deaneries.

In the course of the three years of the life of the forum there are to be at least five meetings a year and the constitution envisages that decisions will be on the basis of consensus or, if necessary, by a majority of two thirds of the attendance. At the end of its term of three years there is to be an evaluation of the functioning of the forum. The constitution then caters for the election or appointment of a new forum.

Both the Kilmore Diocesan Congress and the Ossory Diocesan Forum would be well placed to send delegates to a national assembly. The Kilmore model is perhaps more problematic in that to ensure participation from the diocese in an assembly it may require the congress to reconvene. It met only once, in September 2000. With a three-year life span the Ossory Diocesan Forum has the element of continuity that could provide the sort of momentum a body such as a national assembly would require. These are just two examples of the processes of consultation that have been and are being implemented in Catholic dioceses in Ireland. Their differences, however, highlight the uneven nature of what is happening. Another possible difficulty in focusing on these two dioceses is that they are relatively small. Larger dioceses such as Dublin and Down and

Connor present an even greater challenge in making consultation and discussion a significant reality in the life of the Catholic Church in Ireland.

It is worth pointing out that the Catholic Church in Ireland has organised on a national basis for over two hundred years as the Episcopal Conference itself shows very well. Movement and major developments in particular, such as those that came after the Second Vatican Council, have been introduced simultaneously as much as possible. A national assembly would be to develop this tradition and would help ensure that the Catholic community around the country could advance this process together.

A National Assembly

There is a number of ways in which a national assembly might be organised even though it would be unwise to be overly prescriptive when many Catholics have yet to become part of the discussion. Having said that, the structure of the church at present does lend itself to some suggestions. As already noted Ireland has twenty-six dioceses. In Catholic ecclesiology, that is to say the way in which we speak of the church, the diocese is regarded as the 'local church'. With the bishop, the people of the diocese are the church universal in a particular place. It is not a branch office and neither is the bishop a delegate. This is why the issue of a national assembly is more complex than one may imagine at first. Dioceses are autonomous and in theory need not refer to each other. Since before Catholic Emancipation, however, Irish bishops have conducted the affairs of the church in Ireland as a conference of bishops and in this way gave a lead to the Catholic Church around the world, making a significant contribution to the development of the concept of collegiality in the modern church. Thus, without compromise to their individual autonomy, dioceses in Ireland could send members to a national assembly and show that it represents a development in the life of the church here.

The make up of the membership of a national assembly

would have to be co-ordinated to facilitate good order. This is especially important because dioceses are not natural constituencies. Populations vary dramatically. Dublin has 1,041,100 people while Clonfert, which is mostly located in east Galway has 32,600 people. Dioceses are sub-divided into 'deaneries' or 'vicariates', which are groups of roughly ten parishes within a diocese. In recent years a new entity has emerged which is referred to as a 'cluster'. These are three or four parishes grouped together. The model for the Ossory Diocesan Forum shows how these different structures can produce an assembly. It is most unlikely that the parish would be the basic unit from which a membership might emerge, as there are 1,368 parishes in the country. Even deaneries may produce too large a national assembly, as there are some 155 of them. The simplest method may be to ask each diocese to send a group from its own assembly to participate in a national body.

There is also the question of balance in an assembly. If twenty-six dioceses were to send the same number of members, let us say ten lay people, one priest and the bishop, there would be a certain homogeneity but such a model may be seen as unbalanced, giving too much weight to very small dioceses. On the other hand, to give proportional weight to each diocese may result in the membership from Dublin alone being larger than the combined membership from over half of the dioceses in the country. It really depends on whether greater value is accorded to a representational model of assembly or a more collegial model.

One factor that may help resolve this dilemma is the need to avoid 'parochialism', albeit at diocesan level. I have deliberately tried to avoid using the term 'representative' when referring to the membership of the national assembly because in gathering at a national assembly the members are not 'representing' their dioceses in the way politicians represent their constituencies. There is no bounty from which to secure the greatest possible share for people 'back home' for one thing. The membership of an assembly of the Catholic Church is to represent *the church in the country.* An assembly is to be the church in Ireland reflecting on its mission and the issues it must deal with in fulfilling that mission, which is to be Christ to the people of Ireland and, through our missionary tradition, around the world.

The collegial model, in which each diocese would send the same number of members, has the added advantage of setting a manageable number to participate in an assembly. If each diocese were to send ten or fifteen members, at least that number would be fixed and when the participants from CORI and the various canonically recognised groups and other organisations were added, the overall membership could be in or around five hundred.

Conclusion

Other traditions in the church have their assemblies and, while it would be important that a national assembly of the Catholic Church would have its own clear *raison d'être*, there is much for us to learn from the Church of Ireland, the Presbyterian Church and the Methodist Church. The Reformed churches have been in existence since the sixteenth century. They have stood the test of Gemaliel in the Acts of the Apostles who said that if the activities of the apostles were of the Lord they would endure, if not they would disappear (Acts 5:34-39). It may seem that there should be no need to reiterate such views, but the notion that Protestantism has nothing to teach Catholics has not entirely vanished from the earth.

Whatever form a national assembly takes it will have a life of its own. Because it has yet to happen, any prior discussion must be, to some extent, a work of imagination. Even so, the Catholic community in Ireland is very close to such a gathering because our society has changed so profoundly within living memory. There are still elites in the country but the old elites have largely disappeared and the last of these is only now giving up what was its almost universal leadership: the clergy. Within the Catholic community pastoral initiative must become the co-responsibility of the laity in the church. This is not to say that it is necessarily slipping from the hands of the clergy. But, in the same way that we still need schools and hospitals and have accepted that gifted and qualified people, apart from religious or clergy, are able to run them every bit as well as they were run in the past, so we still need the structures and services of the pastoral ministry of the church and will accept that it can continue through lay ministry. The ministry of priests will adjust. There will be fewer of them so that adjustment will have to evaluate the most appropriate use of the ordained ministry. It will have a different shape but it will be no less demanding.

This prospect may be a scandal for some but it is a liberation for others, including clergy. As the number of clergy decreases and those still working realign themselves, the need for the gospel will not diminish. The question therefore is, as it always has been in our tradition, 'Who will go?' Pastoral leadership will compel the entire community to look deeply into itself in order to answer that question. It will make unprecedented demands because the work will require different hands. In addressing this question and others, the laity of the church will influence and shape structures that were used exclusively by clergy in the past. The common ground in all of this may have to be a national assembly of the church. There will be a need for a forum in which this new life for the church in Ireland can be developed and brought to maturity.

The church must still respond to the call to walk with Christ, engaged and gifted in energetic conversation along the way. This may be our road to Emmaus and only in the sort of exchange that took place there will we taste and recognise who Christ is for us and what Christ is saying. The sort of conversation required now to say and hear what must be said and heard goes beyond what has passed for consultation until now. Pope John Paul has stated it clearly enough and indicated what is at stake: 'The capacity for "dialogue" is rooted in the nature of the person and his dignity' (*Ut Unum Sint*, 28).

Select Bibliography

Brady, Ray, 'The Kilmore Diocesan Congress 2000: Setting Our Hearts Upon the Deep', *The Furrow*, 50 (2000) 683-5

Kelly, Liam, 'An Approach to Pastoral Planning: The Kilmore Experience', *The Furrow*, 55 (2002) 484-9

Martin, Diarmuid, 'Parishes Working Together for Mission.' Address to the Priests of the Dublin Diocese at All Hallows College, Dublin, 30 September 2004. www.dublindiocese.ie

Pope John Paul II, *Ut Unum Sint*, Catholic Truth Society, London, 1995

Pope John Paul II, *Novo Millennio Ineunte*, Catholic Truth Society, London, 2001

Scallon CM, Paschal, 'A Workable Idea ...' *Doctrine & Life*, 54 (2004) 4-19

Twomey SVD, D. Vincent, *The End of Irish Catholicism?* Veritas, Dublin, 2003

The Women's Forum in the Dublin Diocese

Máire Nic An Airchinnigh

It would generally be accepted that women's voices have not been heard in the Irish church – or indeed anywhere else in the Catholic Church. For this reason there was a great air of excitement in the Dublin archdiocese in 1995 when it was announced that Archbishop Desmond Connell intended to take up a proposal from the Ninth Dublin Diocesan Council of Priests 'that a suitable forum be set up whereby women can dialogue with the archbishop and the bishops and with the Council of Priests on issues of common concern'. The proposal attracted a certain amount of media attention, not all of it positive. Those who were involved at the beginning will remember the sense of excitement at the fact that women's voices were to be heard and not alone heard but what was more important, listened to, and not alone listened to but they were to be consulted in a dialogue on matters of common concern. There may have been those who spoke of 'another talking shop' and thought that consultation was one thing; acting on the result was something else, but the overall reaction was positive.

Ten years down the road, I would like now to look back at the Dublin Diocesan Women's Forum with which I was involved at various levels for some six years. Unfortunately in the last few years, when something new is mooted, particularly in the Dublin archdiocese, one is likely to hear someone voice the opinion that is going to join the list of those failed efforts 'like the Women's Forum'. For the record, despite all I will say in the following pages, the Dublin Diocesan Women's Forum is not dead.

Structure of the Forum
Writing elsewhere after the first year, I noted some of the initial

problems as I saw them (Nic An Airchinnigh, 563-6). Some of
these were also taken up by Carmel O'Connell. Firstly, it came
from above. I suspect that after an initial pilot project there was
an eagerness to get something off the ground. It was an initiative
of the then Dublin Council of Priests and structurally it reflected
that. The proposed structure was that each parish would elect
two representatives to deanery level, and each deanery would in
turn elect one representative to diocesan level. There are sixteen
deaneries in the archdiocese and a representative from the
Travellers' parish was also included.

This is the structure of priests' meetings in the diocese. Since
the pilot project had been run in individual parishes, the difficulties this could present would not have been obvious. Priests
at their deanery meetings, however, usually know one another if
only on a nodding acquaintance. Other than those representing
the religious orders, they may have been in Clonliffe or Rome
around the same time, they may have served in the same or ad-
joining parishes or at the very least have friends or acquaintances in common. This did not hold for the women. In urban
parishes many do not know their fellow parishioners. For most
women and indeed for most lay people 'deanery' and 'Vicar
Forane' were terms they had not come across before.

Parish elections were not free of problems. The initial communication to the Vicars Forane (VF), who normally have responsibility for chairing deanery meetings, stated that they were
to ask each parish priest in the deanery to arrange to have two
women elected to represent the women of his parish. These
should be elected by the Parish Council or the PDR (Parish
Development and Renewal) group. Where such groups did not
exist (and there are still many parishes without a parish council)
they should be elected by the women members of some other
suitable group such as eucharistic ministers, although the person elected need not belong to the group in question. Women
were not to be nominated by the priests of the parish.

Inevitably some parish priests were enthusiastic, some went
through with it, some who were not enthusiastic but felt that

they had to do something nominated women (although they had been requested not to do so) and a few simply binned it. The suggested method of election was that those already involved in any of the parish activities mentioned above would be the electorate, but that any woman in the parish could be elected. Some parish priests felt, rightly in my opinion, that this was undemocratic and they opened the election to all women of the parish. Some did not go so far, but at least invited all women involved in any capacity in the parish. In many instances these meetings saw bigger crowds at a parish meeting than had been seen at any meeting since the launch of PDR. This was the case in my own parish and a number of women were prepared to put their names forward as parish representatives. Even at this stage, however, there were intimations of the opposition that was to bedevil the Forum – and this opposition came from women.

Shortly after this, in my deanery the VF called a meeting of the women elected from the parishes throughout the deanery and at this stage there was representation from all parishes. This meeting was to elect someone to represent us at diocesan level. This was a daunting task for twenty-six women who had not previously met. Our deanery, like many others, ran from what the property pages would term the leafy suburbs to areas that were far less affluent. The Celtic Tiger was still young and the economic difficulties of the 1980s were not that far away. Ideally there would have been several meetings of this group where we would get to know one another and the concerns of our areas. Instead we were electing someone after two meetings, when we were adamant that we could not do it at the first meeting. While I write mainly from personal experience, I know that most of what I am saying applied to many of the other deaneries. I would have to add that in spite of these difficulties sixteen very good women were elected to diocesan level.

Further problems arose when it came to replacing delegates. It was not too difficult at parish level, where the approach adopted generally was that in order to maintain a degree of continuity one person would retire after the initial two years, and thereafter one person every year. At deanery level, this meant that half of those voting for a new representative to diocesan level were new themselves and did not know who they were voting for. At diocesan level they decided that, in order to retain continuity, there would be staggered retirements.

A very practical difficulty arose at each level about where and when meetings would be held, both at deanery and diocesan level. This remained a problem. Not all women drove, or even had access to a car. Deaneries stretched over wide areas of the city with no connecting public transport. Diocesan meetings were even more difficult given that the diocese stretches as far as Athy and Wicklow. It was not reasonable to expect people from these places to travel to the city at night, or to ask those from the city without private transport to travel outside. Not many women were free during the day, or at weekends. A request that travelling expenses would be paid to such people met with silence. After a while diocesan meetings came to be held in Clonliffe College as it was seen as reasonably central (for people in the city) and because it was available at no cost. The result was that for these practical reasons parishes and deaneries were gradually lost.

Vision of the Forum

The women at the first diocesan level were fired with enthusiasm (For details of the first diocesan Forum I am indebted to Rosemary Doorley as I was not at diocesan level at this point). They realised that the Forum had not been given any real brief and they saw this as an advantage, feeling that they had the freedom to work out their own vision of the direction the Forum would take. Fairly quickly the women produced their own statement of their vision of the Forum. The main points of this were:

> Our concerns are wide-ranging, from the urgent need for the provision of adult faith formation, to issues of social justice, from the need for inclusive language in the liturgy, to questions of how to involve the youth and win back the disaffected – to name but a few. Underlying all these concerns is the

fundamental and crucial one of improving communication between hierarchy and laity – men and women, young and old.

In order that communication between the women and the
priests and bishops be true dialogue, it is important for all of
us to realise that we are attempting to start a dialogue in a
setting which, up to this point, has been largely monological
… We have committed ourselves to the truth, to speaking
that truth openly at all times so that real life-giving dialogue
can take place.

In the interests of true dialogue, it is important for us to
state at this juncture that the women of the diocese have
taken this call to dialogue with the clergy very seriously indeed. They wish it to be understood from the outset that, in
sharing the burden of responsibility for the revitalising of the
church in their own day, and the handing on of the faith to
the next generation, they wish not merely to inform and contribute towards decision making, but they desire that the
laity (men and women) and, in particular the Women's
Forum, be actively involved in the making of decisions in the
diocese of the future.

The women of the diocese look to the Women's Forum to
make a real difference in the life of the church in the diocese.
The women of the diocese have faith in the Women's Forum
as a means of building the church of the twenty-first century,
a church which is dialogical in nature, a church in which the
strong faith of the people will permeate every aspect of their
lives, a church which will lead the way, not lag behind.

Work of the Forum
The original document said that it was for dialogue 'on issues of
mutual concern'. How would these be discerned? Who would
discern them? Somebody had to initiate the dialogue, so the
women decided that they would do so by going back to the
parishes and finding out what were the issues that concerned
women there. In some parishes this was covering some ground
that PDR had already covered and some of the same topics

emerged, such as youth, communication and the need for *Nurturing the Faith of the Pilgrim People*. Although these were not women's issues, they were, nevertheless, issues on which women would have a particular perspective. Contrary to the view expressed in some places and taken up in some sections of the media, there was not a strong feminist agenda. Two issues were identified which were of particular interest to women: one was the report, *Inclusive Language and Liturgy*, and the other concerned marital breakdown, which led to the report on *Compassionate Treatment of the Marginalised*.

Having identified these five areas, the Forum set about preparing reports on each of them with the idea that they could be the basis of the proposed dialogue. Subgroups were set up and as part of the dialogue members of the Council of Priests were invited onto these groups. A tremendous amount of work was done. (The group working on *Nurturing the Faith of the Pilgrim People* met forty-four times in the course of the two years that the document was in preparation! These people would also have been attending parish, deanery and diocesan meetings.) Because *Inclusive Language and Liturgy* dealt with a single issue this was the first report to be finished. It addressed not alone the use of language regarding humankind inclusively but also the question of addressing God inclusively. Some found this latter difficult. What was more problematic was that, because the issue of the ordination of women had been brought up in a number of parishes, those compiling the report felt that they could not omit it. The archbishop requested that the report be rewritten, but the women felt that it would not then represent what the women of the diocese had said. From that point, those on the Forum felt that the atmosphere of trust, which had existed at previous meetings, was impaired. Some years later a document on the same subject was produced but this was so watered down that it was more a document on the role of the laity, than on inclusiveness.

Arising out of the report on *Compassionate Treatment of the Marginalised*, the Forum made two requests of the diocese. Those who go through the annulment procedure find it a painful experience. Therefore some form of support should be available to them. In addition, women find it alienating that they have to deal with an all-male clerical office. It was surprisingly difficult to convey this. Those who were on the Tribunal felt that they were aware of the delicacy of the situations they had to deal with and did not think that there was any real need for outside support, but did not seem able to grasp that no matter how gentle they tried to be, they were nevertheless always going to be seen as part of the system. There was a certain amount of toing and froing with ACCORD, but this did not really come within their brief. On another occasion it was suggested that the women should bring this back to the parishes. This showed a total lack of understanding of the problem. In spite of the fact that I have stated above that those in urban parishes very often do not know one another, nevertheless in such a situation one would not want to risk meeting a neighbour. For a long time there seemed to be an unwillingness to respond to this request.

The second request was that a review group would be set up to look at the treatment of those in second relationships. On this question it was made plain that the church's teaching was clear.

While this was the position when I left the Forum in 2002 I have learnt recently that there has been progress on both these issues. The services of a counsellor are to be available to those going through the annulment process and all those going through the process will be notified. A diocesan group is to be set up to look at the issue of reaching out to those in second relationships. Two priests have already been nominated; two representatives have been sought from the DDWF. Lay men will also be represented. The importance of this cannot be overemphasised.

While the reports on communication, adult faith formation and youth would have overlapped with other reports such as PDR, they would nevertheless have emphasised further the need for initiatives in these areas. The report on adult faith formation, *Nurturing the Faith of the Pilgrim People*, was seen as very important to many women, as it is now beginning to be realised that the principal religious educators of children are parents. Any major initiative, however, seemed to depend on a decision on the future of Clonliffe College, and this apparently had to be referred to Rome.

Relevance of the Forum

There was an indication that the vision of Archbishop Connell differed somewhat from that of the women when in a homily given to mark the first anniversary of the setting up of the Forum, he said:

> When God plants the seed of his word it may seem insignificant until the life-force within it expands in vigorous growth. Growth is slow but sure unlike the instantaneous productions of modern technology ... Growth has nothing to do with the mere pressing of buttons. Who realises this better than the mother awaiting through long months that cannot be hurried, the birth of her child? And when the child is born, the little one takes years to grow ... But in that time so much has happened besides the growth of the child, so much that rewards the waiting through its influence on the way parents have grown as well. In this case it is clearly not a matter of standing outside the process and waiting impatiently for ever more rapid results, but of a participation essential to the process itself. So it is with our Forum; no pressing buttons or standing aside, but the collaboration that brings us together in a process of growing that will change and enrich us by the participation in which we engage.

The women felt that he was warning them about looking for rapid results. But their whole expectation was that the Forum was going to make a real difference in the life of the church in the diocese. The issues they had identified needed immediate action.

The relevance of the Forum really became clear to me when no plenary meeting was held between October 2000 and March 2002. These plenary meetings were the meetings of the Forum with the archbishop, the auxiliary bishops and representatives of the Priests' Council. (In the first two years of the Forum there had been five such meetings each year.) This left the Forum in a very unsatisfactory situation; all the reports had been submitted but no formal response had been received. Two reasons were given for this delay; firstly the archbishop, now a cardinal, had to attend frequent meetings in Rome. (This raised questions that do not only relate to the Women's Forum: should the pastoral leader of such a large diocese be expected to spend so much time away from it?) The second reason given was that the whole issue of child sexual abuse by priests of the diocese was taking up most of the Cardinal's time. I do not doubt this for a moment but I would have to ask: If the forum were set up to discuss matters of mutual concern, what could be of more concern? I do not think there was a deliberate policy not to discuss this with the Women's Forum. What is more serious is that it evidently did not occur to the hierarchy that it could be discussed. Eventually the women wrote and invited the Cardinal to discuss it inform-ally. Word came from his office, however, that because of the legal situation this could not be done. I would suggest that had the matter been discussed with a group of women, their advice would not have been any worse that that given by civil or canon lawyers. Had the women known at the end of 2000 that they would not meet the archbishop for this length of time, they might have suspended their own meetings. Instead they tried to keep going and to keep the rapidly waning interest of the women at deanery and parish level alive. They were trying to keep alive the idea that the archbishop was committed to the Forum in spite of clear indications to the contrary.

Other difficulties
From the beginning, the Forum met with unrelenting opposition from a group of women who maintained that the Forum did not represent them. In some parishes and deaneries they were so vociferous that it became almost impossible to hold meetings, because all the time seemed to be spent on trying to counter their

objections. Amongst those objections was the fact that the final reports did not come back down to the parishes before they were submitted to the archbishop. Ideally this might have been done, but because of the time taken to prepare the reports it would not have been practical. For this reason, this group submitted their own alternative reports. They also seemed to be unable to accept that there was a need for a woman's view of issues, because they constantly argued for the closing down of the Forum and the establishment of a lay forum so that men would be included. Considering the entire hierarchy of the church is male, it could hardly be said that there is not a male viewpoint in the church! Granted, the viewpoint of the ordained male could hardly be said to reflect that of a man with a wife, children and a mortgage and all the concerns that that entails. There is room for a lay voice, but not at the expense of the Women's Forum.

For the first years at diocesan level, the women were very busy, identifying issues, setting up groups to deal with them, attending meetings, compiling the reports. This meant that it was hard to bring back much more than 'work in progress' reports to the deaneries and parishes. When the reports were finished and submitted, the lack of response meant that there was still very little to bring back. Some of the deaneries and parishes organised lectures and courses but many began to feel that they were overlapping work being done by PDR or other parish groups.

Alternatively

How might things have been done differently? Had there been an announcement that the archbishop would like to have a Forum with which he would discuss 'matters of common concern' and that he was asking the women of the diocese to set up such a Forum, it is possible that women would have come up with a structure which would have worked better. Parishes could have been involved as the best means of spreading the word and maybe in terms of providing facilities. With hindsight it would have been better, when the reports were being drawn up, if more women from the deaneries had been involved, rather than confining it to the women at diocesan level. This would have kept more of a sense of involvement down the line. This would not, however, have overcome the problem of eighteen months without a meeting with the archbishop. It was almost inevitable that those women who were involved to the extent mentioned above were virtually burnt out at the end and felt cynical and disillusioned at the lack of response.

Where now?
There is a new archbishop in Dublin. He has already made very positive statements regarding the position of women in the church. I have also looked at reports of the Listening Day held by the Forum in November 2003 (See *The Furrow,* March 2004, 176-77 and www.ddwf.ie). This meeting was attended by Dr Diarmuid Martin, then coadjutor archbishop, who apparently commented on the general lack of communication that had marked the Forum. Since then there has been progress on various fronts. While new issues have arisen which need to be addressed, it is felt that the method of preparing reports should not be followed as it is too time consuming. Archbishop Martin has suggested that the Forum would prepare guidelines for parishes for dealing with such issues as violence, an aspect of contemporary Irish society that has obviously made a significant impact on him. The task now for the Forum is to regain credibility with the women of the diocese.

Select Bibliography
Nic An Airchinnigh, Máire, 'Dublin Diocesan Women's Forum – A View from the Middle', *The Furrow* 48 (1997), 563-6
O'Connor, Carmel, 'Dublin Diocesan Women's Forum', *The Furrow* 51 (2000) 177-9

Origin and Role of the Irish Episcopal Conference

Jim Cantwell

The Irish Episcopal Conference (IEC) is the world's oldest national assembly of Catholic bishops. It has been meeting regularly since at least 1795. Episcopal conferences were not established universally until after the Second Vatican Council, so the IEC has had a very long pre-history, which can be traced to the failure of the Reformation in Ireland.

Macaulay, the nineteenth century English historian, had no doubt about the reason for the failure: 'The English conquerors neglected all legitimate means of conversion. The government contented itself with setting up a vast hierarchy of Protestant archbishops, bishops and rectors, who did nothing and who, for doing nothing, were paid out of the spoils of a church loved and revered by the great body of people.'

Punitive legislation became the alternative to mass Protestant evangelisation. Lecky remarked that the distinguishing characteristic of the Irish penal code was that 'its victims constituted at least three-fourths of the nation and was intended to demoralise as well as degrade.' The Banishment Act of 1697 required all regular clergy and those exercising jurisdiction to leave Ireland by the following year. Only four bishops remained but some returned later with a price on their heads.

The penal laws, however, were never fully enforced and Froude, another English historian, commented: 'Had the Catholic bishops been compelled in earnest to betake themselves elsewhere, had the importation of priests from abroad been seriously and sternly prohibited, the sacerdotal system must have died a natural death, and the creed have perished along with it.'

With penal legislation reducing the Catholic Church to a

sorry state, there is evidence that bishops occasionally met in secret. When persecution eased after 1745 they were able to meet in relative safety, at provincial level initially. The four archbishops began meeting annually in 1788. From 1793 representative bishops from each of the four ecclesiastical provinces attended meetings of metropolitans.

The closure of French seminaries after the Revolution meant the Irish bishops had to provide urgently for the education of future priests. Here, interests coincided, since the government welcomed the removal of future priests from the influence of revolutionary ideas emanating from France. The result was the endowment by the government of St Patrick's College at Maynooth. Negotiations with the government on Maynooth necessarily involved general episcopal meetings because 'the success of any arrangement made would have to have the maximum support of all the bishops.'

The next major issue erupted in 1815, when the Prefect of Propaganda Fide, Cardinal Litta, instructed the bishops to accept a Crown veto on the appointment of bishops in return for Catholic emancipation. Had the hierarchy not protested vigorously about this, Archbishop Daniel Murray of Dublin told the Synod of Thurles in 1850, many of the bishops then present would never have been appointed.

The legacy of Cardinal Cullen
The issues of Maynooth and the veto gave the early episcopal meetings a clear focus. The pattern of annual assemblies became established. Between 1820 and 1850 they were structured on parliamentary lines, with a chairman elected for each day of the meeting. Although decisions were not binding on the bishops, 'a co-ordinated policy emerged which increased their authority with their clergy and faithful and strengthened their bargaining power with the government.' Cardinal Cullen, however, was to be strongly critical precisely because nobody felt bound by decisions. He believed the spectacle of bishops disagreeing in public weakened their authority, and that those with a facility for

public speaking exercised undue influence within the episcopate.

The hierarchy of which Cullen became leader had been
deeply and publicly divided, particularly on the education questions, for at least a decade. Armed by Rome with the authority of
an apostolic delegate, Cullen changed the nature of the meetings
after the Synod of Thurles. Papal sanction would be required for
bishops to meet, which effectively meant that Cullen could summon them at times of his own choosing. The meetings would
have the formal characteristics of a synod. Cullen, as legate
would preside. No bishop was to express a view publicly at vari-
ance with that agreed at meetings (Cannon, 82).

Cullen established a commanding authority within the Irish
episcopate. As Desmond Fennell has remarked, he 'romanised'
the Irish church, and 'in a sense, gave definitive shape to modern Irish Catholicism, especially the episcopal part of it'.

His authority was put to the test almost immediately when
Cardinal Nicholas Wiseman issued a letter from Rome announc-
ing the restoration of the English hierarchy. Britain saw this as
an act of papal aggression. Wiseman's letter certainly had a tri-
umphalist tone, with 'every conceivable papal claim ... upheld
and elaborated in a flowery Hildebrandine style', as Edward
Norman has observed. About his role as Archbishop of West-
minster, Wiseman declared: 'We govern, and shall continue to
govern, the counties of Middlesex, Hertford and Essex, as ordinary thereof.' Queen Victoria is said to have asked: 'Am I the
Queen of England or am I not?' The government responded
with an act forbidding Catholics to assume ecclesiastical titles
'in respect of places in the United Kingdom'. Although the use
of place names in diocesan titles had never been an issue in
Ireland, alarm bells rang when menacing references were made
in the parliamentary debates about the erection of Galway diocese in 1831 and the restoration of Ross in 1849.

The Irish hierarchy decided to present an address to the
Queen, a petition to parliament, and to issue a letter calling for
constitutional agitation against the bill. 'Their action did not pre-

vent the passing of legislation but helped to ensure that it remained a dead letter from the day it was passed' (Ibid, 73).

When Cullen died in 1878 the legatine powers lapsed. Under Cardinal McCabe episcopal meetings again became less formal. Bishops even felt free to absent themselves. In 1882 Rome had to instruct them to attend and not to leave before business was completed (Ibid, 88). The bishops agreed to hold an annual meeting and to establish a standing committee of the four archbishops and two bishops elected from each province, to deal with business arising between meetings. This set the pattern retained ever since, although plenary meetings are now held four times a year.

Policy issues often involve intense debate, but little of this ever emerges in public, since the minutes of episcopal meetings record only decisions, not discussions. Cullen's time was exceptional for the IEC, so firmly was it controlled within the Dublin-Rome axis. Neither before nor since has the IEC been so tightly directed from the centre. The popular image of the IEC as a monolith is one of the legacies of the Cullen era. This enduring caricature is based on a misunderstanding of the function and powers of episcopal conferences.

Roman attitudes to episcopal conferences
Rome's attitude to 'national' meetings of bishops has always been marked by caution. In the early nineteenth century it opposed them, fearing they might propagate Gallican thinking. In some continental countries, however, the church could not respond effectively to political events affecting it without such meetings. Conferences emerged in Belgium and the German states in 1830, and in parts of Italy from 1848. The origin of the IEC was bound up with political events of the eighteenth century.

The first reference to episcopal conferences explicitly by name was in an 1889 document from the Congregation of Bishops, yet before Vatican II few had been established and these had no juridical status. The Council declared: 'It is often impossible, nowadays, especially for bishops, to exercise their

office suitably and fruitfully unless they establish closer understanding and co-operation with other bishops' (*Christus Dominus*,
par 3), and:

> An episcopal conference is a form of assembly in which the
> bishops of a certain country or region exercise their pastoral
> office jointly in order to enhance the church's beneficial
> influence on all men, especially by devising forms of the
> apostolate and apostolic methods suitably adapted to the
> circumstances of the times (Ibid, 38).

The Irish bishops in the immediate post-Cullen era had actually
anticipated this. They 'had come to a recognition that in order to
exercise their responsibility as pastors of the individual dioceses, they could and should take collective decisions affecting the
whole Irish church' (Cannon, 92-93).

Christus Dominus recommended that conferences be widely
established and laid down general norms regarding them (pars
37-38), later incorporated into canon law (canons 447-458). In addition, because of the variety of conference types, each assembly
also has it own particular statutes, approved by the Holy See.
Most conferences are national, but some – Scandinavia, Arabian
countries, North Africa, Indian Ocean, Pacific – are regional.
Malta's conference has only two bishops, while the US has a ver-
itable parliament of nearly 300. The IEC embraces two political
jurisdictions, whereas in Britain, Scotland has a conference separate from that of England and Wales. The first statutes of the IEC
were approved in 1969, the latest in 2001.

Pope John Paul II and episcopal conferences
During the first decade of John Paul II's pontificate it was noticeable that Rome began to adopt a more 'hands on' approach to
episcopal conferences than in Paul's VI's time. It is probably no
coincidence that this followed the appointment of Cardinal
Joseph Ratzinger as Prefect of the Congregation for the Doctrine
of the Faith in 1981. Four years later a series of interviews he
gave to Vittorio Messori were published in a book called *The
Ratzinger Report*. In a two-page dialogue on 'The Problem of

Episcopal Conferences', he saw them as just that: a problem. They 'have no theological basis', only 'a practical, concrete function'. The Catholic Church 'is based on an episcopal structure and not on a federation of national churches. The national level is not an ecclesial dimension.' The role of bishops 'is restrained, or actually risks being smothered' by their insertion into episcopal conferences.

'It happens that with some bishops there is a certain lack of individual responsibility, and the delegation of a bishop's inalienable powers as shepherd and teacher to the structures of local conferences leads to letting what should remain very personal lapse into anonymity.' The search for agreement between different tendencies within conferences and the effort at mediation 'often leads to flattened documents in which decisive positions (where they might be necessary) are weakened' (Ratzinger in Messori 59-61).

Such unrelieved negativity from the head of the most powerful department of the curia tended to undermine the confidence of conferences and to make them somewhat cautious. In 1998, however, Pope John Paul II articulated an essentially affirming message:

> It escapes no one that issues which currently call for the joint action of bishops include the promotion and safeguarding of faith and morals, the translation of liturgical books, the promotion and formation of priestly vocations, the preparation of catechetical aids, the promotion and safeguarding of Catholic universities and other educational centres, the ecumenical task, relations with civil authorities, the defence of human life, of peace, and of human rights, also in order to ensure their protection in civil legislation, the promotion of social justice, the use of the means of social communication, etc. (*Apostolos Suos*, par 15).

Episcopal conferences are part of a triangle of relationships involving the Holy See, the individual bishop and the conference itself. In exercising authority within his own diocese each bishop is totally independent of conferences, which, in the words of

Pope John Paul II, should not hinder his inalienable responsibility by 'substituting itself inappropriately for him' (Ibid, 24). Conferences can have no say in how he, as diocesan bishop, relates to Rome. Once established by papal mandate, conferences have a juridical status. The curia keeps a careful eye on the conduct of their business, since conferences are required to send the minutes of their meetings to Rome.

The Irish Episcopal Conference and the Second Vatican Council
Long experience of episcopal meetings helped the IEC provide the necessary leadership on church renewal in Ireland after Vatican II. Unlike most other countries the IEC had a continuous existence and settled procedure, which meant it could respond speedily and effectively to changing demands. There is something of a received wisdom that the Irish church still languished in a regressive state well after the Council. This perception is misleading. Consider what went before.

The Irish bishops were totally unprepared for the Council. There is no minute about the Council in the records of IEC meetings during the two-year preparatory period. The only discussion is reported to have been whether the bishops should charter a plane to Rome. In the exhaustive record of the Council compiled by Fr Giovanni Caprile SJ, of *Civilta Cattolica*, the only reference to Ireland in the immediate preparatory phase is that the bishops stayed at the Collegio Irlandese.

The Irish bishops were not alone in being unprepared. Responses to the secretariat during the Council's preparatory phase show that many bishops worldwide were confused. Dom (later Bishop) Christopher Butler, who attended the Council as President of the English Benedictines, looked forward to it 'with more foreboding than hope', fearing 'another dose of authoritarian obscurantism'. His worst fears seemed to have materialised in the early draft texts. Fr (later Cardinal) Cahal Daly, peritus (expert adviser) to Bishop William Philbin of Down and Connor at the Council, found these texts 'dry, academic, negative, apparently more concerned with condemning "erroneous opinions" than with proclaiming the truths of the faith in a language to the people of today's world.' The rejection of these 'pre-packaged schemata', he wrote, 'was to be one of the exciting events of the first session of the Council.'

Cardinal D'Alton had been ailing progressively and Archbishop McQuaid, the dominant Irish churchman of his time, filled the leadership vacuum. He never appreciated the significance of the Council. Desmond Fennell was to write in 1967 that after Vatican II McQuaid 'simply began to carry out the new ordinances and counsels from Rome as loyally as he did the old ones'.

At the first session, with Cardinal D'Alton billeted in the Blue Sisters' Hospital, McQuaid presided at IEC meetings. The fruit of their deliberations came in two brief interventions when he spoke in the debate on the draft text of the liturgy decree in the name of the IEC. Firstly, he requested that the text encouraging the active participation of the faithful at Mass be amended to include the right of the faithful to reflect on the mysteries of Christ, as well as making their own religious exercises and reciting their own prayers. Secondly, he wanted the deletion of any reference to the reception by the laity of communion under both kinds, on the grounds that danger to the faith could scarcely be avoided, even in the limited circumstances proposed in the draft. He also wanted the possibility of concelebrated Mass removed, claiming that people preferred to have priests offering Mass at several altars rather than jointly. The only other member of the IEC to intervene in the first session was Bishop Philbin, who made a sophisticated contribution to debate on the draft of *Lumen Gentium*. But his was a personal intervention.

The bishops did not treat Irish journalists and broadcasters seriously, which was 'an opportunity lost and was to sow the seeds of future problems'. At the time of the Council Ireland was particularly fortunate in having well-informed and theologically literate writers and broadcasters on religious affairs, such as Seán MacRéamoinn, Louis McRedmond, Desmond Fisher and, later, John Horgan. Fr Caprile actually highlighted Mac

Réamoinn's contribution to promoting understanding of the Council in Ireland.

Matters improved after the first session. Aged just 50, William Conway succeeded D'Alton in September 1963. Initially, he encountered great difficulty in asserting his leadership role within the IEC. McQuaid and he were never comfortable with each other. Conway, unlike McQuaid, was very taken with the Council. His contribution to the debate on the priesthood found its way into *Lumen Gentium*.

Conway was a moral theologian who had read the signs of the times. No leader of the Irish church since Cullen commanded the IEC so completely, and he did this through moral authority, whereas Cullen was bolstered by legatine powers. He was only sixty-four when he died in 1977 and is now largely forgotten, which is a great pity. He brought a much-needed dynamism to his presidency of the IEC. He was a gradualist whose vision and leadership skills were of crucial importance in a period of transition. It helped that the Council had energised a fair number of the bishops. Writing in 1967 Desmond Fisher said that in Ireland 'the post-conciliar mood is one of recognition that the Council was a major watershed in the church and a determination to implement it thoroughly in spirit as well as in the letter'. Meaningful lay participation in the church, however, apart from liturgical involvement, remained an extremely neglected area until recent times.

Post-conciliar reform in Ireland

The liturgy was the critical post-conciliar reform. *Sacrosanctum Concilium* gave conferences an important role in the practical regulation of the liturgy. It is a remarkable achievement that the liturgical changes were introduced in Ireland with little of the spirit of acrimony that plagued other countries. The credit for this is in large measure due to Conway's pastoral awareness and his tactical skill within the IEC. Some would argue that in Ireland the liturgy was translated rather than celebrated and there may be some truth in this but it is an exaggeration. Indeed,

Seán MacRéamoinn has described liturgical renewal as 'the success story of Vatican II in Ireland'. A good example of the seriousness with which liturgical reform was regarded by the IEC was the establishment of the Schola Cantorum in Mullingar. Sixty per cent of its graduates pursue a career in the church music.

Catechetics was another major area of achievement. Conway had anticipated the needs of the Irish church by setting up the Mount Oliver Institute of Catechetical Education. A new catechetical programme for primary schools, drawn up by a team answering to Bishop Cahal Daly on behalf of the IEC, was fully supported by Cardinal Conway and successfully introduced.

Trócaire and the commissions of the IEC responsible for advising the conference in areas such as catechetics, justice and peace, social justice, emigration, marriage and family, education, vocations, emigrants, prisoners overseas, and doctrine, all owe their origins to the initiative and drive of Cardinal Conway. The official Irish inter-church talks began in the early seventies following a letter of invitation from him to the other churches.

Church-State relations
Conway was responsible for an important development in church-state relations, with a landmark statement by the IEC in 1973 regarding civil legislation on issues of public morality. While asserting the right of bishops to speak out on such issues, it laid down a principle which has been consistently adhered to in many subsequent statements: 'There are many things the Catholic Church holds to be morally wrong, and no one has ever suggested, least of all the church itself, that they should be prohibited.' Those who insisted on seeing the issue purely in terms of the state enforcing, or not enforcing, Catholic moral teaching were missing the point, the statement declared. The real question for legislators was what effect would the proposed change be likely to have on society. 'That is a question of public, not private morality.' The significance of this statement can be seen when placed beside a declaration of Archbishop McQuaid only two years before, in which he denounced 'the confusion being

spread by an inaccurate use of terms such as public and private morality'.

Of course, most of these church-state issues were in a real sense exclusively of concern to the Republic. Debates on public morality issues in the South must strike bishops of the six Northern dioceses as of little immediate relevance to their pastoral situation, except in those parts of their territories that extend into the South (four have territory on both sides of the border). Contraception and divorce, for example, had long been legalised in the North. To deal with exclusively Northern issues the bishops there meet periodically as the need arises, as it frequently did in the period of violence and political upheaval stretching from the sixties to the nineties.

Whether, and to what extent, conferences have doctrinal authority are questions left unresolved by Vatican II and are still debated by theologians. However, *Apostolos Suos* states:

The concerted voice of the bishops of a determined territory, when, in communion with the Roman Pontiff, they jointly proclaim the Catholic faith in matters of faith and morals, can reach people more effectively and can make it easier for the faithful to adhere to the magisterium with a sense of religious respect (par 21).

It cites canon 775.2, which states that bishops in communion with the head and members of the college, whether as individuals or gathered in conferences of bishops, are 'authentic teachers of the faith for faithful entrusted to their care'. More than most episcopal conferences, the IEC has a tradition of issuing joint pastorals of a doctrinal character. Other IEC documents have covered liturgical, social justice and pastoral issues. Together, they constitute a valuable resource for the Irish church. The prolonged church-state debates over sexual morality in the seventies and eighties, however, though important, helped shape a public perception that it is such issues that define the church's essence, much as fish on Fridays was thought to have done in the past. 'They say they are Catholics but believe in divorce and contraception', ran a headline in *The Irish Times* in February 2004.

Since the mid-nineties the issue of sexual abuse of children by priests and religious has preoccupied the proceedings of the IEC. It is the most serious crisis to confront the Irish church for a very long time. The revelations concerning child sexual abuse by clergy has had a profound affect on people's attitude to the institutional church. Coming so soon after the resignation of Bishop Eamonn Casey, they greatly disillusioned committed Catholics and scandalised the young and 'semi-detached'. The issue also eclipsed, at least for a time, the impact of episcopal participation in the national discourse on a variety of important issues.

Clerical sexual abuse of children is an issue that essentially concerns individual dioceses, since clergy are incardinated into particular local churches or religious congregations and not into the corporate body. Under the leadership of Cardinal Daly as President (1991-97), however, the IEC became convinced that the crisis demanded a corporate response, as the Irish church struggled to confront this ugly aspect of its past. Many dioceses simply do not have the necessary expertise and human resources to respond adequately. Bishops who have had to deal with complaints of abuse are noticeably more deeply affected by the issue than those who have not had to face this problem. This has made unanimity within the IEC difficult to achieve on some issues related to child sexual abuse but, in general, the response of the IEC to a scandal with so many complex dimensions has been constructive. For example, the guidelines, which the IEC issued in 1996, broke new ground on the issue. As a member of the Bishops' Advisory Committee, which drafted these guidelines, I must declare an interest. Nevertheless, it is fair to note that they were widely regarded as a model of their kind at the time. As the first comprehensive set of procedures for responding to the sexual abuse of children from any corporate body in Ireland, the guidelines formed the basis on which other organisations framed their codes – the GAA, for example. When Lord Nolan was drafting guidelines for the English and Welsh bishops he thought the Irish document a good example of what was required and consulted the committee responsible. Of course, it was a document of its time and must be reviewed periodically in the light of experience. Some claim, for example, that it did not give due weight to the rights of clergy suspected of abuse. While it is my personal belief that this owes more to perception than to reality, it is important that the guidelines be subjected to robust critical analysis in the process of revision.

Policy within the IEC is developed out of a rolling agenda. Most decisions are made through consensus and a vote is rarely taken. Experience has shown that this can be the most effective means of reaching an agreed position. But it can have serious disadvantages. If consensus cannot be reached on particular issues the tendency is to leave them floating indecisively in the air, parking them for a future meeting, which effectively means they are unlikely to be resolved. Recent procedural reforms of IEC meetings are unlikely, of themselves, to change this.

The Irish Episcopal Conference and ministry
What value has the IEC for ministry in Ireland? Sometimes the quality of its leadership has been hesitant and uncertain, at other times bold and positive. From its inception over 200 years ago, and despite inevitable and frequent internal divisions, it has responded to crises and new challenges affecting the whole Irish church. The IEC has exercised a teaching role and responded to issues requiring practical pastoral direction. By facilitating the sharing of information and resources, the IEC has helped individual bishops respond to their own particular challenges. Agencies it has established have provided effective service to marriage (Accord), liturgy, emigrants, crisis pregnancies, education and catechetics. In 2002 the IEC moved all its commissions and agencies to a modern HQ at Maynooth and reformed their structures.

They are now grouped into a number of departments based on the model used in the conference of England and Wales. For example, the commissions on education, catechetics, ecumenism, bioethics, doctrine, clergy, and religious are all clustered under the Department of Education and Formation. Each department (including executive heads) meets for an afternoon during IEC plenaries, after which the episcopal chairman reports to the general meeting. This procedure is aimed at greater efficiency in the management of the conference agenda, with the aim of freeing up time for discussion of major policy issues. But, the agenda of the IEC is still weighed down by relatively minor matters that hardly require the attention of the whole body. It needs quality control.

Sadly, in the process of change, the agencies which helped the IEC contribute most effectively to informed public debate on social justice and reconciliation issues, the Irish Commission for Justice and Peace, and the Council for Social Welfare, were effectively abolished, without any indication of how the service they provided is to be replaced. Episcopal silence (or, worse, mere platitudes) on such issues is not an option, since there is a crying need for a prophetic witness by the church's leadership at a time of rapidly changing social, cultural and economic patterns.

And these changes have been extraordinarily rapid. It is only twenty years since the IEC issued a pastoral on *Christian Faith in a Time of Economic Depression.* The Republic's remarkable economic transformation in recent years is a matter for celebration. Thousands who would have had to emigrate in the past now work at home. The population movement has been reversed. This brings new challenges. From being religiously and culturally homogenous the Republic is rapidly becoming multi-ethnic and multi-cultural. We have much to learn from the experience of emigration to Britain and the Continent. The Council of European Episcopal Conferences (CCEE), of which the IEC is a member, has had the issues of immigration into Europe and asylum seekers/refugees on its radar screen for some time. It has highlighted four issues that are particularly relevant if the Irish church is to develop an adequate response: the predictable growth of immigrant ghettos; increasing racism, even where immigrants form a minority; trafficking in women; and the need for ecumenical and inter-religious collaboration in the pastoral care of migrants. The Refugee Project established by the IEC under the directorship of Sister Joan Roddy has provided the Irish church with an important voice at this critical time.

The future

Episcopal conferences are not ecclesiastical parliaments. Their powers are strictly limited. It seems to me that, at this critical juncture for Irish Catholicism, there is a need for collective re-flection and forward planning in the form of a pastoral assem-bly, involving bishops, clergy, religious and laity, to harness ef-fectively the rich variety of gifts and charisms. About consulting priests, religious and people Cardinal Daly has said: '… it must be granted that more structured and organised forms of meeting and of listening are needed now, as society at all levels becomes more complex and more sophisticated.' I believe assemblies at diocesan level would be more effective for this purpose than a national congress or synod. Our dioceses, virtually unchanged geographically since medieval times, are a patch quilt of exotic shapes, some so tiny that they amount to little more than large parishes, some predominantly rural, many urban with rural hin-terlands, and six embracing cities. Two dioceses, as mentioned earlier, are wholly within Northern Ireland and four straddle the border. In the words of Thomas Croke of Cashel in 1878, Dublin 'is no ordinary see'. It has between quarter and a third of all Irish Catholics, which 'is scarcely desirable, but it is a fact', as Archbishop Dermot Ryan once remarked. Its incumbent has al-ways commanded enormous clout within the IEC. So, what suits one diocese may not suit another. In any case, the national con-gresses in Holland and England in the early eighties failed to achieve any lasting impact within the average parish. Just as 'all politics is local', so too is the church, in the sense that real past-oral effectiveness depends much more on the quality of dioce-san leadership than on input at national level. Conferences may propose but it is diocesan bishops who dispose.

In recent years there has been a very interesting development regarding *ad limina* visits, which diocesan bishops are required

to make to the Holy See every five years. In the past bishops reported to Rome individually. Now they go as a conference. The
fact that more former diocesan bishops now head departments
of the Roman curia than in the past probably has something to
do with this development. It offers valuable opportunities for
collective dialogue with those who wield decisive power in the
church's central government. It also means that, in contrast to
the complacency that marked preparations for the Second
Vatican Council within the IEC, the bishops, in anticipating an
ad limina visit, try to develop a concerted approach to issues of
common concern, while still respecting the rights of the individual bishop.

Most diocesan bishops have a robust respect for their office
and do not see themselves as branch managers of a multinational
corporation. *Apostolos Suos* says: '… although conscientiously
respecting the primacy and pre-eminence of the Roman Pontiff,
head of the College of Bishops, they are not acting as his vicars
or delegates.' Conferences are not impotent in their relations
with Rome. From memory, I can recall in my time with the IEC
at least a dozen instances where it successfully confronted
Roman perceptions, judgements and decisions that it considered misleading or unwise. One of the newer cardinals, Stephen
Hamao, a Japanese convert, told the journal *Famiglia Cristiana* in
autumn 2003: 'We of the Roman curia must pay more attention
to, and have more respect for, local churches. We are used to instructing, teaching and correcting. I would like us to be more in-
clined to listen, aid and encourage.' The cardinal spoke from experience, having joined the curia in 1998 after 28 years as a
diocesan bishop. A balance between the centre and the periphery is essential for the good of the church.

Select Bibliography
Macaulay, Thomas, *History of England from the Accession of James
II*, Longman, Brown, Green and Longmans, London, 1852
Lecky, W. E. H, *A History of Ireland in the Eighteenth Century*,
Longman, London, 1892

Froude, Anthony, *The English in Ireland in the Eighteenth Century*, vol i, 1872

Cannon CSsR, Sean, *Irish Episcopal Meetings, 1788-1882*, (abbreviated version, published in a limited edition, Rome 1979). This doctoral thesis, never published in full, is an invaluable source on the first century of Irish Episcopal meetings.

Kerr, Donal, *Peel, Priests and Politics*, Clarenden Press, Oxford, 1982

Norman, Edward, *Anti-Catholicism in Victorian England*, Allen and Unwin, London, 1968

Pope John Paul II, *Apostolos Suos*, Vatican City, 1998

B. C. Butler, *A Time to Speak,* Mayhew McCrimmon, Southend-on-Sea, 1972

Daly, Cardinal Cahal, *Steps on My Pilgrim Journey*, Veritas, Dublin, 1998

Fennell, Desmond (ed), *The Changing Face of Catholic Ireland*, Geoffrey Chapman, Dublin, 1968

Fisher, Desmond, *The Church in Transition,* Geoffrey Chapman, London, 1967

Are Church-Media Relations Stuck?

Simon Rowe

The last decade has been a torrid time for church-media relations in Ireland. Beginning with the Bishop Eamon Casey affair, continuing with the Fr Brendan Smyth and Bishop Brendan Comiskey sagas, and culminating with the child abuse scandals that spanned the 1990s, seldom has the Catholic hierarchy been off the 'back foot', so to speak.

To paraphrase a song by U2, church-media relations appear to be stuck in a moment they can't get out of; trapped in a never-ending news-cycle of bad news – seminary closures, a vocations crisis, clerical paedophilia and broken vows.

Aside from intermittent bouts of good news, the overall impression has been of a church battling against unrelenting negative publicity. The 'drip-drip' effect of TV documentaries such as 'Suing the Pope', 'Cardinal Secrets' and 'States of Fear' saw confidence in the institutional church ebb away. Eventually, over time, the drip-drip effect amounted to a flood that eroded public trust and undermined the authority of the hierarchy. Indeed, such was the scale of the media storm facing the church that it is unlikely even Noah himself could have saved it from running aground on the rocks of child sexual abuse.

When the famous and once very wealthy US writer Scott FitzGerald was asked how he went broke, he replied: 'Slowly at first, and then very quickly.' The same could be said of church-media relations in Ireland.

Arguably it was the church's inability to deal with its own crisis that wreaked the greatest havoc, not the crisis itself. The Catholic hierarchy's inability to match the media's demands for openness and accountability left it vulnerable to unblinking scrutiny from inquiring journalists. As a result, they lurched from crisis to crisis, always guilty until proven innocent in the eyes of the media. Worse, they appeared to lack any defined communications strategy, apart from the tried and trusted approach of 'assume crash positions'.

Furthermore, as the crisis escalated, it became glaringly obvious how much distrust existed between church and media. They were poles apart. In the eyes of the media, the church was mysterious, secretive and Byzantine. In the eyes of the church, the media was superficial, sensational and iconoclastic. And never the twain shall meet, it seemed.

Is it any wonder, therefore, that church-media relations were not what they ought to be?

It would be unfair, however, to suggest that the Catholic hierarchy did nothing to improve church-media relations during this period. They did, and at considerable cost too. The hierarchy invested in media relations, press officers and new modern communications offices in Dublin and Maynooth. In addition, every diocese appointed a media spokesperson (albeit, in most cases, a priest already busy in full-time ministry) to establish channels of communication between church personnel, church agencies and the media.

Yet, in spite of all this investment, it is striking how ineffective the church has been in 'framing' the crisis (specifically the issue of child sexual abuse) and in working to 'contextualise' the problem in the public mind through the media in order to achieve a fairer and more accurate understanding of the problem. Although the church's various communications agencies were undoubtedly bucketing furiously to keep the ship afloat, the hands-on-deck were no match for the task.

Why exactly the church failed to manage its crisis could be the subject of a weighty dissertation let alone a mere chapter. For that reason I want to focus only on what went wrong in terms of church-media relations and suggest how the church can escape this 'moment' it has been stuck in for so long. Why, for example, was the church unable to set the media agenda, rather than being always led by it? And how can the church start to define itself in the media and in the public mind without necessarily having the words 'crisis', 'abuse' and 'scandal' always in close attendance.

Shooting the messenger

In reviewing church-media relations it is common to hear church figures blame the media for the opprobrium heaped on the Catholic Church over recent years. You will hear it said among some that there was a media conspiracy against the church. Regrettably, many church figures regard the mass media as the enemy rather than as a conduit to the public. For most, this is their default position. The media: guilty until proven innocent.

Sometime in the future, in a more light-hearted moment, Irish church leaders may take comfort from a scene in a recent Woody Allen comedy, *Deconstructing Harry*. It could easily have been scripted by them. In it, Woody Allen takes the opportunity to poke fun at the media who in recent years have subjected his personal life to intense public scrutiny. A character descends into hell in search of his wife who has been kidnapped by the devil. As the lift to hell arrives at various floors, the doors open and a woman's computer-like voice says in monotone fashion: 'Fifth floor! Subway muggers, aggressive panhandlers and book critics. Sixth floor! Right wing extremists, serial killers and lawyers who appear on TV. Seventh floor! The media ... I'm sorry, that floor is all filled up!'

Does the Irish hierarchy share Woody Allen's outlook on the media, viewing them in much the same light as subway muggers, lawyers and serial killers? If so, they may indeed feel entirely justified. But such an attitude is not helpful. It only promotes greater mutual suspicion and stifles efforts to bridge the gap in church-media relations. For the record, in Woody Allen's opinion, TV evangelists and escaped war criminals are the only job categories that rank worse than journalists!

When the going gets tough for the church it is too easy to

resort to bashing the media. 'Shoot the messenger if you don't like the news.' 'When it's bad news, it's a media conspiracy.' 'The media don't like us, anyway.' 'They're out to get us' ... and so on and so forth.

But blaming the media is a cop-out. The media, just like the church, is made up of all kinds of people. It is not a monolith. In journalism, as in the church, you will find good people, bad people, hardworking people, lazy people, honest people and hypocrites. All of them have a job to do, and most of the time they have to do it very quickly, working to very tight deadlines. Quite frankly, journalists working in top news organisations do not have time to sit around the water cooler devising elaborate conspiracies to bring down the church.

By blaming the media, however, the church short-circuits self-examination. The very act of doing so, either intentionally or unintentionally, transfers culpability onto a perceived outside enemy. In the long-run though, this approach is self-defeating because as recent history has shown, it was not the enemy outside that the church had most to fear, but the enemy within.

In an address to an Irish media seminar in 1996, British journalist Joanna Bogle succinctly described the problem in the following way: 'Certainly the Irish church was wholly unprepared for what was to hit it in the 1990s. The officers were on watch, the hatches battened down, but there had been inadequate attention to what was in the hold and even to the training of the crew' (Kiberd, 82).

Her comments, because they come from a well-disposed Catholic journalist, are instructive. In effect, she was saying: The media did not cause clerical child sex abuse, they highlighted it. The media did not cause priests to break their vows, they reported it (albeit sometimes gleefully). The media did not cause the church to hide its scandals, they uncovered them.

All this is true, of course. Yes, the media did report those things. Yes, sometimes they appeared to do so gleefully, relishing the opportunity to take to task an institution which (in the eyes of some) had imposed its authority with the aid of a black thorn stick. And yes, the media did not cause clerical sex abuse. But the media did more than that just report the scandals, surely?

Beware of the messenger
Because Irish media coverage of clerical abuse played such a central role in highlighting the problem in the first place (and informing and guiding public debate in subsequent years) it is only right that its role should be assessed too.

In assessing its performance, it is interesting to learn that media coverage of child abuse in recent years has over-emphasised clerical sexual abuse in comparison to other types of abuse. As a result, the public has a grossly inflated view of clergy involvement in abuse. This was one of the key findings of the *Time to Listen* report, a study conducted by the Royal College of Surgeons of Ireland on behalf of the Irish Bishops' Conference. This independent study, which was commissioned in 2001 and published in December 2003, examined the problem of clerical sexual abuse in Ireland – its cause and its effects.

The study found that almost a quarter of the public believes that 30% or more of child sexual abuse in Ireland is perpetrated by priests. As the true figure is closer to 3%, it becomes clear that the public is massively over-estimating the amount of abuse perpetrated by Catholic priests.

Is media coverage to blame for the public's inflated view of the problem?

Professor Hannah McGee, one of the authors of the *Time to Listen* study, said she believed the public was over-estimating the prevalence of sex abusers among priests because high profile cases like those involving priests tended to be emphasised in the media.

For instance, in her analysis of one national newspaper, *The Irish Times*, the term 'paedophile priest' was used 322 times between August 1993 and August 2000. Apart from the term 'paedophile farmer', which was used five times, no other occupation was linked with paedophilia in reports. The authors note: 'It has been argued that such reporting misleads people into thinking that Catholic clergy are the predominant perpetrators of child sexual abuse.' It certainly has. And what would researchers have found if they analysed coverage in the *Irish Independent* or any of the Irish tabloids? Undoubtedly, very similar results – and probably much worse.

Could the Catholic hierarchy have been right all along when they claimed the media was out to get them?

After reading the study, RTÉ broadcaster Vincent Browne confessed on air: 'It's a bit unfair then the way we've ranted on a lot about abuse by clergy.' Then a few days later in his weekly column in *The Sunday Business Post*, under the heading 'Clergy just tiny fraction of abusers' (September 7, 2003), he wrote:

> The phenomenon of sexual crime is by far the most startling of all criminality in the State and yet almost no attention is focused on it, apart from clerical sex abuse, which is a minor, almost incidental, part of the problem, although obviously neither minor nor incidental for the victims of clerical abuse. For those of us who have ranted for ages about clerical abuse, perhaps a more balanced assessment of the phenomenon is overdue.

Arguably, it was not until the hierarchy published its impressive and courageous *Time to Listen* report that there was a perceptible change in public attitudes to the church's position. This report was a 'watershed' moment in church-media relations for a number of reasons.

Firstly, the report was an independent and comprehensive analysis of the crisis that included the views of those most affected by it – abuse victims, abusers, their families, priests and bishops.

Secondly, the hierarchy could no longer be portrayed as failing to face up to the problem. For the first time, Catholic bishops candidly admitted that their response to abuse victims in the past was motivated primarily by a desire to avoid scandal.

Thirdly, while the report was damning in its assessment of church leadership, its publication served to show how the hierarchy was still able to show leadership at a very difficult time.

So, in media management terms it was an over-riding success. It was the corporate *mea culpa* the media had been waiting for years to hear. And they got it. However, for the wider public it was probably too little, too late. By the time the hierarchy decided to 'come out with its hands up' with *Time to Listen* – after defending in the ditches for years – the worst of the damage had already been done. The report had, undoubtedly, the ring of sincerity about it, but with the worst of the crisis over, *Time to Listen* also had the ring of stable doors being bolted.

Yet, for the first time, the church was defining the problem and contextualising it in the public mind. It was doing what the media had been demanding for years: admitting its failures, assessing the full extent of the problem, and putting in place measures to put its own house in order. In doing so, it provoked a widespread debate that, finally, was characterised by greater understanding of child sex abuse as a wider social problem, and raised interesting questions about media coverage of this issue too.

But why did it take so long for the media's volte-face to occur?

Getting the message across

There are two principal reasons for this, in my opinion. Both of them stem from a failure in the church's communications strategy.

Firstly, Vincent Browne expressed surprise at the 3% figure showing clerical sexual abuse as 'a minor, almost incidental' part of the problem of abuse nationally. Yet the figure of 3% for clerical abuse was known since 2002, following publication of the *Sexual abuse and violence in Ireland* report. Why did it take the media so long to refer to this fact? Why weren't church communications strategies more effective in 'framing' the issue around this figure, two years before *Time to Listen*?

This is not to suggest that the church could have lessened the pain of clerical abuse scandals simply by employing slick PR professionals to spin and tame the media. Of course not. Abuse happened. It was a terrible episode in the history of the Irish church and heaped misery on the lives of victims and their families. And no amount of PR and media management can change these facts. However, the church's inability to define and contextualise the problem accurately has exacted a heavy price. This fact was acknowledged by the *Irish Independent* in its editorial published the day after *Time to Listen* was published (December 5, 2003). The newspaper's leader writer concluded: 'It cannot be stressed enough that less than three per cent of priests offend. The tradition and legacy of the church is both proud and honourable. The inability to deal with its own flaws has exacted a disproportionate price.'

A second question arises regarding the failure of the church to inform the public about what it was doing to remedy the crisis. *Time to Listen* highlighted a great lack of awareness among the public of the measures taken by the hierarchy to tackle the abuse problem, stretching from 1994 to 2003. Just one in ten surveyed were aware that in January 1996 the church introduced guidelines for dealing with clerical sex abuse allegations in a proper and adequate manner. Why was there such widespread ignorance? Why, too, did the public not know that in 1994 the Advisory Committee on Child Sexual Abuse was set up to advise bishops on the appropriate response where there was an accusation, suspicion or knowledge of clerical sex abuse? Or that in 1995 the Conference of Religious of Ireland (CORI) established a Child Protection Task Force and a Child Protection Office to assist congregations in dealing with abuse allegations? Furthermore, if they were asked, would the public have known about the child abuse guidelines published for all dioceses and orders in 1996? And what about the Bishop's Committee on Child Protection and the Child Protection Office (CPO) that was established in 2001 to advise the hierarchy on child protection matters?

Why did nine out of ten people surveyed in *Time to Listen* know little or nothing about what the church was doing to help prevent another case of clerical sexual abuse from occurring ever again? This is a serious lacuna. And it is a question that deeply troubles the Catholic primate, Archbishop Sean Brady.

Speaking candidly to journalists at the launch of the study in December 2003, he admitted: 'The lack of awareness of the positive measures which the church has taken on the issue of child sexual abuse is disappointing, and something that requires careful examination.'

A good place to start this 'careful examination' is the church's communications offices and church leaders' attitudes to the media. They must ask themselves to what degree they still view the media as the enemy rather than as a conduit to the people for its message.

Conclusion

This is no time for the church to retreat from the media space and lose its nerve. Such an approach would consign the Catholic Church to the sidelines again – aside from the occasional cameo role as 'pantomime villain'.

At a time when sound bites and 'ducking and diving' appear to be the *lingua franca* of public discourse, and where virtually every position is assumed to be negotiable, the church's message of 'eternal truths' is arguably most needed.

Pope John Paul II, in his 1990 encyclical *Redemptoris Missio*, recognised this fact and outlined the need for the church to see evangelising culture through the media as being at the heart of its mission.

At the time when the Irish church was about to head into a ten-year media storm, the Pope was writing this advice:

> The means of social communication have become so important as to be for many the chief means of information and education, of guidance and inspiration in their behaviour as individuals, families and within society at large ... In particular, the younger generation is growing up in a world conditioned by mass media. To some degree perhaps this Areopagus has been neglected.

Just as the Pope was warning the entire church in the 1990s to neglect the media at its peril, the Irish church today, too, will neglect the media at its peril as it advances towards a 'New Evangelisation'.

Only if the Catholic hierarchy stops seeing the media as its enemy, and engages with the modern-day Areopagus, namely the public square, in a professional and transparent way, then church-media relations should never again become stuck in a moment they cannot get out of.

Select Bibliography

Damien Kiberd (ed), *Media in Ireland: The Search for Diversity,* Open Air, Dublin, 1997

Time to Listen, Liffey Press, Dublin, 2003

The Sexual Abuse and Violence in Ireland Report, known as SAVI, commissioned by the Dublin Rape Crisis Centre and conducted by the Royal College of Surgeons. Published by Liffey Press, 2002

Conversation: A Key to Relationship for Action

Dan O'Connell

Introduction

Conversations have the potential to change people. They can influence our perspective, inspire us to action, help us to love and be loved. When individuals have a chance to talk with others about what matters to them and opportunities are given to act on this, people and communities are transformed. This essay reflects upon the dynamic of conversation in making connections with others. It outlines a successful methodology for actually getting people into conversation about what matters to them. The second part of the essay summarises a process to move the interests identified through the conversations into action.

Conversation

There is much to be reflected upon when we have conversations with others. They can give us energy, connecting us to others in new or deeper ways, help us to become more authentic, ourselves, and even see the world in a new and life giving way. When we talk to others about what we care about, we can come alive. When someone listens carefully and critically to what matters to us, the world begins to change. Change happens when people talk together about things that matter to them. These conversations take place at the kitchen table, while out walking, in the pub, or leaning against a wall somewhere. It happens in some almost invisible ways. Change can begin with words such as 'Well, a few of us were talking ...' This is as true for both international movements as it is for the setting up of the local homework club. Change comes about when a few people begin to talk about what matters to them. True and authentic conversation builds the relationships with others that enable us to act on what is cared about. David Tracy, an American theologian defines conversation this way:

> Conversation is a game with some hard rules: say only what you mean; say it as accurately as you can; listen to and respect what the other says, however different or other; be willing to correct or defend your opinions if challenged by the conversation partner; be willing to argue if necessary, to confront if demanded, to endure necessary conflict, to change your mind if the evidence suggests it (Tracy, 19).

The dynamic of conversation is quite a complex one. It does not simply imply 'speaking with someone' or having a chat. Chats can be important as a prelude to conversation. Authentic conversation has more to do with the type of encounter that enlarges one's sense of connection and responsibility. At its best, it can forge a recognition of a shared capacity 'for the feelings that lie at the core of our essential humanity: fear, joy, yearning, delight, suffering, hope, love' (Parks, 70). When this happens, we have a connection with the other, one that is enlarging and energising. This kind of honest conversation is one that can transform the participants and energise them to work towards what is good for all in society. In the same book, the authors say that 'The single most important pattern we have found in the lives of people committed to the common good is what we have come to call a constructive, enlarging engagement with the other' (Ibid, 63). This is the kind of engagement that helps people move outside their own social location and see things from the perspective of another. This 'seeing' can help us realise that we only see partially, we do not ever see the full picture and so our actions are at best, always limited. We have all had the experience of talking to someone else and saying, 'Oh, my God, I never saw it like that … I had no idea.' This enlarging can help us to realise that we need others in order to better understand our world and our place in it. Conversation is our way to the other and their perspective and experience.

Blocks to conversation

It is not easy to see things from the perspective of another. There is often some work to be done to do this. We need to become aware of our own beliefs and assumptions, which often reveal themselves in what we do. One has operative and stated beliefs and they may or may not always correspond with one another. There are beliefs that I am conscious of and am able to articulate when asked, these are my stated beliefs. Then there are my operative beliefs, which are often revealed through my actions. These are beliefs that I am not aware of but act out of them from time to time. I might like to think I am quite liberal minded. This is my stated belief about myself. When I hear a white, middle class conservative man speak on a topical moral issue, however, I can find myself reacting to whatever he says, regardless of the content or merit. My operative assumptions about such men are that they do not know that they are talking about, they are paternalistic and controlling, poorly informed, seeing things from a very narrow point of view. The effect of these unconscious assumptions is to hear nothing of what is being said. This is my operative stance. Or I might like to think of myself as a good Christian – my stated belief. When the local authority, however, reveal plans to build a halting site for members of the Traveller community not far from my house, I am quick to join with others in resisting this development. This is without wondering what my faith tradition has to say to this situation or what God is doing in and through this initiative. The resistance in myself is revealing of my operative stance. This stance curtails any desire for conversation with the local authority and even less with the Traveller community. We often contradict ourselves, saying one thing and doing the other. However, this is often not done in a deliberate way. We simply find ourselves doing the very things we would rather not do. Where these inherent contradictions between what is stated and what is operative go unexposed, we are not in a position to do anything about them. We continue on as before. When we do become aware of the dissonance, however, the space between what we really believe and what we think we believe, we now have an opportunity to make a choice. This choice can help us become more consistent, less closed and more genuinely open to see and hear another.

Along with the inherent contradictions between what we say and do being an obstacle to conversation, our use of labels often gets in the way also. Being conscious of how we describe or label other people is critical to being in conversation with them, making them less of a stranger and beginning to see the world from their perspective. Appreciating the importance of context and the existence of multiple perspectives on things is one way to do this. We need to be conscious that our perception of another's skills or difficulties changes constantly, depending on our situation and social location. Such awareness prevents us from equating someone's difficulties with their identity. Instead of 'cripple' or 'homeless' or 'diabetic', we would see a man with a lame leg, a woman without adequate accommodation and a child with diabetes. The use of labels tends to influence every other judgement of, or reaction to, the person or community who have been so named.

To test the impact of labels, psychologists Robert Abelson and Ellen Langer (1974) designed an experiment using a videotape of a rather ordinary-looking man being interviewed. He and the interviewer spoke about work. The tape was shown to psychotherapists. For half of the therapists, the man being interviewed was called 'job applicant'. For the others, he was called a 'patient'. The researchers found that when the man on the tape was referred to as a 'job applicant', he was perceived as well adjusted. When he was labelled a 'patient', however, many of the therapists saw him as having serious psychological problems. On the strength of this study, psychologist Ellen Langer, fifteen years later, makes the point:

> Because most of us grow up and spend our time with people like ourselves, we tend to assume uniformities and commonalities. When confronted with someone who is clearly different in one specific way, we drop that assumption and instead look for more differences. Often these perceived differences

bear no logical relations to the observable difference (Langer, 156).

She goes on to refer to the unusual gestures of a person with cerebral palsy, and in that case we might assume a difference in intelligence, which is clearly not the case. The point is the same for meeting people from different groups. We need to be careful when we name or label a person or community: homeless, immigrant, Traveller, married, gay or lesbian, disabled, Catholic etc, that this label does not become the only lens through which we see or meet another. Labels can be both accurate and misleading at the same time. When we are told that someone is a Traveller, it is true that they are a member or not a member of the Traveller community. The use of the label 'Traveller', however, is a term that evokes many feelings and images that are negative and off-putting for many members of the settled community. This is in spite the fact that very few settled people actually 'know' Travellers except for what we see on the television or meet at our doors or drive past on the road. So much of what the label is based upon is broad generalisation and negative stereotyping. There is a similar dynamic in operation when we label others. We can lose sight of the person under the label, hindering our ability or desire to engage in conversation with them.

Interpretation
Each of the previous points, which highlight the blocks to conversation, centre around the difficulty of not really seeing ourselves and others as we and they are. I think one thing about myself, while I act in a contradictory manner and sometimes label others in a narrow, generalised and misleading fashion. This is all a matter of interpretation. Before we are too hard on ourselves, we need to realise that in conversation, we are at all times engaged in interpreting and being interpreted. There is no unmediated access to the experience of the other and even of ourselves. All our perceptions of others are interpretations. Hans-Georg Gadamer, in *Truth and Method*, refers to this as our 'prejudices'; these are the pre-understandings we bring with us into

conversation. Based on these pre-understandings or pre-judgements we have perceptions of the people we meet and this affects how we converse with them. If I only use the label 'teacher' in understanding someone else and make assumptions about the particular individual based only on my previous experience and view of teachers, I will not see her for who she really is. It is just not possible, my experience is too limited. I need to realise that this label, 'teacher', is not the full picture and so remain open to new information and experience to enlarge my understanding. This requires a deliberate choice and is not easy.

As Gadamer says, 'It is impossible to make ourselves aware of a prejudice while it is constantly operating unnoticed, but only when it is, so to speak, provoked do we notice' (Gadamer, 299). So, possibly, when I get talking to this 'teacher', I might begin to see her in a new light, I might be surprised at her interest and passion for the GAA, exotic art, bungee jumping and travel. This experience can offer me the chance to enlarge how I think, feel and behave towards teachers. It fleshes out the label, and gives other descriptors that contribute to a more accurate and real picture of who this person is.

The poet David Whyte says, 'we should not emerge intact from a conversation.' A conversation requires the ability or willingness to be disturbed. It should at times challenge our beliefs and ideas about ourselves, others and the world. A good way to do this is to listen to what surprises, startles or disturbs us in our conversations with others. This is not easy to do. If we notice that we have been surprised, startled or disturbed, however, some of our invisible beliefs and assumptions are revealed to us. For when I am taken aback by what you say, I must have been assuming something else. Here is an opportunity for learning more about our own beliefs and gaining a deeper insight into ourselves. 'We are all biased; it is important to acknowledge bias as a condition for interpretation. There is no uninterpreted fact' (Cowan & Lee, 31). And so if we seek to improve the quality and capacity for genuine conversation with another, we must be open to the fact that untarnished objectivity is not a possibility

and that we bring much by the way of baggage to the conversation. In order to help people engage in conversation that gives
life, Cowen and Lee suggest some commitments that are helpful:

- When I speak I will do it in a way that gives you the best
  chance at understanding exactly what I hold and why I hold
  it. I am speaking so that you will understand me, not in order
  to convince you.
- When I listen my sole intention is to hear you in order to understand you. I will have to let your words mean what they
  mean to you, not what they perhaps mean to me. I will not
  listen in order to refute, but to understand.
- I promise up front that I will not withdraw from the conversation, no matter how difficult it might become. I will not go
  away.
- It will be OK for us to disagree, to argue, and to challenge but
  not until our achievement of the first three points is accom-
  plished (Ibid, 32).

It is through such guidelines and reflection on our own experience that we can move beyond fearful civility in our relationships with others into relationships that are enlarging and life
giving.

Bringing people into conversation
In this section I will look at ways to bring much of what I have
been explaining into practice. It is a methodology I have seen at
work in parishes and organisations in Ireland, England and
North America. It is influenced by the work of Saul Alinsky, a
community organiser in North America and developed by the
Industrial Areas Foundation, an organisation that seeks to help
people find ways to 'translate their values and dreams for themselves and their communities into concrete reality.'

  For the purpose of clarity, the following outline will be taken
from the context of a parish. The process is also used in communities and organisations. The process is in two parts. Part I concentrates on organising people to have conversations with many

others, in pairs, over a given period of time around two questions: what do you care about? what are you doing about it? These questions are designed in such a way as to get someone to become intentional and mindful about what matters to them. The answers are not something that we have much opportunity to articulate, we just 'do' what we care about. We do not talk about it. And we do not give much time to listening to what it is that others care about either. The second question helps identify the congruence, or lack of it, between what we say and what we do in regard to what we care about. The use of these questions widens and builds relationships in a very non-threatening manner. Part II of the methodology outlines a process to move from identifying what is cared about to definite action carried out by the participants themselves. This is done following the *Open Space Technology* model as outlined by Harrison Owen.

Generating conversations

In the first part of the process, everyone in the parish was invited to come and commit themselves to a process that would widen and deepen relationships, generate energy and creativity, identify interests and provide a way to act strategically on these in an ongoing manner. In brief, people were asked to commit themselves to weekly meetings, lasting no more than an hour, over a given period of time. The key action of the meeting was for each participant to identify two other people they were to meet in the intervening week for a conversation. These conversations were to happen in pairs, and to last no more than an hour. The pair were asked to talk about the two questions referred to earlier: what do you care about? what are you doing about it? Depending on the level of the relationship, those involved were to discuss what they cared about at an appropriate level with the other person. When everyone arrived for the following meeting (which was open to all), there was no reporting back of what was said or heard. At this stage, the content was not as important as the conversation. Part II was to pick up the implications of the conversations. The following is an outline of the agenda for some of these meetings, which tended to follow a certain pattern:

- welcome
- opening prayer
- round of introductions
- input on a topic, e.g. community, church, leadership etc.
- sharing experience of previous week's conversations
- selection of partners for coming week
- announcements
- volunteers to take responsibility for above tasks next week
- closing prayer

Initially, people are often unsure of 'how' to go about having a conversation with another person and so the weekly meetings provide a good space to talk about the experience and to get some 'tips' from others. Sometimes, they can get a little stuck in the conversations with another and just begin to use it as a space to 'give out' about all that is wrong with the world. This defeats the purpose of the exercise on a number of counts. It is hard to listen to, exhausting at times, it does not make connections, generate energy nor identify what is cared about in a straightforward manner. The conversations must deal with what the participants care about, what is it that someone has a passion for: one's children, work, a sick aunt or racism. When listening to someone talk about what matters to them, connections are made, energy is created and something new emerges between these two people. Along with looking at 'how' to have an appropriate conversation with others, the weekly meetings can provide a space to look at other pertinent issues for the parish community.

Something else that often crops up at these weekly meetings relates to 'outcomes'. Some will ask, what is the likely outcome of all these conversations, where are they going? Once a woman asked if more young people would be going to Mass as a result of this whole procedure? I replied, if that is what they care about, then it is likely that that would happen. I could not say, however, at this stage, nor was it something that was planned for. She did not return to any more meetings. The process is organic and non prescriptive. People have a chance to identify what they care about and act on that at the end of the process. It is not about finding volunteers for projects or filling churches. It is not possible to set specific outcome like improvements in Mass attendance. It is about providing an opportunity and mechanism for people to identify what they care about through many conversations and helping them to act on it in a strategic manner. Also, it is not about people identifying work for others! We have all heard someone say at parish meetings, 'There should be something for young people in this parish.' They have no intention, however, of doing something about it themselves. The process that I have outlined, in broad strokes, helps prevent this sort of thing and promotes participation through intentional and mindful conversations.

As the weeks go by, energy begins to emerge from within the group (whose membership will hopefully be growing all the time). The conversations that take place between people connect them together in a new way. People are getting to know one another. The connections, along with a new sense of belonging and greater awareness of what others care about, give a new impetus that can be directed towards action.

Moving the interest to action
Once all the weekly meetings have taken place the participants have a choice. They must decide whether or not to continue. If they do they must meet again and identify things that need to be done in the parish and by the parish. Those who chose to move to action, have generally used a methodology based on the writing of Harrison Owen, as mentioned earlier. It outlines a method to link interests and action.

The process takes account of the conversations, the relationships that were built and deepened, and seeks to apply the energy generated in practical and useful ways for the good of the parish. It involves people meeting for a morning or a day, depending on the size of the group. There are the usual welcomes,

and introductions to one another and an outline of the day provided. The heart of the process centres on individuals identifying actions and ideas relating to what needs to be done. The
ideas they suggest need to be ideas for which they are prepared
to take some responsibility. This is not the time to think of good
ideas for others!

At the meeting, all the ideas are recorded, written on large
sheets of paper and hung on the wall. The names of those who
bring up an idea are also recorded. When there are no more
ideas, everyone is asked to put their name beside an idea that interests them and on which they are prepared to work. Most people will put their names beside two or three ideas. These groups
then meet to talk about what attracted them about the idea and
what they might do about it (the logistics of this are too detailed
to go into here, but Harrison spells them out step by step in his
book). This initial meeting has a number of functions: identify
who will bring an idea forward; tease out the idea and set a date,
time and place for another meeting. The planning day finishes
after all these groups have met, many will have met simultaneously during the day. The kinds of ideas that have emerged
from this sort of exercise concern: Bible study, social action for
refugees, work with altar servers, promoting welcome in the
parish, training for those who want to work with the bereaved,
perpetual adoration, youth club, parish resource centre, information booklet for the parish listing local services, recycling and a
film club.

Following the planning day, the information gathered is dis-
tributed throughout the parish. The ideas, dates and places of
next meetings are all included. This is to keep the whole parish
involved and informed. It also provides an opportunity for others
to join at this stage. Some will not have become involved earlier
because the process will have appeared a little too 'touchy, feely'
for them. They are much more adept at rolling up their sleeves
and doing something practical. Now is their time!

The individual groups will then move off and begin to make
some plans around their ideas. They may need some help for

this; they need to identify clearly the issue they are engaging with, how they will answer it, who is going to do it, when this will happen and how they plan to evaluate their work. After the groups have met a few times, it is important that the organising group find a time to speak with the convenors of these new groups.

The establishment of these new groups and the strengthening of older ones, provide an opportunity for the leadership in the parish to identify, recruit and train future leaders. This methodology helps people to identify what they care about, join with others, work out a strategy and act together on particular initiatives. Its success rests on the quality of the relationships that have been built through the many conversations that began the process.

An example of success

In various places throughout North America, this method of organising intentional conversations between as many people as possible, identifying interests and acting on them together, has been used very successfully in various Christian communities across the denominations. These communities go through the process as outlined above individually. Then conversations are held between different communities. This was a very good way for groups from different denominational, cultural and socio-economic backgrounds to build meaningful and inclusive relationships. The Greater Boston Interfaith Organisation (GBIO) grew out of this process. It is a coalition of various Christian communities, Jewish temples and other community groups. They have over 100 member groups. A number of years ago, the member organisations identified 'affordable housing' as a shared interest across the membership. A strategy was identified and in the following two years, the membership acted in a strategic and organised way on this issue. At the end of the campaign, they had raised $100 million towards affordable housing. Their power came from their ability to mobilise thousands of people. This was an issue that people cared about and were prepared to act on it. It was successful because of the relationships that were built through thousands of conversations that were held earlier.

Conclusion

I have seen the power of conversations, properly organised, to change groups of individuals with individual interests, into mindful, participative and active communities. When people take the time and are given a chance to talk about what they care about, they become more intentional about their own interests and mindful of those of others. And when they act successfully on what they care about, their confidence grows and their interests widen. The challenge now is to create the time and opportunity for courageous conversations between all sorts of people and communities.

Select Bibliography

Alinsky, Saul, *Reveille for Radicals*, Vintage, New York, 1960

Alinsky, Saul, *Rules for Radicals*, Random House, New York, 1971

Bellah, Robert N. et al, *Habits of the Heart: Individualism and Commitment in American Life*, University of California Press, Berkeley, 1996

Cowan, Michael A. and Bernard J. Lee SM, *Conversation, Risk & Conversion: The Inner and Public Life of Small Christian Communities*, Orbis Books, Maryknoll, New York, 1997

Gadamer, Hans-Georg, *Truth and Method*, 2nd Revised Edition Continuum, New York, 1999

Gula, Richard M. SS, *The Good Life: Where Morality & Spirituality Converge*, Paulist Press, New York, 1999

Langer, Ellen J., *Mindfulness*, Addison Publishing Co, Wesley, 1987

Owen, Harrison, *Open Space Technology*, Berrett-Koehler Publishers, Inc., San Francisco, 1997

Parks Daloz, Laurent A. and others, *Common Fire: Lives of Commitment in a Complex World*, Beacon Press, Boston, 1996

Taylor, Charles, *The Ethics of Authenticity*, Harvard University Press, Cambridge, 1991

Tracy, David, *Pluralism and Ambiguity: Hermeneutics, Religion, Hope*, University of Chicago Press, Chicago, 1994

Wheatley, Margaret J., *Turning to One Another: Simple Conversations to Restore Hope to the Future*, Berrett-Koehler Publishers, Inc., San Francisco, 2002